Hardcover Bonus Materials By

Win Scott Eckert

Will Murray

John Allen Small

Keith Howell

Rick Lai

Arthur C. Sippo

Christopher Paul Carey

DOC SAVAGE
His Apocalyptic Life

As the Archangel of Technopolis and Exotica
As the Golden-eyed Hero of 181 Supersagas
As the Bronze Knight of the Running Board
Including His Final Battle Against the Forces
of Hell Itself

PHILIP JOSÉ FARMER

DOC SAVAGE: HIS APOCALYPTIC LIFE

AS THE ARCHANGEL OF TECHNOPOLIS AND EXOTICA

AS THE GOLDEN-EYED HERO OF 181 SUPERSAGAS

AS THE BRONZE KNIGHT OF THE RUNNING BOARD

INCLUDING HIS FINAL BATTLE AGAINST THE FORCES

OF HELL ITSELF

COVER BY

JOE DeVITO

DEFINITIVE EDITION EDITED BY

WIN SCOTT ECKERT

METEOR HOUSE • 2013

DOC SAVAGE: HIS APOCALYPTIC LIFE
Hardcover Print edition ISBN: 978-0-9837461-4-0
Published by Meteor House
First Meteor House edition: July 2013

Designed by Matthew Moring/Altus Press

Special Thanks to Christopher Paul Carey, Condé Nast, Michael Croteau, Joe DeVito, Win Scott Eckert, Philip Laird Farmer, Keith Howell, Kristan Josephsohn, Rick Lai, The Lotts Agency, Ltd., Matthew Moring, Will Murray, Art Sippo, John Allen Small, and Paul Spiteri.

Cover illustration commissioned by Win Scott Eckert

This biography is dedicated to Lester Dent,

the Revelator from Missouri,

and his wife, Norma Gerling Dent

Acknowledgments

I AM especially grateful to Condé Nast Publications, Inc., for permission to write this biography of Doctor Clark Savage, Jr. I thank Random House, Inc., for permission to use the extract from *In Cold Blood* by Truman Capote, Random House, Inc., © 1965; Grove Press, Inc., for permission to use the quotations from *Tropic of Capricorn* by Henry Miller, Grove Press, Inc., © 1961; and *Nova Express* by William Burroughs, Grove Press, Inc., © 1964; and Houghton Mifflin Company, for permission to use the quotation from *Raintree County* by Ross Lockridge, Jr., Houghton Mifflin Company, © 1947, 1948. I owe Jack Cordes much, for without the loan of his complete collection of the *Doc Savage* magazines, this project would have been impossible. I thank the main reference department staff of the Peoria Public Library for their co-operation and efficiency in answering my many questions on many subjects. The staff includes the Mses Jane Burch, Betty Roberson, Nona Dutton, Bernhardine Gagneron, Elizabeth Hilderbrand, Velma Gorsage, Alma Rosser, Gloria Shoup, and Mildred Ruch. Gratitude is due Mrs. Lester Dent for her time and information during my two visits to her home in La Plata, Missouri. I thank Mr. Lawrence A. Wien for permission to print his letter replying to my request for information about the eighty-sixth floor of the Empire State Building. I am grateful to Judy-Lynn del Rey for her efforts in ascertaining the identity of the true owner of the Empire State Building.

Table of Contents

Addenda

Limited Edition Hardcover

Tributes

Call up the fiends.
—Prometheus Unbound

But first I mean
To exercise him in the Wilderness;
There he shall first lay down the rudiments
Of his great warfare, ere I send him forth
To conquer Sin and Death, the two grand foes…
—Paradise Regained

Up from Earth's Centre through the Seventh Gate
I rose, and on the Throne of Saturn sate,
And many a Knot unravell'd by the Road;
But not the Master-knot of Human Fate.
—The Rubáiyát of Omar Khayyám

An Extension of the Wold Newton Family Chart of *Tarzan Alive*

Raphael Hythloday

The Scarlet Pimpernel*

Sir Hugh Drummond*
see page xxi

Sarah Frobisher

Solomon Kane

Micah Clarke

Gervas Clarke

Mavice Blakeney

Bruce Clarke Wildman
The Time Traveller

Richard Hannay

Sir Nigel Loring

Captain Blood

Arabella Blood

Tabitha Clarke

Mercy Blood

Sir John Clarke Wildman

Sir Patrick Clarke Wildman

Alexander Clarke Wildman

Patricia Savage

Matthew de Pierson

Matthlette de Pierson

Allan Quatermain

Manuel of Poictesme

Niafer

1st Viscount Castlewood

Lorna Esmond

Lord Tiverton

Armand Chauvelin

Marie Chauvelin

Ned Land

Arronaxe Land

Wolf Larsen

2nd marriage?

Philip Marlowe?

Mr. Moto?

Edwina Land

Ebenezer Cooke

Micah Clarke

Thomas Carslisle?

Mary Brandon

Joshua Spade

Samuel Spade

Reuben Clarke

Eliza Shawnessy

Thomas Duff Shawnessy

Faith Shawnessy

John Spade

Sam Spade

Mary Spade

Joseph Jorkens

Henry Burlingame

Anna Cooke

Juno Cooke

John W. Shawnessy

Eva Alice Shawnessy

Natty Bumppo?

Gideon Root

Kilgore Trout

John Bumppo

Fern Bumppo

Esther Root

Wesley Shawnessy

Allegra Shawnessy

Leo Queequeg Tincrowdor

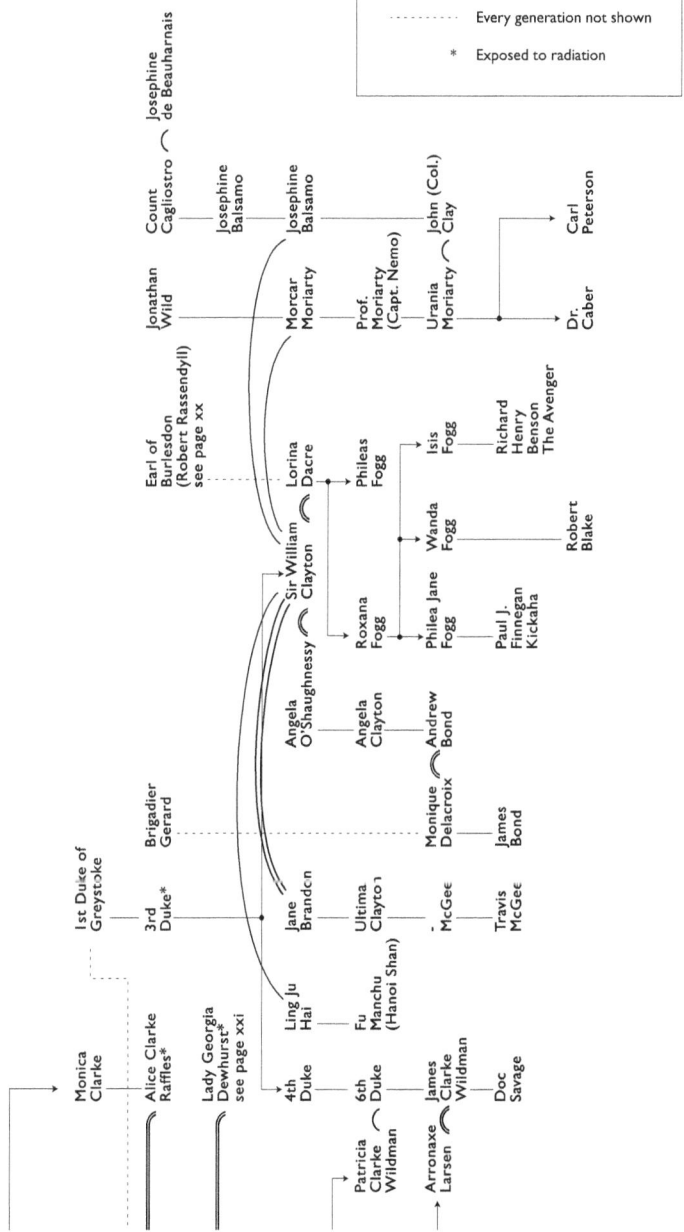

Married

Unmarried

Siblings

Every generation not shown

* Exposed to radiation

Josephine de Beauharnais

Count Cagliostro

Josephine Balsamo

Josephine Balsamo

Jonathan Wild

Morcar Moriarty

Prof. Moriarty (Capt. Nemo)

Urania Moriarty

John (Col.) Clay

Carl Peterson

Dr. Caber

Earl of Burlesdon (Robert Rassendyll) see page xx

Lorina Dacre

Phileas Fogg

Isis Fogg

Richard Henry Benson The Avenger

Wanda Fogg

Robert Blake

Sir William Clayton

Roxana Fogg

Philea Jane Fogg

Paul J. Finnegan Kickaha

Angela O'Shaughnessy

Angela Clayton

Andrew Bond

Monique Delacroix

James Bond

Brigadier Gerard

Jane Brandon

Ultima Clayton

McGee

Travis McGee

1st Duke of Greystoke

3rd Duke*

Ling Ju Hai

Fu Manchu (Hanoi Shan)

4th Duke

6th Duke

James Clarke Wildman

Doc Savage

Monica Clarke

Alice Clarke Raffles*

Lady Georgia Dewhurst* see page xxi

Patricia Clarke Wildman

Arronaxe Larsen

Robert, Earl of Burlesdon Extended Family Tree

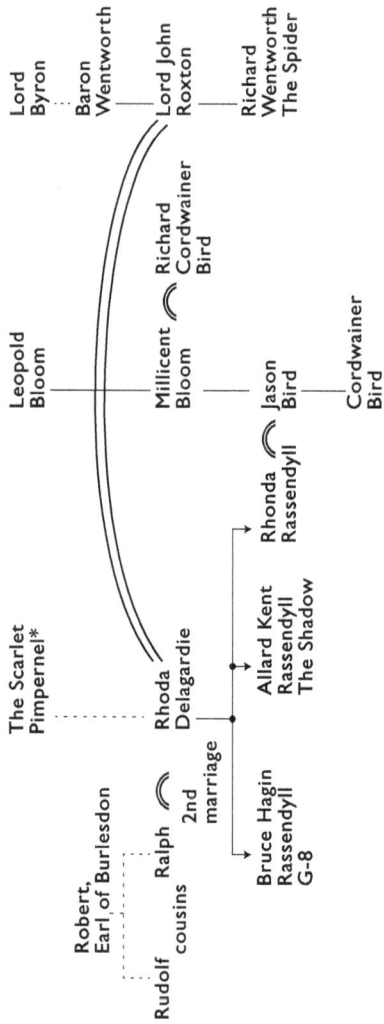

Rudolf
Robert,
Earl of Burlesdon
Ralph
2nd
marriage
cousins

The Scarlet
Pimpernel*

Rhoda
Delagardie

Bruce Hagin
Rassendyll
G-8

Allard Kent
Rassendyll
The Shadow

Rhonda
Rassendyll

Leopold
Bloom

Millicent
Bloom

Jason
Bird

Richard
Cordwainer
Bird

Cordwainer
Bird

Lord
Byron

Baron
Wentworth

Lord John
Roxton

Richard
Wentworth
The Spider

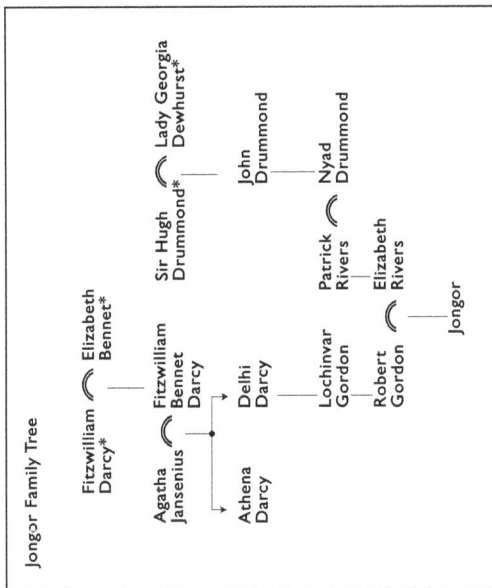

Jongor Family Tree

Fitzwilliam Darcy* ⚭ Elizabeth Bennet*

Agatha Jansenius ⚭ Fitzwilliam Bennet Darcy

Athena Darcy

Delhi Darcy

Lochinvar Gordon

Robert Gordon

Sir Hugh Drummond* ⚭ Lady Georgia Dewhurst*

John Drummond

Patrick Rivers ⚭ Nyad Drummond

Elizabeth Rivers

Robert Gordon ⚭ Elizabeth Rivers

Jongor

Names on same level may not be in same age group.

See this chart and that of *Tarzan Alive* for more detailed lineage of inset.

Foreword

BOOK OF MAGIC

by Win Scott Eckert

IT'S SUMMER, 1975. I'm in the back seat of a silver 1970 Pontiac Grand Prix, on a cross-country trip. We've been visiting family friends in Washington, D.C., where we used to live, and are headed home for Colorado.

Mounted on the center hump running between the back seat and front bucket seats is a custom-installed, state-of-the-art 8-Track player. I'm in charge of the tapes: Elton John's *Madman Across the Water* and *Honky Château*, Harry Nilsson's *Nilsson Schmilsson*, and America's *Homecoming*, and many others.

In a pile in the back seat with me are a bunch of Doc Savage paperbacks and a copy of the Bantam Books edition of Philip José Farmer's *Doc Savage: His Apocalyptic Life*—books recently given to me, a dubious, even skeptical, eight-year-old, by the aforementioned family friends.

Among the Doc novels are *The Living-Fire Menace*, *The Devil Genghis*, *Meteor Menace*, *The Pirate's Ghost*, *The Crimson Serpent*, *Devil on the Moon*, *The Mystery on the Snow*, *Mad Mesa*, *The Polar Treasure*, *The Mystic Mullah*, *The Lost Oasis*, *Murder Mirage*, *The King Maker*, and *The Man of Bronze*.

Magic.

As is the tantalizing back cover copy on the Farmer book:

HE IS THE GREATEST HERO OF OUR TIME!
The golden giant who fought 181 separate battles against the forces of evil!

Now, at last, his incredible life story can be told. Including:
A detailed family tree relating Doc to Tarzan, Sherlock Holmes, Sam Spade, James Bond, Fu Manchu, and Travis McGee.

The background of his most devilish opponents—John Sunlight, the Mystic Mullah, Mr. Wail, and Dr. Madren.

Biographies of the Fabulous Five—Monk, Ham, Renny, Johnny, and Long Tom.

Plus hitherto unknown information on Doc's most fantastic inventions.

The most authoritative account of this remarkable man's astonishing career you will ever read!

I'm familiar with James Bond from the movies (severely edited for airing on ABC television; I'm too young for the theatrical releases) and have heard of Sherlock Holmes.

A whole new world opens up, and the rest of the 1970s and most of the '80s are consumed with eager trips to the bookstore in search of the latest Doc paperback, as well as books featuring the other wonderful characters whom Philip José Farmer described as being related to Doc in a brilliant construct called the Wold Newton Family: Sherlock Holmes, Tarzan, James Bond, The Avenger, The Scarlet Pimpernel, Nero Wolfe, Allan Quatermain, The Spider, Sam Spade, Fu Manchu, Solomon Kane, Philip Marlowe, Wolf Larsen, The Shadow, Professor Moriarty, Travis McGee, and many more.

Along with a regular diet of Doc books, I'm also drawn to Burroughs' non-Tarzan series. The Pellucidar tales are my favorite (a preference influenced, no doubt, by the 1976 feature film *At the Earth's Core* and the corresponding Ace paperback edition), followed closely by John Carter of Mars. I'm particularly enamored of the fact that Burroughs crossed-over two of his primary series, sending his most famous creation, the lord of the jungle, to Pellucidar in *Tarzan at the Earth's Core*.

At this point, of course, I have no idea that Farmer has ingeniously tied John Carter to his Wold Newton mythos through Burroughs' *The Outlaw of Torn* ("The Arms of Tarzan," *Burroughs Bulletin* No. 22, Summer 1971). Indeed, I won't even find a copy of Farmer's companion biography, *Tarzan Alive: A Definitive Biography of Lord Greystoke*, until the Playboy Books edition is issued in 1981.

I have barely scratched the surface of Farmerian scholarship, and, in fact, have no idea how deep Farmer's waters run.

IT'S late 1981, and I'm at the Mile High Comics on Tejon Street in downtown Colorado Springs. It's Saturday, and my dad has taken me for my weekly comics fix. I mostly read superhero comics, but I scan everything on the racks, and I'm also on the lookout for number ones.

Number ones are going to be really valuable someday!

I pick up a new mag, *Starslayer*, from an independent publisher called Pacific Comics. I'll give it a shot.

Inside is an ad for a new series called *The Rocketeer*. The art looks amazing. I'm having a love affair with the 1930s and '40s—inspired by the Doc books, other pulp novel reprints I've found, the 1973 feature film *The Sting* (one of my all-time favorites), and various Golden Age comics reprints such as those found in Jules Feiffer's *The Great Comic Book Heroes*—and this Dave Stevens guy, whoever he is, has nailed it.

In the ensuing months, I pick up Chapters One and Two, and I'm not sorry. It's the first pulp novel in comic format I've ever seen. My journey beyond superhero comics has begun.

But it's *The Rocketeer* Chapter Four (*Pacific Presents* no. 2, 1983) that really sends me for a loop. Who are these mysterious guys who have dealt themselves into the storyline?

One of them is the picture of sartorial perfection and carries a black cane. Another is squat, but massive, an ugly ape with red hair. He calls himself "Colonel May—"

My mind blown, I check Farmer's chronology at the back of *Doc Savage: His Apocalyptic Life*. *The Rocketeer* takes place in April 1938. The timing works. It could certainly be an untold Doc adventure. Doc himself (unnamed) appears in last panel of Chapter Four, and in Chapter Five.

I realize, for the first time, that I'm not alone. Someone else has read this magical book, this biography of Doc Savage.

Someone else is adding to this magical world, this universe, and they're following Farmer's framework in which to do it.

THE late 1980s see the advent of authorized Doc Savage comics from DC Comics, and although the first writer's attempt is flawed in execution and continuity (Long Tom, a traitor? Come on!), the subsequent writer tries to repair these errors and gives a good college try at capturing the spirit of the pulp novels. The 1930s tales he pens also fit into Farmer's chronology (as do subsequent stories published by Millennium Comics in the 1990s) and it's clear to me that the Doc Savage biography is being used as a reference source.

That fact becomes glaringly obvious to anyone else who may not be following as closely as I am, when an "annual" issue from DC features an origin tale of Doc and the amazing five's meeting at, and escape from, a WW I German prison camp called Loki. This origin tale is described by Farmer in *Doc Savage: His Apocalyptic Life*—and in fact is Farmer's contribution to the Doc mythos. It's extrapolated by Farmer from information and hints provided in the original pulps by Lester Dent and the other Doc writers, but the idea is original to Farmer.

Farmer goes on to pen the story—his way—in 1991's authorized novel *Escape from Loki: Doc Savage's First Adventure*.

Meanwhile, I'm seeing more and more crossover stories featuring characters Farmer identified as Wold Newton Family members. Many of these are Sherlock Holmes crossovers. *Sherlock Holmes vs. Dracula* and *Dr. Jekyll and Mr. Holmes*, both by Loren D. Estleman, and *Ten Years Beyond Baker Street* by Cay Van Ash (Holmes and Fu Manchu) are but a few examples. I'm keeping a rudimentary list of these on a Commodore 64 (an outgrowth of a handwritten list), along with updates to Farmer's chronology, adding in the newly published comics.

I'll later decide that these 1980s DC comics just don't fit in, but right now, a Wold Newton Universe is being born.

IT'S 1996. I get on this thing called "the information superhighway" and finally manage to complete my run of Bantam Doc Savages with the double edition #114/#115: *Pirate Isle / The Speaking Stone*. I had acquired all but the one double book through years of scouring used bookstores in Colorado Springs and Denver.

I'm a completist, and this magical moment has been twenty-one years coming, although a part of me regrets not getting over the finish line the hard way.

I START the *Wold Newton Universe* website in 1997 and it takes off. I begin to hear from Farmer fans all over the U.S., and the world. I'm amazed that there are so many others like me, with similar experiences: finding the Doc and Tarzan biographies, being introduced to the amazing characters and literature described in the Wold Newton Family, and creating handwritten extensions of the family trees and chronologies.

I put online my chronology of crossovers which expands the Wold Newton Family into the Wold Newton Universe, and in short order I'm receiving speculative essays similar to Farmer's, with proposed expansions of trunks and branches of the Wold Newton Family Tree.

I soon discover that I've missed an aspect of fandom: Doc and Burroughs fanzines. Through the magic of the internet I'm introduced to two of those who have already published Wold Newton and Farmerian speculative essays in pulp fanzines: Rick Lai and Christopher Paul Carey, two men who are experts in pulp lore as well as Farmer and his works.

Lifelong friendships begin, all traceable to one little book.

SUMMER 2005. Thirty years after that magical summer cross-county trip in the back seat of a Pontiac Grand Prix.

In the midst of preparing my first book for publication (*Myths for the Modern Age: Philip José Farmer's Wold Newton Universe*), I get a spur-of-the-moment invitation to meet Farmer and his wife Bette in Peoria, IL., over the Fourth of July weekend. I drop everything and fly out. Not only will I get to meet the Farmers... I'm to stay overnight in a guest room. They wouldn't hear of me getting a motel room.

Mr. Farmer—Phil—and Bette are lovely people. I can't believe I'm relaxing at their home in Peoria, eating such unassuming Midwestern fare as fried chicken, ham sandwiches, and Bette's special Jell-O salad, and loving it.

My first evening there, I'm allowed into the basement to go through Phil's files, along with Michael Croteau. Mike is the webmaster of Phil's official website, and publisher of the newly-launched *Farmerphile: The Magazine of Philip José Farmer*.

I end up discovering the partial manuscript and complete outline for *The Evil in Pemberley House*—a Wold Newton novel about Doc's daughter taking place in the early 1970s.

Later that year, a dream comes true with the publication of *Myths*, collecting the best of the essays from the *Wold Newton Universe* site and elsewhere, presented alongside Phil's previously uncollected Wold Newton articles; the book is a 2007 *Locus* award nominee.

IN 2006, I finally make the long overdue pilgrimage to La Plata, MO., home of Lester Dent, along with other Doc and Farmer fans Mike Croteau, Chuck Loridans, Rick Lai, John Small, Dennis Power, and Art Sippo. We then make for Peoria for the first "Farmer-Con"—which later becomes an annual tradition.

I show Phil the Wold Newton Family Tree extensions I've drafted, based on the *Pemberley House* manuscript, and he's enthralled.

I'm thrilled.

AT 2007's FarmerCon, I express to Bette my desire to reissue Phil's *Doc Savage: His Apocalyptic Life* in 2008, and make a big splash to coincide with the 75th anniversary of the publication of the first Doc Savage novel. Unfortunately, plans for the book don't pan out. During this time I continue to write short stories, contribute to *Farmerphile* (eventually joining as coeditor later in the run), and write *Pemberley House*, sending bundles of chapters of the latter to Phil and Bette for their review and approval.

JULY 2009. Mike Croteau and I, and our families, make the pilgrimage to England and spend two weeks with our good friend Paul Spiteri and his family. The trip is peppered with Farmerian highlights: London (Sherlock Holmes, Sir Richard Francis Burton, and a special showing of the Wold Newton meteor at the Natural History Museum), Derbyshire (the location of "Pemberley House"), the Lake District (the village of Greystoke, in Cumbria), and of course, the village of Wold Newton, in Yorkshire (including staying at the Wold Cottage and sampling Wold Top Brewery's Falling Stone Bitter).

Phil never made it to visit Wold Newton, but as Paul and Mike and I gather around the brick obelisk erected in 1799 by Major Edward Topham in commemoration of the meteor which fell at the site on December 13, 1795, we can't help but feel that we've brought a part of Phil with us.

The Evil in Pemberley House is published in autumn, after the passing of both Phil and Bette earlier in the year.

Bittersweet.

IN 2011, Titan Books reissues Phil's classic Lord Greystoke-Sherlock Holmes crossover *The Adventure of the Peerless Peer* (as *The Peerless Peer*) as a part of the "Further Adventures of Sherlock Holmes" series, and I open discussions with them about bringing many of Phil's works back into print under a "Wold Newton" series banner. Time blurs by, with more short stories published, coediting three anthologies of Green Hornet tales for another publisher, assisting with Meteor House's *Worlds of Philip José Farmer* series (a logical outgrowth of *Farmerphile*), and coordinating and contributing bonus materials for the Titan Books reissues.

MIDWAY through a weeklong mountain vacation in the fall of 2012—finally having time to decompress—I jolt out of bed one morning and realize that Doc Savage's 80th anniversary is next year.

Matt Moring of Altus Press has dropped me a note or two in the prior months about reprinting *Doc Savage: His Apocalyptic Life*, but there hasn't been any movement (not through any lack of interest or initiative on Matt's or my part). But now, we're nine months out from next year's FarmerCon and reissuing the book is still a wisp of a dream. If we want this book out in time to celebrate both Doc and Phil with the appropriate fanfare, we'd better get moving.

I shoot off a detailed proposal to Mike Croteau and Paul Spiteri at Meteor House, and shortly thereafter we reach back out to Matt at Altus Press. The next nine months are a frenzy of activity.

IN the end, we came up with an unusual deal. Meteor House would publish a deluxe hardcover with bonus materials. Altus Press would bring out the trade softcover edition and eBook. The book would contain significant revisions, making the new 2013 reissue unique.

There are four prior English language editions of *Doc Savage: His Apocalyptic Life*: the 1973 Doubleday hardcover, 1975 Bantam paperback, 1975 Panther paperback (UK), and the 1981 Playboy Books paperback. The Meteor House/Altus Press edition is an amalgamation of the paperback editions.

Following are the revisions Phil made to the 1975 paperback editions (Bantam and Panther); these were carried forward in the 1981 Playboy Books edition.

• Some of the text in Chapter 2 was updated to reflect the forthcoming *Doc Savage: The Man of Bronze* feature film.

• Addendum 1: "The Fabulous Family Tree of Doc Savage (Another Excursion into Creative Mythography)" was revised, and Phil abandoned some of the genealogical theories he expressed in the 1973 edition. Specifically, he altered his prior theory that The Shadow, The Spider, and G-8 were all the same person. In his revised theory, The Shadow and G-8 were full brothers; both were half-brothers of The Spider.

The 1975 Panther edition (UK) was unique in that it contained an index. An index is included in the new Meteor House/Altus Press edition.

The 1981 Playboy Books edition added the recently-published *The Red Spider* (1979) to Addendum 3: "List of Doc Savage Stories"; however, the rest of the text, referring to the original supersagas, was not altered from 181 to 182. "181" has been maintained throughout the text of this edition, to refer to the 181 novels actually published during the pulp era.

Following are the revisions made to the 2013 Meteor House/Altus Press edition:

• The list of stories published to date by Bantam Books was updated in the 1981 edition. This has been eliminated completely, as Bantam completed reprinting the novels in 1990 with *Doc Savage Omnibus #13*.

• Research on the various Doc Savage authors has continued in the intervening forty years since the 1973 edition was published; the information which Phil originally presented in Addendum 3: "List of Doc Savage Stories" has been has been updated in the Meteor House/Altus Press edition; readers can also find the updated information in Will Murray's "The Secret Kenneth Robesons" in his collection *Writings in Bronze* (Altus Press, 2011).

• The genealogy in Addendum 1 has been updated with additional information discovered in Phil's files (known among the cognoscenti as "the Magic Filing Cabinet"); it was inexplicably left out of the genealogy as originally published (both the 1973 and 1975 versions).

• The authorized novels by Phil and Will Murray have been added to the Addendum 3: "List of Doc Savage Stories."

Finally, it should be noted that Phil was never happy with the chronology (Addendum 2). He writes at some length in the introduction to Addendum 2 about the travails involved in writing a workable and realistic chronology. And he says, in the essay "Writing Doc's Biography" (reproduced in the deluxe Meteor House edition), "I had a hell of a time with this," acknowledging that dedicated Savageologists would take issue with it, or with certain aspects of it.

When confronted with non-constructive criticisms by that "crabbed and cracked minority that always finds fault," it's worth remembering that Phil reworked the chronology at least twelve times, without the benefit of a word-processor, or access to online search engines that we take for granted in 2013. He worked from a complete set of pulps lent to him by his friend Jack Cordes; Phil's had been lost in a flood. It's a remarkable achievement.

Despite his own dissatisfaction with it, Phil's chronology is reproduced in the Meteor House/Altus Press edition for historical purposes. He suggested in Addendum 2 that a longer chronology, with detailed notes justifying the placement of each and every supersaga, would "… take at least twenty thousand words, and only the most zealous Savageologist would care to tackle an essay of that length." Rick Lai is that zealous Savageologist. His *The Revised Complete Chronology of Bronze* (Altus Press, 2010) honors Phil's chronology and its premises, while revising and expanding upon it.

Once again, Phil's biography has worked its magic, and rather than a mere twenty-thousand-word essay, a definitive book-length work has sprung from its loins.

IT'S my honor and pleasure to help birth this latest, and hopefully definitive, 40th anniversary edition of *Doc Savage: His Apocalyptic Life*. Phil was one of Doc's biggest fans, and he'd get a big kick out of the book being republished as a part of the celebrations for Doc's 80th anniversary.

Somewhere, I hope that Phil and Bette Farmer are smiling.

I miss them.

Phil was an unassuming man. I believe he had no idea the huge and lasting impact he had made on so many people.

As my friend and fellow Doc and Farmer fan, Chuck Loridans, has put it: "A bunch of little boys, all over the country finding the same book, changing their lives forever. *Magic!*"

Win Scott Eckert
Denver, Colorado
June 2013

Win Scott Eckert is the coauthor with Philip José Farmer of the Wold Newton novel The Evil in Pemberley House *(Subterranean Press, 2009), about Patricia Wildman, the daughter of pulp hero Doc Wildman, the bronze champion of justice. Pat Wildman's adventures continue in Eckert's sequel,* The Scarlet Jaguar *(Meteor House, 2013). His short fiction tales of The Green Hornet, Zorro, The Avenger, The Phantom, The Scarlet Pimpernel, Hareton Ironcastle, Captain Midnight, Doc Ardan, and Sherlock Holmes, can be found in the pages of various character-themed anthologies from Moonstone Books, as well as anthologies such as* The Worlds of Philip José Farmer *(Meteor House),* Tales of the Shadowmen *(Black Coat Press), and* Tales of the Wold Newton Universe *(Titan Books). His critically acclaimed, encyclopedic* Crossovers: A Secret Chronology of the World 1 & 2 *was released by Black Coat Press in 2010. His Wold Newton Origins short stories, "Is He in Hell?" and "The Wild Huntsman," can be found in the first and third volumes of* The Worlds of Philip José Farmer, *while his Honey West/T.H.E Cat crossover* A Girl and Her Cat *(coauthored with Matthew Baugh) is the first new Honey West novel in over 40 years. He holds a B.A. in Anthropology, a Juris Doctorate, and lives with his wife Lisa and a menagerie of three cats and two dogs near Denver, Colorado. Find him on the web at www.winscotteckert.com.*

1

THE FOURFOLD VISION

I COULD find out how the weather was on Friday, February 17, 1933, by checking an almanac. But it doesn't matter whether it was cloudy or snowing or clear and sunshiny. That day will always be bursting with a golden light. That is the day the first issue of the *Doc Savage* magazine hit the stands. That is the day I first saw *The Man of Bronze*, put down a dime (which I was lucky to have in that depth-of-Depression time), and walked out of Schmidt's drugstore quivering with anticipation. That day is indeed golden—much like the day the Reverend Charles Lutwidge Dodgson rowed up the Isis with three little girls and there composed for their pleasure a story about Alice and a white rabbit and a hole which led to earth's center. It was actually rainy that day, but Dodgson remembered it as "a golden afternoon."

That is the day I accompanied Doc and his five eccentric aides on the first of his 181 supersagas. It was a long journey, lasting until the summer of 1949. And it ended, sadly, where Alice's adventures began—in the earth's center.

I was twenty days past my fifteenth birthday when I first saw the bronze man with the strange golden eyes, in his torn shirt, clutching a little black idol, shadowed by three Mayan warriors peering from behind an ancient Mayan pillar.

I never knew Lester Dent, but thirty-nine years after I my first encounter with Doc Savage I met the widow of the man who had written most of the supersagas under the house name of Kenneth Robeson. Mrs. Lester Dent told me and my companion, Jack Cordes, that the Doc Savage stories had been written with the fifteen-year-old male in mind. It was presumed by the publishers that the majority of the readers (at first, anyway) would be near that age group. I chuckled and replied that Jack and I still loved Doc, so we obviously hadn't grown up yet.

This, in a sense, is true. There is a fifteen-year-old in my brain, and he loves Doc. There is also a seven-year-old who still loves Billy Whiskers, a nine-year-old who still loves Oz and the heroes of ancient Troy and Achaea, a ten-year-old who still loves John Carter of Mars, Tarzan, Rudolf Rassendyll, King Arthur, Og, Son of Fire, Umslopogaas and Galazi, the Ancient Mariner, Captain Nemo, Captain Gulliver, Tom Sawyer, Hiawatha, Jim Hawkins, and Sherlock Holmes.

"Smitty's" drugstore was half a block, if you cut down the alley, from the little old white house (it had once been a country school) at 609 Hanssler Place, Peoria, Illinois. Smitty's stood on Sheridan Road and Loucks Avenue, on a triangular, boat-shaped intersection. It was truly a vessel for me, one which I boarded for many a fabulous voyage down the Mississippi of a boy's mind. It was here that I came across my first science-fiction magazine, the glowing first issues of *Air Wonder* and *Science Wonder*, published by Hugo Gernsback and illustrated by Frank Paul.

The Gernsback magazines came out in 1929. In 1931, I first saw, amidst the odors of ice cream and chocolate sauce, the dark broad-brimmed slouch hat and the pale burning-eyed hawk face of the Shadow. And it was here that I dipped my line into the waters and brought up the fabulous *Argosy* magazine once a week. In those days, it featured short stories and serials about those heroes, Jimmy Cordie, Cohen the Fighting Yid, Singapore Sammy, Peter the Brazen and his archenemy, the Man with the Jade Brain, old Thibaut Corday and his fellow Foreign Legionnaire, Elephant Bill, the lawyer Gillian Hazeltine and his beautiful red-haired, green-eyed wife, the dark Norse witch, Lur, and her white wolf, and my greatest love, the Snake Mother. Those were golden days. At least, they had their golden moments, and these are what I've treasured up in my memory.

By the time I was fifteen and had met Doc, I had read the Revelations of St. John the Divine. Aside from Genesis and Jonah and parts of Job, I had read Revelations more times than any other book in the Bible. I had even had a number of terrifying dreams which sprang, in imagery, anyway, from Revelations. And I knew, of course, that Revelations was also called the Apocalypse. Webster's definition of this is "apocalypse, noun [Middle English, revelation, Revelation, from Late Latin *apocalypsis,* from Greek *apokalypsys,* from *apokalyptein,* to uncover, from *apo+kalyptein* to cover—more at HELL.] 1: one of the Jewish and Christian writings of 200 B.C. to A.D. 150 marked by pseudonymity, symbolic imagery, and the expectation of an imminent cosmic cataclysm in which God destroys the ruling powers of evil and raises the righteous to life in a messianic kingdom; *specifically, capitalized*; the biblical book of Revelation. 2: something viewed as a prophetic revelation."

Apocalypse is also used in a sense not quite that of 1. It is sometimes applied to writings, or paintings, in which great forces—supernatural or natural—are at work, usually evil work, and great things are occurring. Cities are toppling, the earth is opening vast mouths and swallowing up armies, huge and hideous monsters stride the world, the sun is turning black or expanding into a giant star, hordes of half-human, half-beast things are torturing naked people, the stars are dripping blood. In short, things on a vast scale are threatening the world.

And there is always the feeling—even in the non-biblical writings and paintings—of good and evil in earthshaking conflict. Hell has broken loose, and only an archangel, or a hero, or God Himself can defeat it. Nowadays, there is the feeling that the archangel or hero won't show; it's all over with the world. But in the earlier days of apocalyptic works, the savior would appear when needed.

At no time during my childhood and youth did I think of the Doc Savage stories as apocalyptic literature. In my young manhood and beginning of middle age, between 1949 and October 1964, I rarely thought of Doc Savage. Such childish things were behind me. I was reading Joyce, James (both Henry and William), Dostoyevsky, Balzac, Freud, Jung, Henry Miller (in smuggled editions at first), Shakespeare, Hooton, Cummings, Chaucer, Russell, Vaihinger, Wittgenstein, Camus, Sartre, Boswell, and the critics: Johnson, Wilson, and Fiedler. But the reprinting of the Doc Savage series by Bantam Books resurrected the buried fifteen-year-old. This was in 1964, when I was just beginning to turn back to the "classics" of my childhood and the poplit of my youth. And as the Bantams came out, starting with *The Man of Bronze,* I re-experienced the delights of my juvenile days. This nostalgic joy was tempered by a recognition of literary faults which I'd not noticed during the original readings.

However, by then I had gotten over my snobbishness. I knew that much of the "great" literature of the world had, along with the great virtues that made them classics, great flaws. Dostoyevsky, Dickens, Melville, and Twain are splendid examples of this. Examples in poetry are Shakespeare, Milton, and Blake.

The "ungreat" literature, the poplit (mystery, romance, adventure, gothic) was put down or ignored by most of the literary critics (and, hence, the intellectuals) on the grounds that they had no merit whatsoever. This is just not so, and perception of this has begun to filter into the academic community. The French were the first to realize it, just as they were the first to appreciate that Poe was more than a mere poplit writer. There are elements in poplit other than just entertainment. Perhaps the first to state this was Nietzsche, who said he'd learned more about the human psyche from the hack Dostoyevsky than from any psychologist then living. (Yes, Dostoyevsky was a hack, though Nietzsche did not use that pejorative. He wrote at great speed to meet deadlines, seldom re-wrote, was paid near-starvation wages, was popular with the masses, and appreciated only by a few critics.) It was Jung who pointed out that there was more to be learned about the archetypes and symbols of the unconscious from H. Rider Haggard than from any hundred of self-consciously psychological *artistes*. And Henry Miller seconds this.

Just so, there is much to be learned from the works of the poplit writers, past and present. And the reader, even the Ph.D., can enjoy himself, if he puts himself into the proper frame of approach. First, he has to be able to enjoy the art of telling a rattling good story. Second, on rereading, he has to be able to abstract the elements that make them psychologically valuable. This requires a somewhat schizophrenic mind, but most scholars have this. Third, he has to be able to fuse one and two if he is going to emerge with the pearl of great price from the depths.

Why is it that A. Conan Doyle and Edgar Rice Burroughs, mere romance-adventure writers, are so vastly read today, while hundreds of their contemporary colleagues, so lauded by the critics, have dropped into oblivion? Why is it that these two, along with Haggard, will continue to attract larger and larger audiences, while so many so highly praised today will be forgotten? What are the ingredients of their appeal? Why is it that Burroughs, for one, has had a larger readership, and far more influence on literature, than has Henry James, a hyperconscious "psychological" writer?

This latter statement will drive the literati far up the wall (where they should stay), but an objective study would confirm it. This judgment, by the way, comes from Robert Bloch, a mystery-horror writer, author of *Psycho*, and a keen literary critic. He is widely read, knows the classic psychologists well, but brings up his stories from his personal psyche, which has an umbilical attached firmly to the collective unconscious.

Whether my argument is valid or not, I am convinced that poplit, despite its massive flaws, is worth a serious study. About this time I became aware of the body of people, many of them distinguished in their widely varied professions, who were devoted to the study of Sherlock Holmes. And I came across the biographies of so-called fictional characters. These included the lives of Sir Percy Blakeney (*The Scarlet Pimpernel*), Mister Ephraim Tutt, Nero Wolfe, Sherlock Holmes, and perhaps Count Dracula. (I haven't got my hands on the latter yet.)

I began writing a "biography" of Lord Greystoke, or Tarzan, based on the premise that he is a living person. While I was doing this, the first of the biographies of Harry Flashman (the chief bully in *Tom Brown's Schooldays*) and *The Life and Times of Horatio Hornblower* came out.

After finishing *Tarzan Alive* (not my choice of title), I started on this, *Doc Savage: His Apocalyptic Life*. I borrowed all 181 magazine editions, having lost my Doc Savages during my many moves around the country. Beginning with the first, I read the entire series. Usually, I read one in two evenings, but when I got to the later and much shorter novels of 1945-49, I could read two in an evening. After I'd made this sweep, I reread each one more slowly, taking notes as I went along. The third time, I picked some here and there for a complete rereading. And while writing this book, I reread a score or so completely and a number partially.

This continuous traveling through a Savage land enabled me to see what I might otherwise have missed. The Savage supersagas are apocalyptic.

They shake with cosmic nightmares. And they have strange bedfellows. One is the early and primitive (in a Grandma Moses sense) space operas of Dr. E. E. Smith. His Lensman series is the best example of his work. Another is the series by William Burroughs: *The Nova Express* (my favorite), *The Naked Lunch, The Soft Machine,* and *The Ticket that Exploded.* The third is Henry Miller's *Tropic of Capricorn.*

William Blake, himself an apocalyptic poet, could have said of these, "I a fourfold vision see."

Smith, Dent, and Burroughs have only their apocalyptic visions and a science-fictional background in common. Miller is not a science-fictional author. He is, if anything, a combination of a verbal Dadaist, an anti-Noble Savage Rousseau, and an explicitly sexual St. Augustine. But his visions have suckled the same early-twentieth-century nipples as the others. They are, perhaps, the most awe-inspiring and certainly the most poetic. Smith and Dent steer wide of any explicitness about sex, though even the tabus of pulp-magazine fiction did not keep them from a few hints about the sexual. (The Lensman series ends in incest between the Gray Lensman's son and daughters.) Burroughs and Miller have not only their roots in sex but their pistils and blooms as well. Their sexual language is that of the masses—even if the masses are offended when they see it reproduced in the works of Henry Miller and William Burroughs.

Burroughs is a bridge, a sort of perverted Bifrost or Al Sirat, between Miller and the two science-fiction writers, Smith and Dent. Burroughs uses the cliché beings and gadgets of old-time science-fiction, and some modern pseudosciences, in his works. Though he is not technologically oriented in the same sense as are Smith and Dent, he is concerned with technology.

Miller, of course, wants nothing to do with Technopolis, the vast many-cubed city of machines and electricity, of automatons that run like men and men that run like automatons. He is its citizen, and he doesn't want to leave it for the country, but he ignores or curses technology and its sons: robots out of the womb by the piston or the TV set.

He shares with the others a male chauvinism, though he is able to portray three-dimensional females in *The Rosy Crucifixion.* (And Patricia Savage, after all the supersagas are read, emerges as complete, except for her sexual life, and this can be inferred from various intimations.)

Smith's epics are closest in spirit to Dent's. They are, however, in a space and time remote from here and now. Unlike the opera of the others, his mostly take place in the galactic depths, on planets of far-off stars, or in the fourth dimension. His visions are the most cosmic because they're not confined to this earth and this age. The howling winds of Aldebaran I push along the bloodthirsty Wheel-men, a sentient race with hub-heads and dozens of arms and hands radiating out like spokes. The personnel of an immense fort blow their minds on *thionite,* a psychedelic from the storm-ridden planet of Trenco. (This was published in 1939.) A superneedle-beam that slices a small planet in half. The hyperspatial tube which enables you to traverse light-centuries in seconds—if you survive. The super-evil Boskonians, using more than 200,000 such tubes to simultane-ously attack Arisia, populated by the most colossal minds that ever existed, and they're eons old. The world of Ploor and its sun going supernova when two planets, traveling fifteen times as fast as light, are hurled from Nth space by the devices of Kimball Kinnison and son. A mind-controlled spider disconnecting a villain's thought-screen so his mind can be read without his knowing it. The Hell Hole of Space. The Sunbeam, which uses an entire solar system as a vacuum tube and planets as its grids and plates. The Material Cosmic All, in which every inhabited world in all of space is to be conquered and enslaved by the Boskonians, as opposed to the Cosmic All of the ultragood Arisians. An inertia neutralizer, enabling spaceships (and even planets) to attain faster-than-light speeds instantly with no disturbance to the passengers.

These and many other mind-bogglers fill Smith's apocalypse. His visions, however, are too vast, too far-off, to concern us much here. And he is, of the four, the most borglumian. His characterizations do not even deserve this comparison; they are not sculptures but paper dolls. Still, he doesn't come off badly when compared to William Burroughs. Dent is the best of them in this respect, if a consideration of Miller is confined to *Tropic of Capricorn.* The reader, however, has to travel through all of the Savage stories before he sees the major characters as round and complex.

But this doesn't matter. An apocalyptic writer has no need to characterize people; he is out to characterize the universe. Or, if he stays on earth, the earth. And this is what Dent, Burroughs, and

Miller do, though the world of each differs considerably from the others.

Before we leave Smith, we should note certain similarities between his hero and Dent's. Doc Savage and Kimball Kinnison are both supermen whose goal is defeating evil. Kinnison is the result of centuries of human breeding, secretly controlled by the Arisians. Doc's superior genes are the result of accidental matings, but his ancestors, like Kinnison's, have inbred to some extent. Both have been trained from infancy for the conquest of vast evil forces.

Doc's hair is a dark bronze, and his eyes are light tawny with many striking golden flecks. Clarrissa MacDougall, the superwoman who marries Kinnison, has a peculiar shade of red-bronze hair and striking gold-flecked tawny eyes.

Kinnison and MacDougall first appeared in *The Galactic Patrol*, in the September through December (1937) issues and the January through February (1938) issues of *Astounding Stories* magazine. Doc first appeared in the March (1933) issue of Street and Smith's *Doc Savage* magazine. Doubtless, the similarities noted before are coincidental.

Doc's headquarters are on the eighty-sixth floor of the tallest and most impressive skyscraper in Manhattan (hence, in the world). His three rooms occupy the entire floor, an area almost as large as the city block which the base of the building nearly covers. Here are his small reception room, the much larger technical library, and the laboratory. The latter takes up two thirds of the floor space. From the windows of the eighty-sixth floor, Doc can see over fifty miles in any direction on a clear day. (Not much smog then.) Sometimes the clouds cling to his windows, and he can see nothing. Then, if he wishes, he can bring out his ultraviolet projector and his special "blacklight" goggles. With these, he can pierce the clouds.

Never mind whether or not he can see the city. He is master of all he surveys (though frequently challenged), and he surveys Technopolis often enough. He sees the greatest megacity in the world, laid out in orderly fashion, the trains and subways running on time, the machines pumping as regularly as a cheetah's heart, the machines' products issuing in orderly and satisfying numbers, the street traffic obeying the stop-and-go lights and cops' whistles, the electric lights everywhere turning off and on as bidden, all highly efficient.

Then—Chaos enters. Chaos and her sister Evil, or perhaps Evil is the big mother. And Doc and his aides, the Famous Five, are busy combating Chaos and Evil. And then Law and Order are restored. But only momentarily. After all, the universe is entropic, and everything is going downhill, and at the bottom of the hill is Hell. Down there, at the bottom of the hill, and often below its surface, Chaos and Evil are breeding.

Fortunately, Doc is independently wealthy—in fact, is the wealthiest individual in the world. So what goes on below doesn't bother him much except when Chaos and Evil come after him, and he has to leave his experiments in the Wizard's Den. Then the mountaintop sorcerer comes down. Bronze lightning strikes. The minions of Hell pick up the mangled body of their latest black witch and retreat into their holes. Sometimes they flee without the body. Doc has taken their leader on his trimotored magic carpet to his "college," where he disassociates them from their evil past and re-educates them. And they often go to work for him.

Still, no matter how often criminal disorder and sickness intrude, Technopolis maintains an outward unchanging regularity. The esthetics of civilized order keep the geometries straight, and from his stone-and-aluminum eyrie, the golden-eyed eagle sees beauty. For the time being, all's right with the world, and Doc Savage is on the eighty-sixth floor.

But one of the dwellers below, Henry Valentine Miller, sees Technopolis as "… the highest form of madness…" He cries, "… the scaffold of the city's mad logic is no support." And "The city grows like a cancer… it is an insatiable white louse which must eventually die of inanition…" He means "to die as a city in order to become again a man."

Doc has nothing of what he would call sick pessimism. If the world isn't right, he'll set it right. He stands on the running board of his limousine (or a taxi, or a stolen bakery truck) while his trollish assistant, Monk, drives, and the wind whips over his hair, which moves not, and his gold-flecked eyes miss nothing. The streets are cleared for him by NYPD's finest, because Doc has an honorary commission, and the cops respect and admire him. (In his early career, anyway.) Traffic gets out of the way, and the drivers and pedestrians gasp with wonder at this giant mental and physical marvel, the Man of Tomorrow.

The bronze knight of the running board is on another quest. Good men can breathe easier, and the knees of the evil men turn to water. Nor is Doc always so intent on the battle that he has no time to dispense philanthropy. Hot in pursuit, he halts to give an old blind woman a card which will get her into a hospital owned and run by Doc and an operation which will cure her. (Possibly the knife wielder will be Doc himself.) He gives a man down on his luck fifty bucks to tide him over while he is working on the job Doc will arrange for him with one of the several hundred factories, airlines, shipping lines, and trucking lines he owns. Bob Cratchit would have loved him, and Scrooge would have mended his ways sooner if Doc had been in the neighborhood. Fagin would have left town.

Henry Miller, the penniless Brooklynite, sees the city's night as "incalculably barren, cold, mechanical… in which there is no peace, no refuge, no intimacy… to be of a great city… is to become oneself… a world of dead stone… of the secret perfection of all that is minus…"

He talks of the "door which the body wears." Opened out onto the world, it can lead to nothing but annihilation. Opened inward, it reveals an infinity of trapdoors. And there are no horizons, no airlines, rivers, maps, or tickets in his world.

Doc Savage, of course, seldom opens the inward door for us, and he travels always with a map unreeling from a photographic memory. If there is no map, he makes one.

Miller goes from restaurant to movie to tavern to dancehall to beach, but all these places are "like abortive explorations of a myth."

Doc generates full-grown myths wherever he is. He is, literally and figuratively, the Hero with a Thousand Faces.

Miller—and most of his fellow dwellers on the pavemented surface—cannot take root. The moment they think they have, the earth shudders, prelude to a dissolving of the universe, the stars float loosely, the self implodes, and Miller, along with Dante, is sitting at the lowest level of Hell. It is "a dead center from which time itself is reckoned."

Doc, as we'll see, began his career with certainty, with a self that is neither implosive nor explosive but rigidly contained in the magnetic field of his unique education. But we get glimpses of a loneliness which must have equaled, or surpassed, Miller's or that of any other citizen of Technopolis.

However, Doc has the Great American Formula: Keep Moving. Motion, busyness, whether purposeful and productive or not, enables the self to avoid the self. And so Doc is busy in the laboratory or studying or lecturing or, mainly, in furious battle with the supervillain. But his actions are always productive. He, at least, doesn't move just for the sake of motion.

There was little time for Doc to consider Miller's question of "on what the tortoise stood." Just as well. Miller says a study of this problem only results in madness.

Doc would doubtless have thought Miller contemptible, a potential candidate for his "crime college." He would have abominated Miller's shiftlessness, parasitism, callousness, and his incessant keenness for quim. But he would have agreed, in part, with Miller's apocalyptic observation: "The whole country is lawless, violent, explosive, demoniacal. It's in the air, in the climate, in the ultragrandiose landscape, in the stone forests that are lying horizontal... in the over-lush crops, the monstrous fruits, the mixture of quixotic bloods, the fatras of cults, sects, beliefs, the opposition of laws and languages... the continent is full of buried violence, of the bones of the antediluvian monsters and of lost races of man, of mysteries which are wrapped in doom... America is pacifistic and cannibalistic... Superficially, it looks like a bold, masculine world; actually it's a whorehouse run by women... Nobody knows what it is to sit on his ass and be content. That happens only in films where everything is faked, even the fires of hell. The whole continent is asleep and in that sleep a grand nightmare is taking place."

True in 1939, and many would say that that is still true in 1975.

Doc, though agreeing with much of this, would have rejected its pessimism and its whorehouse theory. The human brain at birth has the potentiality for good or evil; usually, the adult psyche is permeated with both, but the largest content is good. And as long as babies are being born, we have hope. He also knew that whorehouses are owned by men; the America of his time was patrifocal.

Doc lived in the Olympus of the skyscraper, while below the Depression did its work. When he went down into the streets, he was able to act forthrightly and vigorously to solve his problems. If he had to act outside the law to do it, and he generally did, he got away with it.

But the people of Miller's world, the poor, the underprivileged, the sick, the demented, the perverted, the persecuted, came to Henry Miller looking for salvation. Henry, the poor man's savior, was personnel manager of the Cosmodemonic Telegraph Company of North America. His stories of the woes of the unfortunates who crowded daily into his office are a minor apocalypse. And, no doubt, the would-be employees sometimes looked up at Doc's skyscraper and thought of pulling it down and the wealthy in it. Doc must have had a controlling interest in Cosmodemonic, since he seems to have had huge blocks of shares in companies all over the world. Doc would have been appalled if he had known what was going on in Cosmodemonic, but it's doubtful if even he could have straightened out that mess.

Miller must have been thinking of Doc's skyscraper and perhaps of the frequent dashes Doc and his pals made around the globe in their battles against evil when he wrote, "From Apis"—the great bull-father god—"sprang the race of unicorns, that ridiculous beast of ancient writ whose learned brow lengthened into a gleaming phallus and from the unicorn by gradual stages was derived the late-city man of which Oswald Spengler speaks." And Miller says that from the dead phallus "of this sad specimen arose the giant skyscraper with its express elevators and observation towers."

Certainly, the latter phrase is a description of the building which housed Doc's superspeed express elevator and on top of which was a dirigible mooring mast-observation tower.

Miller then says, "Now for the aluminum wings with which to fly to that far-off place, the bright country where Apis, the father of fornication, lives."

Substitute "supervillain" for "Apis," and you have a description which fits Doc's flights across earth to tangle with the great fathers of crime.

Time and time again, in the Savage stories, a cataclysmic weapon is turned on New York City by a supervillain. The city panics, and thousands flee while more thousands cower in their homes. Dent shows us only the exterior of public alarm, the newspaper headlines and the jammed bridges and tunnels out of Manhattan. Miller shows us the city suddenly caught in a Vesuvian eruption, the deadly gases rolling in, the lava covering everything. And everybody, including the great financier J. P. Morganana, is caught literally and figuratively with his pants down. Though the derivation of the name of the financier is obvious, Miller may also have had Doc in mind when he described "J. P. Morganana sitting on the toilet bowl" when trapped by the volcanic gas.

Which leads us to the next apocalyptic, William S. Burroughs. He, like Miller, also deals out many hands onto the auctorial poker table. But whereas Miller's sexual interest is in women only, Burroughs is compulsively interested in sodomy. The main themes in all of his books are male homosexuality, drug addiction, and a cosmic paranoia. Like E. E. Smith, he describes many kinds of extraterrestrial creatures. But since Burroughs' stories are confined to this planet, he can be put into the same category as Miller and Dent.

He presents us with a series of horrifying images, all the more horrifying because the style is disjointed, broken, as if the mind of the narrator is in the tertiary stage of syphilis, corroded with heroin, or ridden by delirium tremens. Or as if he had blacklight goggles enabling him to see past the stable appearance of things into the blooming buzzing confusion at the subatomic level. Ignoring the language and the style, his stories do have certain similarities to Dent's. There are the super-villains, the extraterrestrial invaders, the Nova Mob. And there is the Nova Heat—who could be Doc and his aides. The visions are scary; even listing the themes can have a spooking effect.

The Cancer Deal with the Venusians. The Orgasm Death. The Nova Ovens. The Reality Studio. "To live is to collaborate." The Intolerable Kid. A Rumble in the Crab Galaxy. Another Twilight of Your Tired Gods. "… that black nova laugh." The Venusian Gook Rot. The Caustic Enzymes of Woo. A Monster Crab with Hot Claws at Your Window. The Thing Police. K9 in Combat with the Alien Mind Screen. Magnetic Claws Feeling for Virus Punch Cards. Staked out under the White Hot Skies of Minraud Eaten Alive by Metal Ants. "Blast-Pound-Strafe-Stab-Rill." Mayan Codices and Egyptian Hieroglyphs. "This, Gentlemen, is the Death Dwarf." "I'll Cook You Down to Decorticated Canine Preparations." All the Pain and Hate Images Come Loose. His Metal Face Moved in a Slow Smile as He Heard the Twittering Supersonic Threats Through Antennae Embedded in His Translucent Skull.

Comes on Honest and Straight, and the smart operators all think they are conning him. How could they think otherwise until he slips on the antibiotic handcuffs.

The Nova Mob slide in and out of human bodies, control their hosts, suck the delight of life itself out of them, make them do all sorts of hideous things. It's as if Dent's supervillains had anticipated Burroughs' Life Form A invading a series of Life Form B.

The Nova Police move in on the Nova Mob, and the parasites leave their dead hosts behind as they flee. They have wild names, as wild as those of Dent's villains. Hamburger Mary, Uranian Willy the Heavy Metal Kid, the Brown Artist, the Subliminal Kid, the Green Octopus, Iron Claws.

The Nova Fuzz slip on the antibiotic cuffs and haul Willy's heavy metal ass off to the rehabilitation center. (Reminiscent of Doc's crime college.)

Neither the work of the Nova Fuzz nor Doc is ever finished. The supply of hosts and parasites is endless.

And the judge in the Biologic Courts? Isn't he Doc? "The judge, many light years away from the possibility of corruption..."

Lester Dent's nightmares reel through scenes of cataclysm, terror, and carnage.

The skyscraper, groaning, leans, and blocks of masonry leave it to sail across Manhattan. The dirigible mooring mast on top of it falls off while the citizens run screaming into the streets.

Large ribbons of flame crash across the heavens.

These are tied in with the man kidnaped in San Francisco and found dead in New York City three hours later. (This was in 1939, when air travel was much slower.)

The world is faced with the possibility of the dead being brought back to life, and an ancient Egyptian Pharaoh is loose on the streets.

A terrible weapon turns men into smoke. No man is safe.

A substance buried for eons in the earth's bowels is being released by a volcanic eruption. Anything in its vicinity not tightly attached to the earth is hurled high into the skies. A two-ton palm tree sails through the night. Coconuts rain.

An island blows up and sinks, taking with it the last of the dinosaurs.

Mile-long tongues of flame leap into the skies.

In New York City, anyone who tries violence on another dies mysteriously, his eyes popping out. A mass evacuation seems imminent. Who dares to be angry?

Snowflakes the color of blood materialize and fall hissing on people, and these become dust.

Deep in earth, an ore turns its miners into walking lightning streaks. The earth opens up and swallows a glass factory.

Battleships are picked up and hurled far by some sinister force.

Giant invisible amoebae threaten the greatest of cities with their paralyzing stings.

A statue of a man a mile long lies on its back in the jungle. Panther tracks, the toes larger than washtubs, are seen in jungle mud.

People turn into blue clouds. All radio transmission, the world over, is turned off by an unknown genius. All powered vehicles are stopped by a push of a button. Crimson snow burns on Mount Shasta.

The Gulf Stream will be diverted, and Europe will freeze.

All over the city, men are turning into automatons. (This sounds like Miller's description of the night denizens of New York City.)

The Inca in Gray scatters his deadly Dust of Death.

Huge holes are ripped in earth's crust. The bodies of weird men float in the air while a strange melody plays.

A dying green man gasps that he's been a prisoner on the moon.

A dagger two hundred feet high hangs in the heavens.

A monstrous spider stalks through a valley during thunderstorms.

"A rose-red city, half as old as time," rears out of the Arabian wastelands.

Deep in the earth beneath Maine are strange beings, looking exactly like *Homo sapiens*, but they have frightening psychic powers. Either they are extraterrestrials or they are the demons of Hell itself. The first encounter between Doc and devils is a draw. But other conflicts are inevitable, with the odds heavily in favor of the "devils." Doc has met and defeated the greatest of the human hosts of evil. Now he is faced with the origin of evil itself.

And there the tales end.

2

LESTER DENT, THE REVELATOR FROM MISSOURI

LESTER DENT was born 12 October 1904 in La Plata, a small village in northeastern Missouri. He was the only child of Bernard Dent, a farmer and rancher, and Alice Norfolk, a school-teacher before her marriage. His paternal grandparents came from Lancaster, Ohio, in 1858. Though Lester's birthplace was in the Show Me state, his parents had been living for some years in Wyoming. Mrs. Dent had returned to La Plata to stay with her parents during the birth.

At the age of two, Lester went with his parents to Wyoming. Part of the trip in Wyoming was in a covered wagon, which took weeks to travel through country that a car can pass through in two hours. The elder Dent ran a ranch near Pumpkin Buttes.

Lester attended a country grade school and paid for his tuition by trapping animals and selling their furs. He had few companions and so was more often by himself than not. Mrs. Dent thinks that it was isolation and loneliness which drove him to make up fantasy companions and the adventures in which he and his imaginary pals were heroes.

Whether the ranch failed or the parents just got tired of the emptiness of Pumpkin Buttes is not known. About the time Lester was in eighth grade, the family moved back to La Plata, where his father dairy-farmed. Here Lester completed the eighth grade in a little white schoolhouse near the farm. (Today the building is visible from U. S. Route 63, about twelve miles south of Kirksville, but it has been converted into a farm storehouse.)

In 1923, Lester Dent went to Chillicothe, Missouri, to attend business college. He had meant to be a banker, but while waiting in line to apply at the college, he got to talking to another applicant. Dent was informed that, as a bank clerk, he would make a starting wage of fifteen dollars a week. A graduate of the telegraphy course, however, would begin at thirty-five dollars a week. That was enough for Dent, who switched his goals then and there.

After finishing his courses, Dent taught at Chillicothe Business College. In the fall of 1924, he went to work as a telegrapher for Western Union in Carrollton, Missouri. (The Cosmodemonic Telegraph Company is Henry Miller's name for Western Union in *Tropic of Capricorn*. Dent, however, did not have Miller's Hieronymus Bosch-like experiences with Western Union. But, then, Dent did not work for Western Union in Depression New York City, nor was he a personnel manager.)

In May 1925, Dent became a telegrapher for Empire Oil and Gas Company in Ponca City, Oklahoma. Here he married Norma Gerling, the daughter of Louis Gerling and Dora Weber, on 9 August 1925. They went that day to a movie, the title of which Mrs. Dent does not remember. She will, however, never forget that Lester was so flustered that he tried to give their tickets to a wooden Indian in the lobby.

The Dents moved to Chickasha, Oklahoma, in 1926. Here he was first a telegrapher for the Associated Press and then a teletype operator. Later, he worked for the Associated Press in Tulsa, Oklahoma.

One of his co-workers sold a story to a magazine for four hundred and fifty dollars, big money in those days and not so bad today. This intrigued Dent, who read a number of blood-and-thunder pulp magazines and thought he could do as well and probably better. While on the unbusy night shift, he wrote a number of stories. The first to sell was a novel for which *Top Notch* magazine paid two hundred and fifty dollars. Titled *Pirate Cay*, it came out in the first of the two September 1929 issues, on sale 1 August. He was startled shortly thereafter by a telegram from Dell Publishing Company in New York. It offered to pay his passage to New York and give him a five-hundred-dollar-a-month drawing account if he would write exclusively for Dell.

After recovering from his astonishment, Dent asked a friend in New York to check up on Dell. Was its owner, and perhaps its editor, insane?

On finding that both seemed to be as mentally balanced as any Gothamite could be, Dent got a leave of absence from AP. He and Mrs. Dent arrived in New York City on 1 January 1931, one of the coldest and bleakest days in Mrs. Dent's memory. Things soon became rosier, however. Dent quickly taught himself the craft and discipline of turning in a required number of words in a certain format on schedule. He did not remain Dell's exclusive property for long. He was soon writing for a number of pulp-magazine chains. This genre was demanding and tiring for writers, and only the sturdiest could survive in it. Dent had energy, and he ensured that the reservoir of his fertile and vivid imagination would not dry up from lack of pumping. He read omnivorously, from poetry to the literature of the latest advances in technology and science. He was not content to get all his knowledge from books. He got a first-class radio operator's license and would, years later, build his own powerful ham radio set. He passed the rigid electricians' and plumbers' examinations. He got a pilot's license and flew his own plane. Instead of just reading about climbing mountains, he climbed them.

His inflamed inventiveness, his expertise at pulp plotting and characterization, and his technical knowledge brought him to the attention of all the pulp-magazine publishers. Among these was Henry Ralston, a business executive of Street and Smith. Ralston had hired Walter Gibson in 1931 to write *The Shadow* stories. The success of this encouraged Ralston to hire Dent in 1932 to write a new series, the *Doc Savage* magazine.

Ralston was at that time credited with having invented the characters of the Shadow and Doc Savage. Now, however, we know differently. Ralston was an influential man with many sources of information for making good contacts. He got permission from the man who was the real Shadow to publish his exploits in fictionalized form.

Ralston struck another coup by getting permission from "Doc Savage" to publish stories based on his adventures. Ralston approached Dent on the project. Since Doc was the greatest gadgeteer of all times, and Dent had many qualities Doc possessed, and so could empathize with him, Dent eagerly accepted. Dent was himself the greatest gimmick writer in the field, according to Frank Gruber in his *The Pulp Jungle*. What better choice than a man who knew gadgets?

In fact, Dent wrote a string of novelettes for the Street and Smith *Crime Busters* magazine which were known as The Gadget Man Series. The first appeared in the November 1937 issue and was so well received that he continued the adventures of his gimmick-minded hero for three years.

According to Mrs. Dent, Lester did not like the name picked for the hero of the new series. He thought he had a much better name, which, unfortunately, Mrs. Dent can't recall. It doesn't matter now. Doc's name has been so hallowed by long usage that anything else is unthinkable.

Dent also wanted to write under his own name, not the house name of "Kenneth Robeson." He felt that he could do much better if his own name were on the masthead. As usual, however, the executives and the editors had their own way. But Dent did get at least some revenge years later. Somebody goofed, and the March 1944 issue contained *The Derelict of Skull Shoal* by, not Robeson, but Lester Dent. This caused some consternation and not a little hell among the editorial staff, and the error never again occurred.

In the beginning, Dent got $500 for each Doc Savage story. Later, this was increased to $750. These were, in the early years, about 65,000 to 70,000 words long. Often, he'd write two a month, which meant he was putting out 130,000 to 140,000 words a month, two complete novels, and getting $1,500 a month. This was $18,000 a year in the Depression, when eggs were ten cents a dozen. Moreover, Dent was augmenting this amount by writing at the same time and at a comparable rate for other magazines. There were times when Dent, writing under pseudonyms, could, and did, fill an issue of a magazine with his own stories. These often required eight or nine stories.

At times, he would write eighteen hours a day, day after day. Dent, being human, even if a pulp writer, had to stop to eat and go to the toilet. When this happened, he used a trick to make sure he'd continue with the same thought with which he had quit. He would stop in the middle of a sentence.

His usual hours, however, were from 9 P.M. to 3 A.M. He would then sleep until 10:30 A.M. He ate only two meals a day.

His favorite drink was milk, of which he could drink a quart at a sitting. Hard liquor was no problem for him, as it is for many writers. When he did drink, he preferred Irish whiskey. He did not know much of music and seems to have been tone deaf. The only tune he could carry at all was "The Whistler and His Dog." His parents had a gramophone but only one record, which accounts for his ability to half-master that one song.

The *Doc Savage* magazine, like *The Shadow* magazine, was a great success. Six months after the first issue, it had a multitude of imitators on the market. All were short-lived.

There was good reason for Doc's popularity, aside from a writer who seemed born for the job. The Depression had put almost everybody down and millions out. But the man who picked up a *Doc Savage* could become for an hour or so the wealthiest man in the world. Doc had a never-failing supply of gold from a lost valley in Central America. (Heroes often seemed to have a secret source of precious metal and jewels which enabled them to live well without working. Tarzan, the Shadow, and Richard Benson, the Avenger, are three examples.) The average citizen, a miserable creature in those days, was feeling frustrated, anxiety-ridden, and diminished in manhood and womanhood. But for ten cents he/she could be a superman/woman in both brain and body. The average man felt that vast evil forces beyond his control were responsible for his plight. And he was suffering, while the criminals were certainly prospering. In Doc he had a hero who battled the insidious forces of evil. And who won. Moreover, Doc could take his reader away from his grim world into the most exotic of places around the world.

Ralston himself is said to have stated that Doc was four great people all rolled into one. He had Sherlock Holmes's marvelous deductive genius, Tarzan's perfect physique and herculean strength, Craig Kennedy's knowledge of science, and Abraham Lincoln's messianic qualities.

Despite the incessant requests for his stories from editors, Dent and his wife managed vacations. In 1933, on the very day that Franklin Delano Roosevelt closed all the banks in the country, the Dents left on a cruise to the West Indies and South America. They took a trip to England and Europe, along with Dent's secretary, in 1938. In Prague, Czechoslovakia, Dent was questioned by the Nazis for taking unauthorized photographs.

Dent purchased a two-masted, forty-foot schooner, the *Albatross*, and he and his wife lived in this for several years. They sailed up and down the Atlantic coast of Florida and through the Caribbean islands, wintering in Florida. Dent became an expert deep-sea fisher and swimmer, and he also did some serious treasure hunting in the Bahamas. All that time, however, he was pounding away at his typewriter, turning out many stories.

Tiring of the ship, Dent sold it in 1940. He felt that he had mastered sailing and had learned all he could about treasure hunting and the West Indian and Caribbean seas. So he wanted no more to do with them. His nature was to learn a subject thoroughly and then drop it.

After the ship fever was over, Dent went to Death Valley to prospect for gold. He found little but he did learn much about the desert. He also met and visited with Death Valley Scotty.

His travels and search for gold earned him a membership in the Explorers Club, of which two distinguished members were Admiral Byrd and Doc Savage.

The same year that he sold his ship, he decided that he would "retire" to La Plata. Perhaps he had squeezed New York dry, too, and now wanted to re-establish his roots in his native soil. His retirement meant no slackening of work, however. He continued to turn out fiction, though he took more time at it. In between writing stints, he designed his new house and supervised its construction to make sure that it was done properly.

The Dent's home was widely known then as the House of Gadgets because of the many devices he installed in it. These have become standard now, but in 1940 they were ten or more years ahead of their time.

As a prognosticator, Dent's record beat that of Jules Verne. The list of gadgets that first appeared in print in the Doc Savage stories and only came into existence years later is a long one. Doc used radar, for instance, in 1934, though this was something the electronic scientists were then only messing around with in the laboratory. Ten years before they were actually used in the U. S. Navy, Dent had put shark repellent and sea trace (colored dye to mark the location of pilots downed at sea) into his stories. Dent wrote of nerve gas, supersonic dog whistles, anesthetic gas grenades, and ultraviolet "black light" photography before the general public, and many scientists, knew of their potential existence. Twelve years before wire recordings were offered to the public, Doc was using them.

In 1935, Dent designed a magnetic treasure-hunting device. He hired a man in Miami, Florida, to build it for him. Some years later, the U. S. Army developed a mine detector from the data provided by the same Miamian.

Dent also went in, successfully, for dairy farming, was a partner in an aerial photography business, lectured, and spent much time on community projects. He especially enjoyed working with youths and was a Boy Scout leader. His lecture tours made a profit which he donated for lunches and spectacles for grade-school children. He had been a member of the New York chapter of the American Fiction Guild. In 1946 he received from the Missouri Writers Guild the award for the most successful Missouri writer of that year.

Although he was very busy at other activities than writing, he worked at polishing his style, plots, and characterizations. The early Savages are splendid examples of pulp writing in all its potential spectrum. They have a great but loose epic sweep. They are shot through with red for blood, white with the purity of the heroes' motives, black with the vileness of the villains' motives, green with comedy, blue with terror, and purple with science-fictional-adventure apocalypticism. The characters are mainly caricatures, not people. Yet, there is a certain thread of realism throughout, yellow and hot as sunlight.

The quality of prose and realism in the early Savage novels do vary, sometimes widely. Generally, they are at a high level for the pulps. Some, such as the ridiculous and badly written *The Yellow Cloud*, read as if plotted and typed in one day and sent out by midnight messenger directly to a drunken printer with literary aspirations.

Jim Harmon, author of *The Great Radio Heroes* and *The Great Radio Comedians* and a Savage fan, thinks that much of the renaissance of Doc in the Bantam editions is due to their very badness. They are considered camp by the young. He reports seeing young people at airports laugh uproariously while reading them. Since he did not question them as to why they were laughing, he could be wrong. They might have been amused at the clowns, Doc's aides, Ham and Monk, or at Doc's chasteness. Admittedly, there is much corn among the gold in the early epics. But if the youths and Jim

Harmon were to read the Savages from 1941 on, they would have little cause for ridicule. These became progressively shorter, more tightly plotted, more sharply characterized, and began to explore the psychology of the main characters. The dialogue became more realistic, and the style was enormously improved. The villains were still not run-of-the-mill, but they were not the supervillains of old. Doc seems to have cleaned out most of that breed before World War II, though he is engaged in combating the minions of those Luciferians, Tojo and Hitler.

With the gain of better writing and more realism, however, purple romance and gusto are lost. We are not reading epics; we are reading mystery stories. In fact, for five issues, from late 1947 to mid 1948, the magazine is renamed *Doc Savage, Science Detective*. Doc is only half a superman, more Dr. Thorndykish or Craig Kennedyish than the Man of Bronze. Beginning with the 1945 issues (if not before), the mature reader of spy-detective-mystery stories can read with satisfaction almost all of the stories.

Dent did his most "literary" work in the mystery and Western fields. Some of his mystery novels were published by the Doubleday Crime Club. One of his mysteries attracted the attention of the F.B.I. One of its agents came to Dent and requested that he please make the ransom notes in his stories less realistic. A Kansas City kidnapper had clipped one out of a magazine and mailed it in unchanged.

He was also an excellent Western writer. The last new story of his to be published was of this genre. This was *Savage Challenge* in the *Saturday Evening Post* of 22 February 1958. The story is about the conflict between a group of pioneers in a wagon train and a band of Indians. The problem is solved by a frontiersman who knows the ways of the Indians and uses humor, not violence, to settle the issue. Both the whites and Amerinds are depicted as real human beings, not stereotypes.

Another Western, *River Crossing*, appeared in *Collier's* magazine and was later adapted for an episode in the *Wagon Train* TV series.

Both *Savage Challenge* and *River Crossing* demonstrate that Lester Dent was more than "just a pulp writer." When he finally got the time to polish his tales, he became a writer who may have developed a stature equal to that of Raymond Chandler or J. G. Guthrie.

In February 1959, Lester Dent had a heart attack. Though hospitalized for three weeks, he continued to write. Then the Ender of Tales, on 11 March, wrote *The End*.

He was buried in the family plot at La Plata cemetery.

The citizens of La Plata are considering putting up a sign on the main highway: THIS IS DOC SAVAGE LAND.

Moviegoers will have their first chance to view Doc Savage and gang in action in the summer of 1975. George Pal, producer of those visual epics, *Destination Moon, War of the Worlds, The Time Machine,* et al., has filmed DOC SAVAGE... The Man of Bronze. This is based on the first Savage novel, *The Man of Bronze*, and parts of it were filmed in Central America, the location of the latter part of the supersaga.

Pal, after an intensive search for physical counterparts of Doc and his aides, chose Ron Ely as Doc (Ely was the Tarzan of the TV series); Michael Miller as Monk Mayfair; Darrell Zwerling as Ham Brooks; Eldon Quick as Johnny Littlejohn; Paul Gleason as Long Tom Roberts; William Lucking as Renny Renwick. Pamela Hensley, a model who has been a cover girl for *Harper's, Vogue, Paris Match* et al., plays the romantic female lead. The director is Michael Anderson, and the writer is Joe Morhaim.

The movie was originally scheduled for the spring of 1974, but, as Pal reported to me, "We made it too good." Warner regards it as one of its major pictures, and so it has rescheduled it for the summer of 1975. A world premiere, however, will be held over the Easter holidays in 1975.

3

SON OF STORM AND
CHILD OF DESTINY

MONK MAYFAIR and Ham Brooks, two of Doc's aides, are on the American passenger liner *Virginia Dare*. Loaded with World War II refugees, it is on its way from Portugal to New York. The night is cloudless; the sea, smooth. Ham and Monk are the first to see the strange star. It's black but outlined by a blood-red light and is five-pointed like a Christmas-tree star. Directly under it, an area of the ocean is lit with a steady fiery brilliance. In the center of this luminosity floats the golden man.

The Golden Man (April 1941) starts with this weird episode and becomes more and more mysterious. The golden man himself, picked up naked and unconcerned in the middle of the ocean, knows things about the passengers which he should not know. About himself he knows almost nothing. He has no name as yet and doesn't need one. His mother, he says, is the sea, and his father is the night.

He predicts that the *Virginia Dare* will sink at eleven. It does sink, though seven minutes after eleven.

When he finally meets Doc in New York, he says, "Since that stormy night you were born on the tiny schooner *Orion* in the shallow cove at the north end of Andros Island, you have done much good and many things that were great."

For one of the few times in his life, Doc is flabbergasted. As far as he is aware, he's the only one in the world who knows where he was born. His birth has never been recorded, and everyone aboard the *Orion* is now dead. His father, Hubert Robertson, and Ned Land were the only other survivors of the wreck of the *Orion*, which occurred when Doc was less than a year old. They would not have talked.

This deepens an already deep mystery, which Dent never explains. Why wasn't this birth registered in the ship's log? The answer must be that Doc's father had good reason to leave it unrecorded. And even if he had entered it, the log was lost when the schooner sank.

Dent never says exactly when Doc's mother died, but we know from a number of supersagas that she died shortly after his birth, though his exceptional memory has retained vague impressions of her. It's reasonable to suppose that she drowned when the *Orion* was driven onto a reef.

What prevented Doc's father from registering the birth again? The answer is that he did so but at a later time and with faked data. Both of Doc's parents were British citizens, and Doc was born in British waters. The baby was, therefore, also a British citizen. The elder Savages, however, would have been using faked papers at this time. Doc was, according to all official records, a native-born American. When Doc thinks that no record of his birth exists, he is thinking of his birth on the *Orion*.

The Golden Man, like most of the supersagas, has a rational explanation of its mysteries. What concerns us here is that the golden man was head of the intelligence section of an unnamed country. The evidence is that this country was Germany, not as yet at war with the U.S. He states that his department had a complete dossier on Doc and his men. Doc was wrong in thinking no record of his true birthplace existed. How the German intelligence got their information is not disclosed.

Doc's father named the schooner *Orion*. It was an appropriate name for the birthsite of the future Man of Bronze. Orion is the most striking and the brightest of the constellations (to the naked eye). It is represented on some astronomical charts as a giant who carries a shield or a lion's skin on his left shoulder and a sword in his belt. In ancient Greek mythology, Orion was a great hunter. The Egyptians of the Fifth Dynasty called the constellation Sahu, the hunter of gods and men. One of the ancient Hebrew names for Orion was Gibbor, the Giant. In some Greek versions, he is the son of Poseidon, the greatest of the sea deities. He is large enough to walk through the deepest waters, and he originates the tides in the Aegean Sea.

Doc's father was thinking of the role he had planned for his son when he christened the ship. Orion—the hunter, the walker in deep waters. Doc was to be a great tracker of evil men and was to walk in very deep, very dangerous waters, both in his exploits against crime and in his scientific devices and inventions.

Fortunately for the plans of the elder Savage, Doc was not a girl. And if he had been puny or had just decided not to go along with his father's project, he would have nullified everything. But he wasn't puny in mind or body. In fact, as Doc's aides said, even if he had not had this special training, he would have been great. His father must have banked on the chances of his being exceptional because of his heredity. He had many extraordinary ancestors and relatives; his family ran to both brains and brawn, as will be shown.

But first, why did the elder Savage have to fake his identification papers? And why did he shape his son into a superman nemesis of evil?

As I've demonstrated elsewhere,* Doc's father was a fugitive from English justice. The details of the events leading up to his flight are to be found in an almost entirely true story by a Dr. John H. Watson (issued under his agent's name, A. Conan Doyle): *The Adventure of the Priory School.* Watson and Sherlock Holmes are called into this case by a Dr. T. Huxtable. He is the author of two books now considered collector's items: *Huxtable's Sidelights on Horace* and *Sidepaths of the Midlands.*** However, he becomes Holmes's client, not as an author but as owner and supervisor of his exclusive boys' educational institution, the Priory School. He is only a temporary client because he is actually bringing Holmes into the case without authorization. His pupil, the only son of the sixth duke of Holdernesse, has disappeared from the school. When Holmes and Watson meet the duke, they find him angry because the duke did not want a private investigator. With the duke is his secretary, a young man whom Watson calls James Wilder. During the investigation, Heidegger, the German teacher of Arthur, the duke's son, is found murdered.

Holmes solves the mystery. Wilder is the instigator of young Arthur's kidnaping. Wilder is also revealed as the illegitimate son of

---

*   *Addendum 2 of* Tarzan Alive *(Doubleday, 1972).*

**   *See the Bibliography of* Tarzan Alive *for the latter.*

the duke. His mother, greatly beloved by his father, had died when he was very young. His father has raised him in Holdernesse Hall and given him "the best of educations." The duchess is so incensed by this that she has separated from the duke. James Wilder has tried to get the duke to break the entail of the estate in his favor. (The duke can't do this even if he wants to because the English law would prevent it.) Wilder has plotted with the local innkeeper, the brutal Reuben Hayes, to keep Arthur hidden until his father comes to terms.

Wilder is horrified when Hayes murders Heidegger. Nevertheless, he is guilty of kidnaping and being an accessory after the fact of murder. Holmes finds out where the boy is imprisoned, and Hayes is arrested by the police during his flight on information given by Holmes. The duke tells Holmes that his repentant son, James, has promised to leave England forever. He is going to Australia to seek his fortune.

(I stated in *Tarzan Alive* that Wilder did go to Australia, struck it rich almost at once, and migrated to America. This was based on Holmes's report to the duke three years later when the duke had asked Holmes to find out where his son was and what he was doing. Holmes, however, had not done the actual detective work but had relied on some agents he had hired. He regarded this task as routine and as something lesser beings could handle. Recent evidence now shows that his agents had been bribed by the duke to turn in a false report. The duke wanted no one but himself and a single trusted agent to know where his son was. Wilder, after leaving behind the false story of his intentions to go to Australia, actually went to Canada. Sexton Blake, also of Baker Street, was the detective the duke employed.)

Holmes collects a 12,000-pound fee from the duke. Six thousand pounds of this is either an unsolicited bribe for the silence of the two or Watson's share. Apparently, Holmes says nothing to the police about James Wilder, but this is not the first time he breaks the law in his pursuit of justice. What happened after that is unreported by Watson. Holmes says that the duke should be able to keep Hayes from exposing Wilder's part in the crimes. Just how, he doesn't explain. But Hayes is destined for the gallows, and no amount of silence money from the duke is going to help him. Undoubtedly, if only for revenge, Hayes would have spilled everything.

Since the duke would also have been charged with withholding information from the police and as an accessory after the fact, and since this doesn't seem to have happened, Hayes did not squeal. He may have died of a heart attack shortly after being arrested, or the duke may have added another felony to his list and arranged for the escape of Hayes. In this case, though it's not difficult to tell the good guys from the bad guys, there is no question about the good guys also being criminals.

Sexton Blake's report should have pleased the duke. His son had discovered treasure, though in the West Indies, not in Australia. He was now entered in premedical school at Johns Hopkins University. The duke would have been shocked to find that his son had been married while the events of *The Adventure of the Priory School* were taking place and that his wife was pregnant. He might have been pleased to learn that he was the grandfather of an extraordinarily handsome and strong infant. If he could have looked into the future, he would have been thankful for him. At least one fruit of his loins was going to survive, since his legitimate son would die in his twenties in Africa.

What the duke thought about the strange career his son had designed for his grandson, we don't know. He may have had the same thoughts that Monk and Ham, and Doc himself, had. This was that guilt had worked a moral screw loose in the head of Doc's father. He would pay society back a thousandfold for his crimes. In a sort of *Magnificent Obsession* state, he would himself become a medical doctor and surgeon and heal sick people. He would, also, and this was by far the strongest impulsion, fight evil. His overreaction, we may be sure, was caused by his own criminal impulses. The duke had said that his son had a taste for low company. The duke's son dedicated his own son "to go here and there, from one end of the world to the other, looking for excitement and adventure, striving to help those who needed help, punishing those who deserved it." But his son, if he were to get an education in all the professions he needed for his work, would have to have millions. Though Doc's father was famous enough as a surgeon to become wealthy, he still would not have nearly enough. So out he went with Hubert Robertson and others to search for the pot of gold at the end of the jungle rainbow. And he found it.

Later, undoubtedly under Doc's influence, the goal is modified. Though Doc is always the archenemy of crime, he wants most of all to rehabilitate the criminal. He wants to keep him alive, if possible, cure him, and return him to society as a useful citizen.

As I've shown in *Tarzan Alive*, the true name of "James Wilder/ Doctor Clark Savage, Sr.," was actually James Clarke Wildman. Clarke Wildman was one of the many compound family names of the English landed gentry. Most of these are hyphenated (as in Smythe-Jones), but some are not. Dent, in his fictionized versions of Doc's exploits, was compelled by both Doc and Street and Smith Publications to use a fictional name for Doc Savage.

Heredity dumped all her cornucopia into the cells of the infant Savage. Doc was descended on his paternal grandfather's side from a very ancient and extremely distinguished family of British nobility. This lineage and many of his extraordinary relatives are described in detail (some say too much detail) in Addenda 2 and 3 of *Tarzan Alive*. Doc's ancestry on his mother's side (and some distant relatives) is in Addendum 1 of this book.

According to a letter written by Doc himself (in *No Light to Die By*), his training toward supermanhood started when he was fourteen months old. From then until he was twenty, he was in the hands of a board of scientists. His education was so demanding, so rigorous, that it would have broken a less gifted and sturdy child. At that, it left psychic scars.

For one thing, his father seems to have been absent most of the time. While attending medical school and during internship, he was too busy to see much of his son. Afterwards, he was off around the globe in his quest for more gold. Even after he found all he needed in the lost Valley of the Vanished, he seems to have devoted himself to archaeology and lion hunting. Toward the end of Doc's training, he returned to New York and there planned with his son for their crime college. But Doc had no father—in its fullest sense—for all of his formative years.

He had a steady succession, of father substitutes. And this invalidates the speculation of some Savage scholars that he was a suppressed homosexual. According to modern psychology (admittedly a discipline that keeps changing its mind), male homosexuality is often caused by a weak or absent father. Doc's tutors, however, were strong-minded men who seem to have loved him. Certainly, Jerome Coffern, his chemistry instructor (*The Land of Terror*) had a great affection for Doc which was reciprocated. Of course, the temporariness of such relationships may have caused the young Savage a certain amount of insecurity, and he would have felt grief at the departure of particularly liked tutors. On the other hand, though deserted in the particular, he was never so in general. He always had one and quite often several males as companions, mentors, and fathers.

Doc complains in the later supersagas of being lonely, of having missed a normal boyhood. When he became old enough, he had several boys as companions. But the "play" was restricted to one hour a day. During this time, he was pitting his strength and hand-to-hand skills simultaneously against two or three boys his own size in a roughhouse. It was all competitive, and there was no time for palling around with them, joking, bragging, telling stories and daydreams, or going fishing or to the movies.

It's lonely being a superman; it's far more lonely to be a superboy.

Doc's education was carefully planned down to the least detail. But somehow, probably because the board was composed of male scientists, no provision for females was made. Doc doesn't even seem to have had a female housekeeper or cook. (He ate his meals on the run, grabbing whatever was handy, and, though trained in a hundred skills, he was a bad cook.) And he never associated with little girls.

The great minds that nurtured him forgot that when Doc went out into the world, he would find that half of it was female. And a man who doesn't know women is half a man. Or half a superman.

Fortunately, Doc was too busy most of the time to suffer from loneliness. He studied intensely, and his extremely high I.Q. and almost perfect recall enabled him to grasp and to remember anything he studied only once. And he enjoyed things about which most boys could only fantasize. His travels were extensive enough, long enough, and exotic enough to satisfy even Tom Sawyer. He learned diving and sea lore and the Polynesian tongues in the South Seas. He learned woodcraft from an Amazon Indian tribe and a savage African tribe. A ninety-year-old Ubangi taught him to be awakened instantly from sleep if anything was amiss. In India and Tibet he studied yoga, hypnotism, and the art of emotional control and how to block off from his brain the most intense agony of the body. From these sages he also learned the mysteries of the occult and how to generate a fever in his own body and to put himself in suspended animation through mental means.

It was in India that he picked up his habit of unconsciously trilling in certain situations. At the same time that the yogis, fakirs, lamas, and Zen masters were teaching him the arts of peace, he was learning the Oriental arts of personal combat.

In the Occident, he learned savate from the French, free-for-all tricks from longshoremen, a peculiar form of savate from a Berber tribe in North Africa, fencing from the best Italian, French, and Hungarian masters, sabership from the greatest of the Germans, and archery from the greatest of British and Americans. (Despite the latter, he was only a good, not a great, bowman.)

Along with his athletic and scientific studies went instruction in the arts. His voice was innately unusual—"thunder under control"— and he could have become a great opera singer if he'd continued his training. Like Caruso, he could shatter glass with his voice, a talent which saved the day in at least two sticky situations. He composed pieces for the violin which the blind violinist Victor Vail insisted had touches of genius. Doc also played the violin well enough to appear at the Metropolitan Opera, and afterwards he was scheduled to play the clarinet in a jazz jam session. (His love for the violin was shared by Holmes and Richard Wentworth.) He could sketch and draw well, but his paintings would never hang alongside the masters'.

Doc had a number of unconventional tutors in the skills he would need in his fight against crime. From the retired Jimmy Valentine and Arsène Lupin he learned how to pick locks and open safes. He was a master of quick-change disguise as befits a descendant of the Scarlet Pimpernel. For this exacting field, the price of failure usually bringing death, Doc had Arsène Lupin and several months' tutoring by the retired Sherlock Holmes. From the Great Detective and Richard Wentworth, plus some gleanings from the Indian fakirs, he became able to add six inches to his height or lose several inches. (An excellent talent, considering his conspicuous six feet eight inches.) By controlling individual muscles, he could increase or decrease the distance between the vertebrae of the spine. At one time, such control seemed incredible, but contemporary research indicates this is possible.

In addition to the teaching of scientific deduction by Holmes, Doc was taught by another great English detective, Dr. Thorndyke, and by the greatest of the scientific detectives still in harness, the American Craig Kennedy.

Ventriloquism and vocal imitations were necessary arts. Doc's teacher for these was the Great Lander himself. Excellent though he was in these, he could not imitate a woman's voice perfectly. In one case, he would have to call in his cousin. This flaw was undoubtedly a result of his femaleless childhood.

The best of circus acrobats were hired to instruct young Savage in tightrope walking, tumbling, knife throwing, and trapeze skills. One of these acrobats taught Doc how to tie and untie knots with only his toes. (His aide, Monk Mayfair, could do the same.)

Doc's linguistic accomplishments were marvelous. He could speak fifty languages fluently and a hundred languages and dialects passably. He was willing to bet that he could identify any spoken language after listening to a few words of it. (He would have lost his bet in *The Secret of the Su.*) It was not only living speech that he could master. He could rattle off classical Latin and Old Norse, and he could read Chaldean and Egyptian hieroglyphs as smoothly as if he were reading Polish. The range of his semantic abilities was enormous; he used the deaf-and-dumb sign language in many cases, and he was conversant with hobo signs and symbols.

Young Savage's training suddenly halted on 7 April 1917. The U.S.A. had declared war on Germany the day before. Savage, who wouldn't be sixteen years old until next November, ran off to join the Army. This threw his guardians into a frenzy, since they had no idea why he had dropped out of sight. They hired private detectives to search for him, but even Craig Kennedy and Sam Spade's father (a Pinkerton man) couldn't locate him. The news did not cause the elder Savage any distress because it did not reach him until the war was over. He was in the Amazon hinterland looking for the Maple White Land reported by the Challenger expedition.

Young Clark, fed up with his cloistered life and the never-ending study, had decided to test his extraordinary abilities against the greatest evil of them all—Germany. (At this time, the U. S. public was convinced of the truth of the atrocity stories spread by the propagandists against the "Huns.")

Though Doc was only fifteen years old, he was six feet one inch tall and weighed one hundred and ninety pounds. His mature appearance, plus his faked papers, got him into the Army Air service. He was already an excellent pilot, having been taught by the best pilot in the world, A. K. Rassendyll, who was at that time going under his Kent Allard pseudonym.

In March 1918, while on his seventh flight, he was shot down during a balloon-busting exploit. Though wounded by shell fragments and machine-gun bullets and injured by the crash, he managed to crawl out from the wreckage of his Nieuport. He got away from the German infantry troops but was tracked down by dogs and captured. On his way to a POW camp, he escaped twice, only to be recaptured. Because of these escape attempts, he was sent to a special POW prison of which only a few highly placed Germans were aware. This prison received those who were considered to be too intractable even for the infamous Holzminden camp. It had no national or rank discriminations. British, French, Italian, and American, whether privates or generals, were held here. Its code name was *Loki*, and it was located, appropriately enough, near Berchtesgaden.

Loki was a series of caves inside the mountain with a small fortress built over the entrance. It was deep inside the mountain that the youth met and formed a lifelong friendship with five older men. They were Americans: the intelligence agent William Harper Littlejohn, Major Thomas J. Roberts, Lieutenant Colonel Andrew Blodgett Mayfair, Colonel John Renwick, and Brigadier General Theodore Marley Brooks. "Johnny," "Long Tom," "Monk," "Renny," and "Ham." Ham Brooks was the highest-ranking officer among the prisoners, and so was their official leader. His sidekick, Monk Mayfair, was, however, the one who gave his guards the most trouble. This gorilloid Yank (a relative of Savage's, though neither knew it then) had once ripped up several rods of German barbed wire with his hands. When captured, he was wiping out a squad with the barrel of an empty machine gun. Monk could not be repressed, and so the inevitable happened. Poked in the crotch with a rifle barrel by a guard, he struck the German so hard that he broke the man's spine and killed him.

He was to be sentenced the next day, but Savage hurried up his escape plans and the six, with some French and British, escaped.

It is too bad that Dent never got around to writing of this highly ingenious and exciting breakout. Perhaps someday Condé Nast will give its permission for an author (myself, I hope) to write this very first of the supersagas.*

In July 1918, Savage and his friends rejoined their respective outfits. In the Argonne operation of September—November of that year, Doc met another cousin, Flight Lieutenant John Drummond Clayton, temporarily attached to the U.S. Army Air service. They talked about Clayton's father, the eighth duke of Greystoke, the grandson of the brother of Doc's grandfather. As a result of this meeting, Doc would take some postgraduate training from Lord Greystoke. The arboreal skills learned from this visit enabled Doc, on at least four occasions, to carry a person on his back *à la* Tarzan through the trees and so escape the villains.

And in 1934, Greystoke sent to his cousin some pills he had obtained from the Kavuru tribe. Doc was to analyze and then synthesize this age-delaying elixir, though he refused, for good reasons, to release them for public consumption.

In February 1919, Doc returned to Johns Hopkins. At the time he ran away, he was, though only fifteen, a senior. He had passed all his examinations and so been admitted without going through the regular route. Doc got his M.D. in 1926 and went to Vienna for more study in brain surgery and neurology. While there, he attended some lectures by Sigmund Freud. It is said, though there is no record of it, that he underwent a brief analysis by Freud.

In 1927, Doc made the first of his experiments designed to cure criminals. In 1928, with his father, he built the secret upstate New York "college" for criminals. (See Chapter 8 for details about this singular institution.)

<hr>

* *Phil Farmer finally saw his hopes realized with the publication of* Escape from Loki: Doc Savage's First Adventure *(Bantam Books, 1991).* —WSE

4

THE BRONZE HERO OF
TECHNOPOLIS AND EXOTICA

UP **ABOVE** the world so high, Doc Savage lives.

His headquarters and home are enormous. They consist of the entire uppermost floor of the tallest building on earth. There is a small reception room, a vast library, and a laboratory that covers two thirds or more of the available floorage. When Doc isn't out nemesizing criminals, he's usually in the lab, the Wizard's Den, working his white magic of gadgets and scientific amulets. Despite the many inventions he gives to humanity, and a number of others he conceals for its good, science, or magic, is not his main profession.

Sammy Wales, in *No Light to Die By*, asks a bellhop what Doc does. The bellhop replies, "Savage? He rights wrongs and punishes evildoers."

Sammy comments, "He shouldn't lack for business in this world."

Sammy, usually wrong, is right this time.

Pat, Doc's beautiful cousin, says that somebody tries to kill Doc at least once a month.

Pat underestimates. Some months, at least a dozen villains, major and minor, attempt to kill him. He is their object of murderous desire. Get him, and the going will be smooth. Whether in luxurious suites or crappy tenements, they turn pale when Doc's name is mentioned. He is a "great bronze bird of vengeance," "a metallic specter of violence," "a golden-eyed juggernaut." Monk describes him as "a blend of ghost, magician, and bobcat." He is "...nobody to be in the same woods with if he doesn't like you."

Yet this is the same man who says, "Violence isn't going to show anyone a profit, either in human rights or money."

However, if he had refused to meet violence with violence, he would have been dead at the very start of his career.

Doc also says, "It's unfortunate that the moral enlightenment of the human race isn't keeping pace with its scientific discoveries."

But he makes a peculiar statement which runs counter to this. Or does it?

"Society prepares the crime, and the criminal only commits it."

On reflection, this sounds very much like an indictment of the structure of his society. Doc, however, makes no effort to change that structure, perhaps because he believes it is the best available or because any effort to do so is foredoomed.

In any event, he is too busy defending himself from and attacking the practitioners of black magic to try to alter the bases of society.

And who and what is this Nimrod of the Tower of Babel, the deadly Harun-al-Rashid of Baghdad-on-the-Hudson, the Merlin of the Fifth Avenue Camelot, the Galahad of tubes and gadgets, the guardian of Manhattan's Carbonek?

Doctor Clark Savage, Jr., at twenty-nine years of age, stands six feet eight inches high and weighs two hundred and seventy pounds. At least that's what Dent's notebook says. In the first supersaga, *The Man of Bronze*, he is six feet tall and weighs two hundred pounds. His height and weight vary throughout the tales (as do Monk's, Renny's, and Johnny's). Generally, he is almost seven feet tall. The discrepancies can be attributed to the hastiness and forgetfulness of Dent and the other occasional writers of the supersagas.

Doc, according to Monk, is "as conspicuous in a crowd as a fig leaf on a fan dancer." Sammy Wales says that he moves as easily as if he were on oil bearings. Mr. Weed describes him as "all lion and a yard wide."

He is handsome; his forehead is unusually high; his nose is straight; his lips are mobile and not too full; his cheeks are lean; his chin is square; his jaw is strong but not massive. His hair is a beautiful bronze, straight and close to his scalp. It, along with his bronze skin—"deeply tanned by many tropical suns"—has the peculiar property of shedding water as if it were a penguin's back. Possibly Doc coats himself with a water-repellent substance, though Dent never says so.

He has "weird golden eyes," "hot aureate pools," "radiating a hypnotic magnetism." They're a very light tawny brown with golden flecks that seem always to whirl, like some sort of protean Goldwasser.

He is a giant but so perfectly proportioned that he doesn't look big unless he is near some object of known size or standing next to you. His muscles are not gorilloid but like bundles of thin piano wires covered with a bronze lacquer. When he bunches them, they coil like pythons.

These muscles are the result of a daily two-hour exercise taken since he was fourteen months old. Part of these workouts consist of a Charles Atlas-like contest of pitting one set of muscles against the other. (Now used in modified and restricted form by the Canadian Royal Air Force.) This 120-minute stint is never neglected by Doc (well, hardly ever). While he is working out his muscles, he exercises his brain by multiplying, dividing, and extracting square roots and cubes. Given a hundred-digit number, he can repeat it in exact sequence hours, or even days, later.

He listens to sound waves of frequencies too high or too low for the ordinary human ear to detect, and so improves his auditory sense. He has exercised his eyes in the dark to the point where he can see almost as well as a cat can in the dark. (These last two abilities must really have come from chemical preparations, since the human eye and ear have innate limits that no amount of exercising can extend. Or maybe Dent was exaggerating.)

He names "scores of different odors after a quick olfactory test of small vials packed in a case." This is credible, but his sense of smell is also equivalent to that of an ape's. This superhuman, or, rather, subhuman, ability must have been due to a genetic mutation. It is shared by his relatives, Lord Greystoke and Lew Archer.

Doc improves his sense of touching by reading braille. And many other devices are used by Doc in his high-speed, highly involved exercising. It leaves him tuned up, ready to go, but people break into a sweat just watching him do it.

He knows no leisure and feels ill-at-ease when he tries to take a vacation. "Hazards are his heritage," and so also is the compulsion of probing into the unknowns of science—of, in fact, almost everything. Almost everything but cooking and female psychology. Until 1946, he doesn't know how to dance. But this can be forgiven in a man whose technical books are in the libraries and laboratories of every great institution of education in the world.

Just a listing of all his designs, developments, and inventions would fill pages of this book. They range over a hundred fields. Designs for airplanes, dirigibles, motors, elevators. Quick-growing lumber trees. A cure for paranoia. New brain-surgery techniques. An electric method for bonding plywood. A radar for differentiating between metals at a distance. A shoulder-holstered ram's-horn-shaped submachine pistol shooting .24-caliber bullets, 786 a minute, 66 in a magazine. The first wire recorder. Dissolvable parachutes. A cigarette case which shoots darts (later used by Russian secret agents, according to Ian Fleming). A wristwatch-sized TV receiver. A true autogyro. A spray-on plastic skin for resisting 60°-below weather. Pills for diving which supply oxygen to the blood for half an hour. A bleach to change a black car to gray in a few minutes. A gas to neutralize poison gases. The first telephone message recorder. An epoxylike glue for repairing breaks in bone very quickly. A cure for the common cold.

Not all of these inventions worked. Though a superman, Doc wasn't perfect. His new cableless pneumatic elevator was described by Monk (rather gleefully) as a lemon. And in *Mad Mesa* the only result of his experiments to cure the common cold is that he himself catches one. His trinitromite, a thousand times more powerful than dynamite, is too unstable to be safely used. His atomic disintegrator is only effective a little over twenty feet. His truth serum sometimes works on criminals and sometimes doesn't. In its strongest form, it is very effective but can kill. Thus, in *The Men Vanished* Doc refuses to use it on three captives.

When he is dressed to kill—literally—he is a walking dreadnaught, a human minefield. He wears bulletproof metal-alloy underwear and a skullcap which simulates his own hair. His leather vest is so loaded with gadgets that he must often have looked like a walrus. His fingers are sometimes tipped with false nails at the ends of which are tiny needles covered with an anesthetic drug. A hollow tooth contains a tiny coiled saw. Other hollow capped teeth contain explosives. He has an artificial scar on his back which hides a tiny flat box of explosive powder or a flare with which to blind his opponents. He carries, usually inside his belt, a long slender silk cord with a collapsible grapnel at one end. His quiet brown business suits are impregnated with various chemicals for various uses against criminals. The lining of the outside breast pocket is a thin elastic transparent material easily torn out. Put over the head and tightened around the neck, it makes a short-term gas mask. In conjunction with the oxygen pills, it is good for half an hour.

His shoes have hollow heels containing anything from a short-range radio transmitter with a tiny battery to radioactive pieces of metal to enable his aides to track him, or they contain explosives, flares, or lock-picks and drills. The vest always holds small explosive grenades or thin-walled glass balls full of anesthetic gas or chemicals to release smokescreens. He also wears under his shirtsleeves flat glass cases of anesthetic gas strapped to his arm. By tensing his bicep, he breaks these. While he holds his breath, his unsuspecting enemies keel over.

But Doc doesn't wear all these gadgets at the same time. He is usually equipped for the particular occasion.

Even when some knowing villain strips him of clothes and skullcap and uncaps his teeth and tears off the artificial scars, he is as dangerous as a bull moose in rut. Six men armed with billy clubs might get him, but most of them will be down and out before the sap descends on the unprotected head.

Doc is—in a sense—a Boy Scout, always prepared. He can only survive through a never-ending suspicion and many measures for preservation. He never stands where he is in the line of fire from a window. If he has an appointment, no matter with whom, he checks out the person and the site before the meeting. "His foes were legion," and if they became less during the years, it was not because he got there first with the most, or showed up late or not at all. Sometimes he allows himself to be captured. That is the only way he can get a lead onto the villains or to his captured aides. This takes supreme confidence, and Doc has it.

He often depends on gadgets, but he hates to use a gun. For most of his career, he refuses to wear one. During the later years, he loses his interest in gadgets, which he once said were "his principal vice." Even so, he carries the line-and-grapnel for sentiment's sake.

This divesting of technological devices parallels an increasing loss of self-control. Either he is slowly breaking down under the never-ending strain or he has an unconscious reliance, deeply rooted, on the gadgets. For some reason, psychological probably, he has to give these up. Perhaps he realizes he is more machine than man as long as he clothes himself with them. To become more human, he sheds them, however reluctantly. But as they depart, he feels less and less secure. He can't admit this to himself, so he continues the scaling off, layer by layer, of metal and chemical defenses. Thus, the inner Doc, the one deprived of his mother at fourteen months of age, the one who knew no females during his formative years, becomes more and more the abandoned baby.

In his early exploits, Doc rarely smiles. He never takes part in the juvenile but therapeutic horseplay of his aides. He endures silently Monk and Ham's incessant chatter, corny jokes, loud quarreling, and their often cruel practical jokes on each other. When he does reprimand them, he doesn't do so vigorously. More by tone than word, he makes it obvious they're a drag, or he sighs so deeply they know what he's thinking.

In his first two exploits, Doc is as violent and bloody as any two-handed engine of retribution. It is true that his reasons for the merciless slaying of the villains are enough to make the most pacifistic of us want to kill in a most violent way. In *The Man of Bronze,* his father is purposely infected with the horrible Red Death and dies. In *The Land of Terror,* his beloved chemistry tutor, Dr. Jerome Coffern, falls victim to the terrifying Smoke of Eternity. In both cases, Doc, while on the trail of the murderers, slays right and left with his bare hands and anything else handy. He leaves a trail behind him that surely must have brought some questions and reprimands from the police. In both exploits, however, Doc can plead self-defense against known vicious criminals, many of them wanted for murder. But the crooks are often trying to get away from him as fast as possible because they realize what they have aroused.

After this, Doc is changed. Revenge has sweetened him. Between *The Land of Terror* and *Quest of the Spider,* he spends two weeks in his Fortress of Solitude. (Chapter 9 describes this Strange Blue Dome on an arctic island.) Here he must have brooded on what had happened in the first two supersagas. He must have been sickened by the ogre that had broken loose from the dark dungeon of himself. Certainly, the murderers of Coffern and his father deserved to die. But he doesn't want to go on killing, killing, killing. If he does, he'll become no better than the murderers. Worse, in fact, because he is far superior to any of the poor sick beings. Criminality is a disease, and he doesn't want to catch, it.

To keep his own health, and because the criminal is sick, Doc adopts a new philosophy. From now on, no antagonist is to be killed unless it's absolutely necessary. And even the necessity will be much regretted by Doc.

Doc lays down the new law to his five associates: Monk, Ham, Renny, Johnny, and Long Tom. They seem to agree. But the irrepressible and violent Monk quite often kills by "accident." Renny, on at least one occasion, openly disobeys Doc. It is only when this ruling is broken that Doc harshly reprimands his associates. The rest of the time, no matter how much they foul up, and the two clowns Ham and Monk often do—"Humpty and Dumpty on a raft"—he never criticizes.

On the other hand, he has the disconcerting habit of seeming to be deaf when he doesn't want to answer their questions. These are usually about the identity of their mysterious assailants or their motives. Doc never guesses, and often it's better to say nothing. If his associates knew what he was thinking, they might later fall into the villains' hands and be forced under torture to give the information.

"Sagacity usually motivates Doc's operations," Johnny says.

"Words have to be jarred out of Doc," Monk says.

Doc has seen the light long before the others are out of the dark. As he tells them, "What you don't know can't hurt somebody else."

After a while, his aides adjust to his failure to answer. But others, especially the women, are upset and angered by this habit. It is one mode of behavior he keeps throughout his career.

He changes others as time's catalysts permeate him.

One is his trilling.

"It was low, mellow... It might have been the alarm notes of some strange feathered songster of the jungle, or the sound of an undulating breeze filtering through a... forest... melodious, it still had no tune, and it was inspiring without being in the least awesome.

"'Doc Savage!' Ham said softly.

"For this was... a part of Doc—a small, unconscious thing which he did in moments of concentration. To his friends it was both a cry of battle and the song of triumph. It would come... in moments of stress—when events of importance impended.

"It had the peculiar quality of seeming to come from everywhere rather than a definite spot. It might have been emanating from the office. Yet Doc Savage was nowhere about."

This habit was to betray him at least once. Perhaps it was this near-fatal incident that determined him to rid himself of it. In almost every one of the supersagas from the beginning until War World II, he trills. But after that started he begins to lose his trademark and eventually he has wiped it out of his neural circuits.

In the beginning, Doc knows no fear, and the most startling and horrifying events fail even to twitch the bronze mask. As the years wear on him, something inside him loses its control. The ego becomes butterfingered. He reacts with disgust, with alarm, sometimes with an almost complete loss of control. He jumps at unexpected noises. He loses his temper and throws away his contact lenses (used in disguises). In *Mystery on Happy Bones* he sweats nervously before a parachute jump. In *The Invisible-Box Murders* he loses his temper and slams Blosser across the room. In *Men of Fear*, while shadowing a suspect, he pulls a thoroughly nonprofessional boner.

He seems to be another person in *The Lost Giant*. Certainly, he's not the Doc we know. He's full of fears and self-doubts and is neurotically subdued. He does come through (locates and saves Winston Churchill, downed in the arctic, from Nazis), but not in the grand old style. James Bond would have done it with more flourish and gusto. And in the final tale, *Up from Earth's Center*, Doc actually screams with horror. Doc screaming?

As the adventures roll on, he makes mistakes. They would be expected and forgivable from lesser beings. But they do show he's human, and we like him the better for them. In wartime London he's almost run over because he's forgotten that English traffic is on the left side of the road. In *The Metal Master*, he forgets that his tied-up captives can get to a kitchen knife and so cut themselves loose. He blames himself, rightly so, for his stupidity. But he evidently still has the superman image to conform to. He ignores the fact that everybody, no matter how intelligent, has lapses. He thinks he should be perfect.

At one time he carries in his head the detailed maps of every large city in the world. Put him down in one, and he'll know where he is. But in a postwar story, his marvelous fluency in even the most obscure Arabic dialect is failing. He isn't as good as he used to be even in the widely spoken Egyptian Arabic. Due to lack of practice, he can't lip-read as well as he once did. (He could lip-read Chinese, among other tongues, which seems incredible, since the meaning of Chinese words depends not only on phonemes but tones.) He's forgotten the subtleties of the Oklahoma dialect. And *The Speaking Stone* reveals that he speaks Spanish with a slight American accent. In the earlier stories his Spanish is perfect. This regression is strange. Once a language is mastered, the vocabulary and grammar may be lost because of disuse. But the pronunciation is ingrained, imbedded in the nerves. Did Dent exaggerate some of Doc's accomplishments in the earlier stories? Did he do so because he had orders from the publishers to build a superman for his readers (supposedly largely in the fifteen-year-old bracket)? And did the publishers decide he should draw a more realistic portrait in the later exploits?

We know that Doc complained (in *No Light to Die By*) that Dent made the exploits overly colorful. And in one story he comments disgustedly on a magazine article about him. "That chap certainly has a lot of imagination."

Did he actually kayo a shark with one fist blow on its snout? Did he really knock out a polar bear with his fists and then break its neck with a half nelson? Did he then tear out steaks from it with his bare hands? Could he turn an automobile back over onto its wheels with his hands only? Could he leap, in street shoes, two feet above the world's record high jump? This, in 1934, was six feet nine and one-eighth inches. Doc was six feet eight inches high, and so his jump was one foot and two and one-eighth inches above his head. Valery Brumel of Russia and N. Chih-chin of China have cleared sixteen and seven-eighth inches above their own heads. Doc didn't do as well as they, but he was handicapped by his much greater weight. And he did not have track shoes on.

The other feats, though marvelous, are not beyond the bounds of credibility. And since it's been verified that Lord Greystoke has performed equal or greater herculeanics, we can accept Doc's as true.

Doc's relations with his aides are those of a big brother to a smaller. They are all older than he, but he is the natural leader. In fact, Doc addresses them as "Brothers" so often that you wonder if they really are. He often gets fed up with Ham and Monk, so much so that in *Trouble on Parade* he is thankful that they're absent from the adventure. He can't take much more of them at this point in his life. Despite this, he would have been deeply grieved if they'd quit the group (fat chance!) or been killed (highly likely). He loves them, and often, when a situation demands a sacrifice of the life of one, insists that he be the one to take the chance. The others love him and will throw away their own lives to save him, and sometimes try to do just that.

On several occasions, when it seems that Doc is dead, the others are stricken. They reminisce about him, and it's significant that they don't dwell on his superhuman feats. No, they talk of the little things they did, Doc's humanity and compassion and the fun they've had when grim things weren't occupying them. Monk once makes a speech to Doc after he's come back alive that brings tears to Doc's eyes.

Also, much as Doc reproaches Monk for his bloodthirstiness and deceit, he must use Monk as a vicar for his own repressed tendencies. He never tells a direct lie, or at least he tries not to. (In a number of cases, including *They Died Twice,* he lies straight out.) Sometimes he needs a liar. In *Meteor Menace* he gets Monk to tell the pretty Rae Stanley that her father has been killed some time before. Actually, he was the mad villain, Mo-Gwei. Monk would rather lie any day than tell the truth, and he does so cheerfully for Doc. In addition, though Doc seldom manhandles a captive himself, he sends in Monk for a softening-up before the basic questioning begins. He knows very well that Monk's technique is to try to scare the crooks with tough talk and then, if that doesn't work, to throw them against a wall, jump up and down on them, and bend legs and arms into painful positions.

This is illegal, and it is cruel. But there is never the slightest doubt that the captive is guilty, and if the information isn't gotten quickly, some innocent will die.

Also, despite a moral position that often makes Ham and Monk uncomfortable, he must get some vicarious sexual stimulation and maybe even relief from their studding.

Doc says, "Understand this, I'm no judge of female character."

He's taken a course in feminine psychology but gotten nothing out of it. He can generally tell if a man is lying, but he wishes that someone would invent a contraption to flash a red light when a woman is lying to him. In *The Terrible Stork* he says he's finally learned to read the female character. Later tales don't bear this out. Johnny thinks that women scare him. Patricia Savage, the only woman who knows her cousin well says that Doc had a "goofy training." It hasn't made him a freak, though he has his "goofy moments." She says that he's afraid of women because his lifelong education has been scientific, and he thus "expects to understand how things tick." Not knowing what makes women tick, he is afraid of them.

Despite regarding women as mysterious time bombs, Doc is "powerfully attracted" to them. He is wise, but he *is* a male. In *Meteor Menace* the Cockney Shrops explains to his fellow villain Saturday Loo that he needs Rae Stanley to vamp the bronze man. Loo replies, "It is said that wise men are not affected by women." Shrops, after laughing, says, "Then there ain't no wise men in this 'appy world."

In *Brand of the Werewolf* Doc is kissed for the first time in his life by a woman. Señorita Oveja gives him a big smackeroo on the lips, which he finds delicious and stimulating. Rae Stanley gives Doc "a resounding and amorous kiss." Doc gets himself into a bind with her because he's gotten affianced to her. He does this just to further his plans against Mo-Gwei, and he knows that she's really not in love with him. He pushes her to get married immediately, so she refuses. But he must have some deep feelings for her, because he blushes when Ham calls her a hussy.

Toni Lash's startling beauty affects Doc greatly in *The Devil Genghis*. In the comical *The Freckled Shark* he takes a few days off from the persona of Doc Savage in the disguise of the bumbling, insulting Henry Peace. He proposes marriage to Rhoda Haven a number of times. When the need for the disguise is over, he's terrified. Ham and Johnny, for the first time, laugh at him. They find his terror ridiculous and, probably, satisfying. Their superman leader has weaknesses.

It is in this tale that we get the first intimations that Doc isn't in love with his role of superman. As Henry Peace, he works off many repressions and irritations, plays stupid, pays court to a woman, and knocks Ham and Monk down. Doubtless the last was the expression of a frequent wish. It is however, he concludes, dangerous being Henry Peace because he's tempted to keep on being him.

Again, in *King Joe Cay* Doc enjoys himself tremendously in disguise. After stealing a purse on a train out of Chicago (for a good reason), he sees an oatfield and desires greatly to forget everything and just lie down in the oats for the sheer pleasure of it. He'd like to loaf and invite his soul, be one with the beasts.

In *The Dagger in the Sky* Doc is captured because he's not as alert as usual. He's been too interested in watching the beautiful Sanda MacNamara.

The Men of Fear states that he was frequently inclined to become attached to a girl. More than one, throughout the tales, has a beauty which makes him "curl his toes."

By the time of *Jiu San* (October 1944) Doc is asking women out to dinner. (And these beauties accept, of course.) In *Strange Fish* Doc is attracted to Paris Stevens "more than a little." And he wonders in *The Terrible Stork* if he's not trying to show off before Ada Nobel.

Patience, a "cute trick," gives Doc a mere glance from her big brown eyes in *Fire and Ice*, and it sends "electric flashes coursing through him."

He is enraged by Susie Lane's accusations of cowardice in *The Exploding Lake*. Certainly, if he did not care for her, he would not have reacted so strongly.

By the time of *The Devil Is Jones* (November 1946) he is interested enough in women to learn to dance.

As for Doc's possible sexual attitude to his cousin Pat, Chapter 16 contains some speculations on that.

Given Doc's unusual vigor and his undoubted desire for women, why did he remain chaste—if, that is, he did? His excuse was that his enemies would strike at him through any women he became involved with. But he made only a weak effort to keep Pat from taking part in his dangerous exploits. Did his all-male childhood make him impotent? Was Monk speaking in more than one sense when he said, "The woman isn't made who can get a rise out of Doc"?

Doc himself, in *The Ten Ton Snakes*, implies that he may need psychoanalysis. He admits being a juvenile.

"He still had the kid stuff in him. He'd never had a chance to work it off."

If he had had, he'd "now be a young settled family man with a wife who dragged him out to bridge parties."

Renny, tickled at the idea of Doc being dominated by a henpecker, gives one of his rare laughs. Offended, Doc shuts up.

But his self-analysis is significant. Juveniles (in Doc's day, anyway) thought girls were sissy stuff. And there is still an active fifteen-year-old in Doc.

After Doc had cooled off from Renny's laugh, he must have agreed with Renny that he is being ridiculous. Such a domestic life could never have been his, even without the peculiar education his somewhat cracked father had arranged for him. There is a taint in the Savage blood, a lust for danger. He is a genius who could never have adjusted to a "normal" lifestyle. He must have remembered his father's quotation, taken from Gibbon. His father had placed it before him shortly after he had learned to read, and it was one of the first things he could remember about his father.

> Conversation enriches the understanding,
> But solitude is the school of the genius.

And as The Man of Bronze, he does far more good than as just a surgeon or businessman. His charities are numerous and far-flung, a listing of which would fill many pages. He has ended the careers of many geniuses of crime. Any one of them, if successful, would have put the world under a tyranny even more unshakable and terrible than that planned by the Austrian Hitler. He owns, or has large shares in, so many businesses that he is the richest man in the world. (For a time, anyway.) He has rescued dozens of big businesses from financial ruin and so ensured employment for thousands. His surgical techniques and many inventions have saved thousands of lives and enriched mankind. His "crime college" has converted hundreds of crooks into honest men and saved the taxpayers much money and canceled many crimes that would otherwise inevitably have been committed.

Doc is indeed the archangel of Technopolis and of far-off jungle-and-desert Exotica. He is the scientific savior. As saviors always must, he suffers loneliness and a sense of isolation from the people.

He has to be ready for those who would daily crucify him.

The price is worth it. Otherwise, he could have quit his role.

Before we close this chapter on Doc, we must consider some puzzling statements by Pat in *The Motion Menace*. She tells a villain, Penroff, that Doc is a man who has always had many enemies. It's remarkable that he's succeeded in surviving. Penroff asks her what that has to do with the present situation. Pat replies, "Suppose that Doc was never the bronze man he appeared to be. You must admit that his big bronze characterization stands out in a crowd. Almost any enemy would recognize him instantly. Think what it would mean if he was never really the bronze man? Suppose he was a totally different individual?"

Penroff likes this idea. It would explain why he has had so much difficulty capturing him. But he wonders about the golden eyes. Pat says that these could be glass caps fitting on the eyeballs.

It's true that Pat seems to say this simply to throw Penroff off the track and make him think that his prisoner is Doc Savage. He's not, and Pat's ruse works.

But what if Pat were really telling the truth? Then Doc's real appearance is never described in the supersagas, and the discrepant descriptions by Dent and the other Savage writers might be explained. Perhaps Dent's initial description and some others, including the police bulletin in *The Man Who Was Scared*—six feet four inches, from 210 to 220 pounds—are closer to reality.

In any event, it's meaningful that it was Pat who suggested that Doc's true appearance was not known. If she were Doc's lover, then only she might have seen him in the undisguised flesh.

The Man of Mystery is even more mysterious than we thought.

5

THE SKYSCRAPER

THE BUILDING in which Doc had his headquarters is never mentioned by a specific name. It is always just "the skyscraper." Many times, it is "one of the tallest in New York," or "one of the most impressive." More often, it is "the most impressive," "the grandest," "the highest," "the tallest," or "the finest." When its location is mentioned, it is always in midtown Manhattan.

In *The Man of Bronze* Dent describes it thus: "A gleaming spike of steel and brick, it rammed upward nearly a hundred stories."

Variations of this run throughout the supersagas. A respectable number, however, stipulate that the building is only eighty-six floors high. One gives it one hundred and two stories.

A few times, the dirigible mooring mast on top of the skyscraper is mentioned. In *The Evil Gnome* it is called "as useful as a pair of tonsils."

The Empire State Building is in midtown Manhattan. It is the only skyscraper in the world to be topped with a dirigible mooring mast (never used), and the building itself is eighty-six stories high; but with the mooring mast added, it is one hundred and two stories high.

There is other evidence which enables us to locate and identify this building precisely.

In *The Man of Bronze* Doc leaves the skyscraper and takes a taxi which goes north on Fifth Avenue, directly from the building. In *The Land of Terror* Doc takes a taxi on the Fifth Avenue side of Central Park and goes south on Fifth to the skyscraper. In the same supersaga, the Sixth Avenue Elevated is close to the building. In *The Red Skull* the villainous Buttons Zortell walks south from

Forty-second and Broadway until he reaches Doc's skyscraper. To do this, he would have to cross Sixth Avenue. In *The Phantom City* four criminals walk down Fifth Avenue and turn onto a side street to observe the exit of Doc's subbasement garage. This side street has to be either Thirty-fourth or Thirty-third Street.

One of Doc's secret tunnels from the skyscraper's subbasement garage leads to a locker in the Broadway subway. *The Land of Terror* notes that Broadway is the only street to run the whole length of Manhattan and that a subway runs beneath it nearly its whole distance. Broadway angles southeastward from the intersection of Thirty-fourth Street and Sixth Avenue (the present-day Avenue of the Americas). It then intersects Fifth Avenue and continues southeastward, straightening out at Tenth to run more or less straight south.

If Doc's tunnel leads to the Broadway subway, and if Doc leaves the building to take a taxi directly up Fifth Avenue, then the building must have Fifth Avenue on its east side and Sixth Avenue to its west. Additional evidence indicates that Thirty-fourth Street bounds it on the north.

According to *The South Pole Terror*, Doc's huge warehouse-hangar-dock—the Hidalgo Trading Company—is at or near the Hudson River end of Thirty-fourth Street. The Hidalgo Trading Company is connected underground to the skyscraper by the great pneumatic tube which Monk Mayfair calls the "flea run," among other things. The tube starts from the eighty-sixth floor, plunges down through the skyscraper deep into the earth, and then curves upward to terminate inside the Hudson River building. The underground length of this tube must be over 6,000 feet. The expense of tunneling through the bedrock and installing the tube had to be enormous. Thus, the shortest distance to the river was the most efficient for operation, considering the amounts of power involved in sending the passenger car at one hundred miles per hour through the tube. (*The Freckled Shark* specifies this velocity.) The shortest distance to the river is also the most economical in terms of time spent digging and money expended. This is why Doc chose the Thirty-fourth Street site for the Hidalgo Trading Company. And this is one of the reasons why we know that Thirty-fourth Street is a boundary of Doc's skyscraper.

What building is it that is definitely in midtown Manhattan and is bounded by Fifth Avenue, Thirty-fourth Street, and Thirty-third Street? What skyscraper is the only one in Manhattan with a dirigible mooring mast? The only one that fits these specifications is the Empire State Building.

The Empire State Building also has other qualifications. The reception room on the eighty-sixth floor has windows on the west and north sides, which would place it on the northwest corner of the building. From there, Broadway, Times Square, and the Hudson River can be seen. The Sixth Avenue Elevated could be seen from there (it's gone now).

The stories are not consistent in specifying the number of elevators in the skyscraper. *The Red Skull* states that it has more than fifty passenger elevators. *The Angry Canary* says that there are forty or fifty elevators in it. Only twenty-two elevators are specified by *The Fiery Menace*. (This story also says that 5,000 people work in the building.) *The Feathered Octopus* counts nearly a hundred elevators.

In fact, the Empire State Building has sixty-three passenger elevators, is 102 stories high (counting the mooring mast), and 25,000 employees of 940 firms worked in it in 1932.

In *The Terrible Stork* the eighty-sixth floor is called the top floor. Above it, however, is a roof restaurant, a night club, an observation tower, a souvenir shop for tourists, elevator machinery, a water tank, and "other stuff." This resembles somewhat the Empire State Building setup of the observation floor.

All things considered, Doc's aerie must have been in the tallest skyscraper in the world. Why, then, was Dent so vague about its identity, why did he even set forth contradictory details concerning it in the various supersagas?

The most compelling reason for the avoidance of the truth is the legal reason. Doc was well aware that Dent and other Street and Smith writers were writing a series of fictional stories based on him. Doc admitted that himself in *No Light to Die By*. Doc wasn't too pleased with the pulp-magazine versions of the exploits of himself and his aides. They were far too exaggerated, too purplish, and, though he doesn't say so, probably contained a number of character distortions. But he wasn't going to be bothered with lawsuits forbidding Street and Smith from publishing these fantasies about him. He did, however, lay down certain rules for the *Doc Savage* magazine. One was that his true name not be used. The other was that deliberate contradictions be made so that readers would believe that the supersagas were fiction. On this latter point Doc could have saved himself his breath. Dent, Donovan, Hathway, and Bogart wrote with such speed and lack of editing that many contradictions were inevitable.

One of the things that must be ascertained, however, is the true location of Doc's HQ. Were they actually on the eighty-sixth floor of the Empire State Building?

We know that Doc would not be content with anything but the best and the highest. And the topmost residential floor of the highest residential building in the world would be Doc's, if it were possible to get it.

From his "skyscraper aerie" he would command a view of the richest city in the world, as befitted a man whose private dirigible had cost him more than the national debt of some small countries. And where else would the Great Wizard (for Doc was such) dwell? Where else but on the top of the tallest artificial mountain, on top of the loftiest tower of Babel? Here Doc would commune with the lightning and talk with the eagles. Here in this Indiana-limestone and granite, stainless-steel and aluminum Olympus, the demigod of the vast Technopolis worked his scientific miracles and planned his campaigns against the demons below.

The dirigible mooring mast (see Figure 1) is familiar to most of the older generation all over the world (and to many of the younger). They know it as the site of the last stand of the Brobdingnagian ape King Kong. Here, at the summit of Technopolis, the great ape fell victim to the Technopolis.

(It's unfortunate that Doc and his aides were not in New York City when the titanic anthropoid escaped his bonds.* What a fine

---

* *According to Farmer's tale "After King Kong Fell," a golden-eyed man, apparently Doc Savage, and his aides arrived in the aftermath of the giant ape's fall from the Empire State Building.* —WSE

supersaga the conflict of Doc and Kong would have made!* Perhaps Doc might have averted the tragic end of the ape by capturing him and taking him back to his native isle. However, Kong was doomed even in this event, since the isle sank about a year or so later anyway.)

It's worth noting that King Kong's capture on the isle was made possible by grenades which released an anesthetic gas. These were provided by Doc Savage, of course. Only pressing business elsewhere prevented Doc from joining the Carl Denham Expedition. Doc was, however, a technical adviser for the film which re-enacted the Kong caper.

No doubt, Doc lived on one of the highest floors of the ESB, but it would not have been the eighty-sixth. This is incontrovertibly the observation floor. I have been on that floor twice, but those who may not care to take my word for it can refer to the opposite page. This is a photostat of a letter from Mr. Wien, a former co-owner of the ESB. His authority establishes that the eighty-sixth floor is not and never has been Doc's HQ.

I have been unable to determine which story Doc actually occupied. The management of the ESB has informed me that this information is unavailable. I suppose that the management means by this that the information is highly confidential. Probably, the management does not want thousands of Savage fans making pilgrimages to the actual floor and so interfering with the business which now occupies it.

I'll guess that since Doc would want to be as highly placed as possible, his HQ were on one of the floors between the eightieth and the eighty-sixth. On the other hand, since his visitors never transferred at the eightieth to go to a higher floor, if we can believe Dent, he may have been in a story between the seventieth and the eightieth.

---

* *The supersaga has finally been told, in Will Murray's* Skull Island *(Altus Press, 2013). The novel identifies a different paternal lineage for Doc than that identified by Farmer, as well as a different mother. Of course, it should be remembered that Farmer was writing a biography about the real man on whom the character Doc Savage was based, Dr. James Clarke Wildman, Jr. —WSE*

For the purposes of this book, and in deference to those who would be outraged if any other were named, the eighty-sixth will be designated as Doc's throughout this book. And it is called out as such in Figure 1.

From the eighty-sixth floor, three pneumatic tubes and three secret elevators lead downward. The two small tubes are in the reception room. One delivers newspapers from the lobby on the ground floor. The other delivers mail from the central post office on Thirty-third Street between Eighth and Ninth avenues. The third tube, the giant, propels its passenger car from a hidden compartment to the Hidalgo Trading Company building on Thirty-fourth Street by the Hudson River. Monk Mayfair called this great pneumatic tube and its car the "flea run" or the "go-devil" or the "angel wagon."

Obviously, the pneumatic tubes and the secret elevators were not afterthoughts. They were planned before the Empire State Building was built, and the shafts and tubes for them were installed during the construction. The mail and newspaper tubes must have been used as soon as Doc's father occupied the eighty-sixth. The secret elevator near the public elevators is first mentioned in *Pirate of the Pacific* (July 1933). But Doc had installed it before this adventure, probably shortly after the events of *Quest of the Spider*.

The first mention of the flea run is in *The Midas Man* (August 1936).* The chronology (Addendum 2) considers this supersaga to have occurred in June 1935. So it took about four and a half years after the skyscraper was built before the great pneumatic tube was ready for operation. During most of this time, digging through the hard bedrock of Manhattan Island from the basement of the Empire State Building westward under Thirty-fourth Street to the Hudson River had been taking place. The bill for this would have given anybody but Doc the blind staggers even to contemplate. He merely sent out another radio signal to the Valley of the Vanished in Central America, and another burro caravan of Mayan gold would wend out of the mountains, headed for the seaport of Blanco Grande.

Of the three hidden elevators, two could go all the way to the subbasement garage. The third went to one of Doc's secret apartments on lower floors. The only one of these which is located specifically is on the seventy-fourth floor. This, however, does not seem to have been one of those to which the second secret elevator led. This was accessible by a regular route from the corridor outside it. The third went to a secret apartment on the thirteenth floor. This apartment is not mentioned in the supersagas but is in Dent's notebook.

The subbasement garage housed Doc's fleet of armored limousines, touring cars, roadsters, a taxicab, and an old laundry truck which contained a chemical laboratory. In the early stories the vehicles are lifted to street level by a special elevator. By the time of *The Man Who Shook the Earth* (February 1934), a ramp had been built for the cars to drive out through the giant steel door. Except for a few building employees, no one knew of the garage. By the big doorway was a smaller one which Doc and his gang sometimes used when on foot. They also used a secret stairway from the garage into the lobby.

---

* *Per Will Murray, the flea run was first introduced in* Mystery Under the Sea, *but the scene was cut, although later restored in the Sanctum Books edition.*—WSE

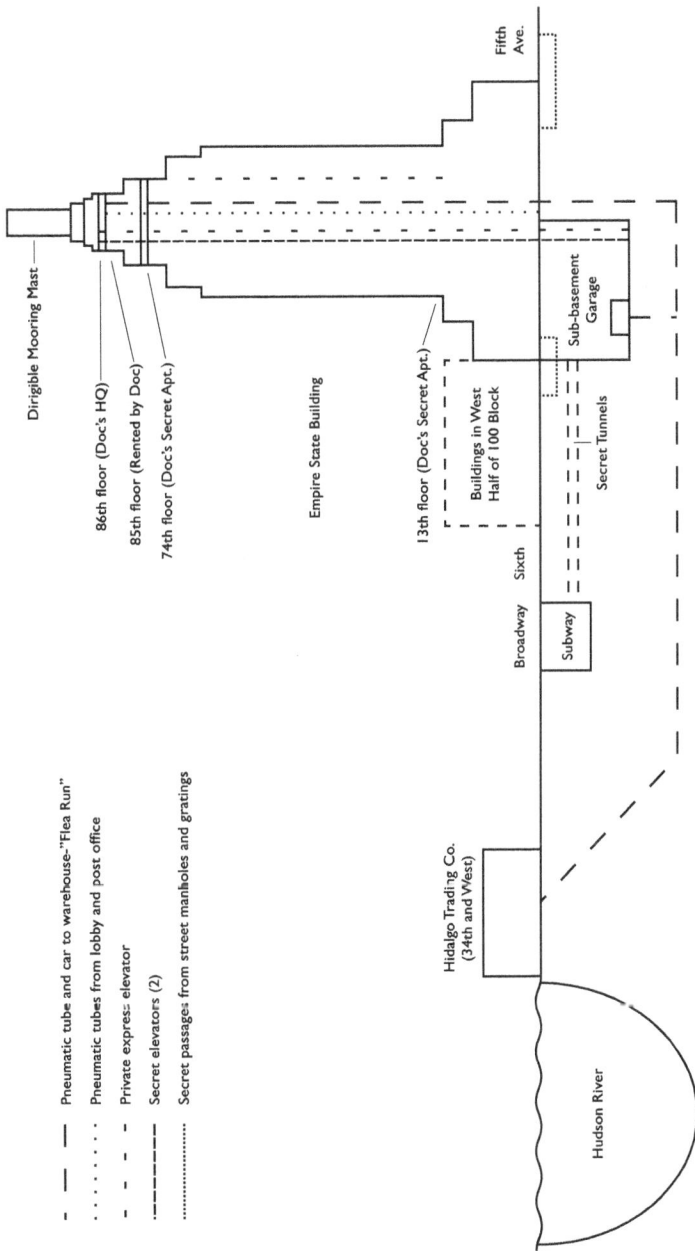

Figure 1. Not drawn to scale

Where was the entrance to the subbasement garage?

I checked out the possibilities during a trip in October 1972. After rounding the ESB several times, I concluded that it could only have been at the southwestern corner of the building. The rest of the ground floor is occupied by entrances to the lobby, a restaurant, and various businesses. It would not have been beyond Doc's means to buy one of the stores and install machinery to open its entire front during ingress or egress. But the vehicle would have had to drive over a sidewalk intended only for pedestrians and mount a curb. He could not have kept that a secret for very long.

The southwestern corner forms the wall of a loading dock, the area for which is in a large recess. A mechanism could have swung out a section of this wall and part of the attached loading platform. The workers there would certainly learn of its existence, but it can be presumed that Doc paid them enough to keep their mouths shut. However, any enemy with determination could have found out about it, and this was indeed the case. Doc's secret exit was really no secret.

The garage doors opened automatically when a button was pressed on the dash of the vehicle that was going out or in. This caused transmission of coded radio signals to a mechanism which opened and closed the door. The code was changed once a week to prevent crooks from learning it. The use of radio signals to open doors is old today, but in the early 1930s it was "hot stuff."

The two elevators which went into the garage stopped near white concrete-walled passages leading to the nearby Broadway subway. In *The Mental Monster* Doc used some secret passages from street manholes and sewer gratings into the building. To cover their retreat into the skyscraper, Doc and his men triggered a device which shot out flaming gas. This prevented their enemies from following them. It also gave them the idea that an accidental spark had caused the explosion of a leaking gas main and that Doc and his pals must have died in the blast. The device was Monk's invention. He had also supervised the installation of the gadgets.

Those who went to Doc's HQ to ask for help or to kill the lion in his den, had to take the public express elevator up. Only twice were attempts made to kill him in the eighty-sixth floor HQ by other routes. In the first recorded supersaga, *The Man of Bronze*, the Mayan assassin shot at him from the still uncompleted observation tower of the Chrysler Building. The first bullet shattered the window on which Doc's father had left a message visible only under a black light. The second punched through several inches of the brick and plaster of the wall and through the steel back of the huge old safe against the wall.

The weapon was found later and turned out to be a double-barreled elephant rifle, a .577-caliber Nitro-Express, manufactured by Webley and Scott of England. Fired from a height of about 1,040 feet, the 750-grain bullets traveled approximately a half mile. The sniper had not hit Doc, but he came close. His shooting was very good, since it was night and raining. Looking up through binoculars, he counted upwards until he came to the eighty-sixth floor. Here was a light in "the west corner of the building." Dent meant the northwest corner, since later stories make it clear that the reception room had two walls of windows. Moreover, only the Chrysler Building would have been tall enough for a sniper to be anywhere near high enough to get a good shot at the eighty-sixth floor.

The Chrysler Building was at that time the second highest in the world, being 1,046 feet high. It had seventy-seven stories, including the spire, which meant that the Mayan had to shoot upwards from a point nine stories lower than his target. Dent says that the building from which the Mayan fired was eighty stories high and that it was topped by a 150-foot observation tower. No such building existed. The only two structures to come close to the ones described are the Empire State and Chrysler buildings. On the other hand, since Doc's HQ were not really on the eighty-sixth floor, they could have been level with or even lower than the sniper, and he would not have had to shoot upwards.

Unfortunately, there is grave doubt that a .577-caliber rifle bullet would punch through many inches of stone and the thick wall of a safe after a half-mile flight. Such a bullet has terrific shock power; it can knock down an elephant inside a quarter-mile range. But the large bullet has a higher air resistance and a lower velocity than rifles designed for sniping at long distances. The truth is that a .577 would not penetrate so much stone and an inch or two of steel at the end of a half mile.

The Chrysler Building had to be the place from which the sniper shot, because it was the only one high enough for the sniper to see

Doc's figure against the lighted window. But the rifle described as the sniper's weapon could not have done the job nearly as well as, say, a Springfield rifle using the Ml cartridge. This expels a 172-grain boat-tailed bullet with an extreme range of 3,500 yards or nearly two miles. Whether or not the bullet would have penetrated so much stone and hard steel is debatable. In any event, Dent described the weapon as an elephant rifle in order to make the scene more impressive. He was free to fictionize, and fictionize he did.

The second attempt using an unconventional route to get to Doc will be described later.

Anybody who wanted to visit Doc through regular channels had to phone him first. Doc's number was unlisted, but the telephone operators always put through anyone who said their case was important. Sometimes Doc himself answered. More often the caller heard a voice that was definitely not Doc's. This was a squeaky voice, a child's. Sometimes a man with a Harvard accent would answer. These two voices belonged to Monk and Ham, who apparently spent much of their time waiting for the phone to ring.

More often, the call would go through a screening agency. In the beginning, this agency was comprised of graduates of Doc's upstate college. Later, it was a private detective agency, though possibly this also was run by the graduates.

Monk and Ham were screening for Doc in a room on the second floor in *The Feathered Octopus*. In *The Awful Egg* they were interviewing visitors in a twentieth-floor room. They had transferred to the fifth floor in *Birds of Death*. The screening room, not open at night, was on the twelfth floor in *The Wee Ones*. A private detective agency questioned would-be visitors on the fourth floor in *Measures for a Coffin*. By the time of *Five Fathoms Dead*, the agency had moved to the fifth floor. In *The Exploding Lake* it was on the seventh floor, Room 710, but apparently Ham was working with them. He was the only one there when fat Orlin Dartlic was attacked by three men with knives.

In the early days, a private elevator with one operator could take the visitor directly to the eighty-sixth floor. This does not seem likely in view of the known facts about the ESB elevator system.

The Otis Elevator Company had installed in the ESB sixty-four express, signal-controlled elevators. These were of the self-leveling type and stopped and started automatically by the pressing of buttons numbered for each floor. Otis had developed and installed for the first time a special device to take the place of human dispatchers. This prevented any two cages from stopping to answer the same signal and so wasting the time of one cage. The device also sent cages from the ground floor at carefully spaced intervals to give a smoothly running and continuous service.

Only two out of the sixty-four elevators went as high as the eightieth floor. The eightieth was the extreme upper limit for any car. None could go any higher because the weight of the cables required for this elevation was too heavy. Thus, all passengers were required to transfer at the eightieth floor to another car. This took them up to the eighty-sixth, where they could get onto the lower observation platform. Or, if they wished, they could take a third elevator up to the 102nd story, which was in the mooring mast (observation tower). The mast was two hundred feet high and had been intended as the mooring for intercontinental passenger dirigibles. The eighty-sixth floor was to be a depot for the dirigible passengers. But the powerful, dangerous updraft had prevented execution of this plan.

Apparently, Doc was responsible for this engineering goof, since he oversaw the plans designed by Renny and authorized them. Why Doc forgot the strong winds is not explained by Dent. But, as we have seen, Doc made mistakes, forgot things, just as all mortal men do.

The requirement for exchange of elevators by the passengers at the eightieth floor throws an unbendable crowbar into the machinery of the Doc Savage stories. So many of these hinge on direct elevator trips to and from the eighty-sixth floor. Perhaps Dent speeded up events, and hence the story, by eliminating transfer from one cage to another. He ignored the facts and had the cage go directly to the HQ. On the other hand, the actual HQ may have been on the eightieth floor or floors below it and so the visitors really used only one elevator.

But what about the bronze man's main secret express? This dropped from the HQ with such speed that the occupants felt as if they were floating a few inches off the cage floor. When it decelerated, it did it so abruptly that even the trollishly powerful Monk was forced to his knees. Only Doc remained standing. And the elevator shot up with equal speed from the depths of the subbasement garage straight to the HQ.

Yet the building laws not only forbade any elevator to exceed the eighty-story-in-one-trip limit, they restricted the elevator speed to twelve hundred feet a minute. A short time before the ESB was built, the legal extreme velocity had been only seven hundred feet a minute.

The Otis Elevator Company had determined by experiments (to its own satisfaction, anyway) that twelve hundred feet per minute was the approximate limit of speed which the human body could endure in an eighty-story trip, considering the acceleration/deceleration factors. It concluded, however, that it was possible to construct elevators capable of traveling nearly two thousand feet a minute. As it was, the ESB express cages could go from the first story to the eightieth in a few seconds over a minute.

To get his private express elevator, Doc had to overcome two obstacles. First, he had to invent a metal alloy to be used for the cables of the cage. This would have to be both strong enough and light enough to lift the cage from the deep subbasement garage to the HQ floor with no danger of cables breaking. Second, he would have to keep the building inspectors from knowing about his express conveyance.

The first was no difficult problem for Doc. He developed a number of lightweight and extremely tough alloys during his career. As for the inspectors, Doc could have arranged matters so that the inspectors never became aware of the existence of the secret elevator. No doubt, an examination of the building blueprints would have revealed to the inspectors that a shaft obviously designed for an elevator cage was hidden in the building. That is, the inspectors would have seen this immediately if they had the true blueprints.

Doc and Renny had been the hidden powers behind the construction of the ESB. The public never suspected their involvement with the ESB. As far as anyone outside the circle of Doc, his father, and his aides knew, Empire State, Incorporated, owned the building. This organization was headed by Alfred. E. Smith, the unhappy Happy Warrior and ex-governor of New York State. It included in its directorate Pierre S. Du Pont, Louis G. Kaufman, and Lawrence A. Wien. Shreve, Lamb, and Harmon was the company responsible for the building's design. H. G. Balcom was consultant for the erection of the steel. Meyer, Strong, and Jones, Inc., was the engineering firm which installed the utilities. Post and McCord, Inc., set up the steel framework for Starrett Brothers and Eken, Inc., the general contractors.

But we know who was really responsible for the design of the ESB and for certain installations and who really owned the building.

Doc would never have stooped to bribing the building inspectors even if they had been bribable. But Doc did not mind bending, or even breaking, the law as long as it was for the abstract quality of goodness or for the specific good of individuals or the people. He needed the express elevator in his fight against crime, and so he got it. How he managed to conceal it and the passenger pneumatic tube from the inspectors is something we do not know. But the richest and the smartest man in the world would have ways and means to do just about anything he wished to do.

The express operated on conventional principles for a long time. But in *Dust of Death* (October 1935) Doc has installed an air-compression device at the bottom of the shaft. This is fortunate, because a short time after the installation, villains cut the cables and the cage fell eighty or more stories into the subbasement, only to be slowed down and halted by the cushion of squeezed air beneath it.

By the time of *The Green Master* (Winter 1949) Doc had removed the cables. The express, like the car to the Hidalgo Trading Company, now operated on pneumatic pressure. Its acceleration/deceleration was so violent that the interior of the cage had to be padded. It threw everybody but Doc to the floor. (Apparently, it never occurred to Doc to install hanging straps or restraining harnesses for the benefit of the passengers.)

This use of pneumatic pressure would have kept the cage from stopping at intermediate floors. Thus, Doc and his aides could enter it only from the HQ floor or the subbasement garage. They could no longer use the ground-floor-lobby exit/entrance, which was behind a wall panel. It must have disconcerted uninitiates to see Doc disappear behind the panel or come out from behind it. This may explain why the secret express was later moved to another shaft (*The King of Terror*, April 1943).

The second location had its ground terminus at the blind end of a small hall which formed a narrow thumb off the main lobby. The first reference to this relocation is in *Birds of Death* (October 1941). Here Benjamin Boot is told by the starter in the lobby to take the elevator *around* the corner. He does so and finds in the cage one control board with one pushbutton. It is simply labeled: DOC SAVAGE. (Doc was often informal.) The cage only ascended five stories, however, and the door opened directly into a screening room. Here Monk and Ham interviewed Boot to determine if his business was important enough to interrupt Doc's electrochemistry experiments.

In earlier days (and again in later days) the cage was occupied by an operator. Those entering or leaving it might have noticed that mirrors across the lobby enabled the elevator passengers to see the entire lobby. Doc had installed these as a safety precaution at about the time of *The Red Skull*.

The controls and the plaque were changed from time to time. In *The Evil Gnome* the cage is in the rear of the lobby and has no operator. There are two buttons: UP and DOWN. Over the UP is a plaque: CLARK SAVAGE, JR. Usually, however, the cage has an operator. In *Return from Cormoral* (Spring 1949), the next-to-last of Doc's recorded adventures, the elevator is run by a human operator. Doc enters it to go up to the HQ floor and speaks to the new man at the controls. This man is obviously a fake, since he does not know the code words that genuine operators in Doc's building are given each week. Doc takes care of the man in a short time without the man ever catching on. Doc puts him to sleep by breaking one of his anesthetic gas grenades, puts a plaster cast on the man's elbow, and then leaves. The man awakes sometime later and is told that he has fainted and wrenched his elbow when he fell.

The crook does not understand what has happened, but he does not like it. However, the three pistols he carries are still on him, so he decides that his disguise has not been exposed. He takes the day off, not knowing that Doc has installed a small radio transmitter in the cast and that Monk and Ham will soon be following him.

This adventure is the last in which the elevator to the HQ floor is mentioned.

6

THE EIGHTY-SIXTH FLOOR

IN *THE EVIL GNOME* Lion Ellison, the beautiful heroine, is directed to the private elevator in the rear of the lobby. She presses the UP button and is shot directly to the eighty-sixth floor. However, as we know, this elevator would not be permitted to go higher than the eightieth. Here Lion undoubtedly transferred to another of Doc's private cages and went on up to the eighty-sixth. This cage was in the bank of elevator shafts called out as (1) Figure 2.

Before Lion can get out of the cage, a voice from a loudspeaker in the ceiling tells her to remove the knife from her purse. Ham Brooks then comes out of a secret room (2) through a small door into the elevator. He has used the X-ray machine in (2) to locate and identify any concealed weapons carried by passengers. In later supersagas, it won't be necessary to keep a man in the secret room. The X-ray pictures will be transmitted by TV to wall screens in the three rooms of Doc's HQ. The X-ray is also used to fog the film of newspaper reporters who try to sneak cameras in.

Lion Ellison goes down a modestly decorated corridor. It has only blank walls. However, in *The Czar of Fear* (November 1933) the corridor is richly decorated and even has a mirror. *The Angry Ghost* (February 1940) states that it's a long plain hallway of rich marble.

From the account in *The Evil Gnome*, it would appear that the door (D) to the reception room could be seen from the elevator. Too many other supersagas make it evident that the door is around a corner of a corridor. *The Phantom City* differs from most in saying that the reception room door is halfway down the corridor. And so it is, as may be seen from Figure 2. The door is halfway down a corridor after you turn the corner from the elevator corridor.

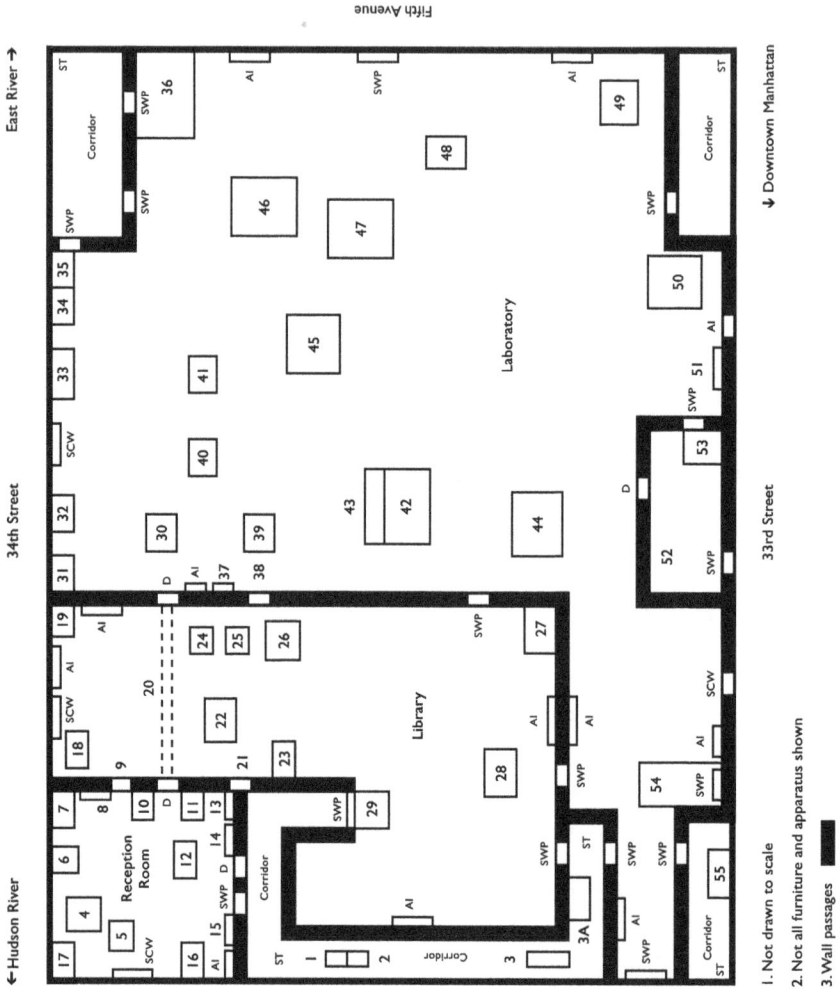

Figure 2. 86th Floor Diagram

Key to Figure 2

AI = basement garage and eighty-sixth-floor alarm indicators
SWP = secret wall panel
SCW = specially constructed windows
ST = stairway
D = doorway

1. Elevator bank
2. Secret room (next to elevator)
3. Secret elevator to basement garage
3A. Later location of 3
4. Inlaid oriental table
5. Old leather chair (wired)
6. Wall safe (and hidden rack for pistols)
7. File cabinet
8. Stuffed fish on wall
9. Concealed clothes locker
10. Open clothes locker
11. Pneumatic mail and newspaper tubes
12. Old walnut desk
13. Concealed televisiphone
14. Wall TV receiver
15. Picture of Doc's father
16. Teletype machine
17. Cabinet for stereopticon, supermachine pistols
18. Big chart case
19. Corner cabinet for guns
20. Aisle formed by bookcases and glass-wall trap
21. Concealed observation niche
22. Chair with restrained, alarms, lie detector
23. Desk containing binoculars
24. Table with telephone battery
25. Case containing ossified young pterodactyl
26. Mounted African lion
27. Bookcase concealing wall niche instruments
28. Medal display case

29. Bookcase and niche with reception room easy-chair lie-detector indicators
30. Disguised steel trap
31. Distilled-water apparatus
32. X-ray machine
33. Fingerprint TV transmitter, teletype, phone robot
34. TV receivers and short-wave transceivers
35. Photographic darkroom
36. Living quarters
37. Wall panel with levers for "ring-heater" transmitters
38. Concealed wall niche with chair
39. Big apparatus concealing 38
40. Table with illuminated top
41. Cabinet with televisiphone
42. Pillar containing mooring-mast elevator shaft
43. Secret stairway to mooring-mast interior
44. Piles of metal cases
45. Huge fishbowl with secret entrance to tiny elevator
46. Big electric furnaces and workbench
47. Giant test chamber
48. Large chest holding gray vapor-trace cylinders
49. Table with typewriter
50. Giant wheeled ray-repeller machine
51. Concealed niche with couch
52. Storeroom
53. Pneumatic "flea run" tube entrance
54. Surgical operating room
55. Corridor pillar concealing tiny elevator

In most of the stories, the corridor floor, when described, is tiled. Apparently, Doc had it luxuriously carpeted for a while (in *The Man Who Shook the Earth*, February 1934). Later, he removed the covering.

Most of Doc's visitors—evil or good—looked up and down the corridor with a keen eye after getting out of the elevator. None suspected that a wall panel down the hallway concealed Doc's superspeed express elevator (3). They could, however, see past the elevator bank to the nearest stairway (ST). This, according to *The Man of Bronze*, was sixty feet from the reception room door. If they had gone south down the corridor and around the corner, they would have found another stairway (ST). Near it was a pillar (3A) containing a secret shaft. This was to hold the express elevator of (3) when Doc relocated it. Presumably, he moved it so he could get to it with less chance of being observed. He could pass through a secret panel (SWP) in the laboratory wall and cross the corridor without being seen by anyone getting off the regular elevator (1).

Lion Ellison, looking at the reception room door, sees a bronze-colored panel bearing in plain letters the legend: CLARK SAVAGE, JR. No doorbell is mentioned, but there is no need to do so since Ham accompanies her. The first description of the door is in *Quest of the Spider*, the third published supersaga. Big Eric Danielsen and his beautiful daughter, Edna, arrive in Manhattan at Grand Central Station. Their taxi cuts over to Fifth Avenue and goes south on it before stopping in front of a towering white skyscraper. (This is one more locative item establishing the ESB as the site of Doc's HQ.) On the eighty-sixth floor they touch a bell button beside a severely plain door with no lettering.

Three stories later, in *The Red Skull*, the door bears, in extremely small bronze-colored letters: DOC SAVAGE. The bell button is still there. Poison smeared on it kills Bandy Stevens when he presses it.

"Bandy had ridden his last bronc, unless they have cow ponies in the hereafter."

By the time of *The Phantom City*, the tenth published issue, the lettering has changed to: CLARK SAVAGE, JR. This is kept unchanged through most of the supersagas.

In *The Man Who Shook the Earth* (February 1934) the bell button is gone. The door has a knob and a lock. The door, however, opens mysteriously when Doc approaches it. So do the library and laboratory doors, the warehouse door, and the release valves of some gas containers. All open when Doc nears them. Monk is mystified—dumbfounded, in fact. But he refuses to comment on these phenomena. Not until he is in a frenzy of curiosity does he break down and ask Doc how he does it.

Doc explains that he carries a piece of radioactive substance in his pocket. The doors and the valves have driving mechanisms which are attached to a relay and a screen sensitive to radioactivity. When Doc is close enough, the radioactive particles strike the screen, even through cloth or metal, and this starts the chain of electrochemomechanical events which results in the opening or closing of the doors.

Today such a device is commonplace. In the early 1930s, the reader of the supersagas was thrilled by this novelty. In later stories, Doc, his aides, and his cousin, Patricia, would carry radioactive tokens which looked like coins to open the HQ and Hidalgo Trading Company doors.

In *The Mystery on the Snow* (May 1934) Doc equips the reception room with a new door. It looks like wood but is of thick steel with a veneer coating. In the panel is a slit for a letter drop. Inasmuch as Doc's mail is delivered directly from the central post office via the pneumatic tube, the reader might wonder why a mail slot in the door is needed. No doubt, Doc installed it for the benefit of those who might not want to use the regular mail service. This is the only mention in all 181 supersagas of a letter drop, and Doc must have got another door, minus the mail-drop slit, very soon thereafter. Chances are that Doc found that more poison and explosives came through the slit than mail.

The door still has a knob in *The King Maker* (June 1934). In *The Terror in the Navy* (April 1937) the knob is gone. In *The Golden Peril* (December 1937) it's back again. This could be because *The Golden Peril* case occurred before *The Terror in the Navy*, even if the latter was published first. It's more likely that Dent forgot that the knob had been eliminated. As has been noted, Dent and other "Robeson" writers sometimes (or perhaps often) made mistakes because of their haste in writing these half-fictional narratives.

Doc's visitor would step into the reception room, and the door would automatically shut behind him. He would find himself in an air-conditioned room forty feet long and twenty feet wide. (The reception room is shown as a square in Figure 2 for the sake of convenience.) The walls of this room were said to be soundproofed, but it could not have been very effective. In several supersagas those in the corridor can hear voices in the reception room. And in *Dust of Death* Doc hears a cry for help from the corridor while he is in this room.

The visitor would be standing on a very beautiful carpet, a gift from the Khedive of Egypt for some unspecified service Doc had once done for him. In *Mystery Under the Sea* (February 1936) part of this rug is cut out by Seaworthy so he can study the writing left on it by a murdered man. Undoubtedly, Doc had a new piece woven into it. In *The Submarine Mystery* (June 1938) the rug is electrified, as the shocked "Prince Albert" discovers.

Across the room, by the north windows, is a massive oriental table (4). This had many exquisite inlays on its top, some of which were disguised controls. Pressing one opens the door. Another can be used as a telegraph key to transmit messages to the subbasement garage. Pressure on another causes a transparent bulletproof glass shield to drop from the ceiling before the reception room door. Another is the control which causes metal gates to block the stairways of the corridors. However, in *The Roar Devil* (June 1935) the stairways are always kept locked. This does not seem likely, since the building inspectors would have forced Doc to unlock them. In case of emergency, the people on the observation floor above would have had to have an open route to safety on the lower floors. Dent threw in this statement about the locked stairway gates without pausing to think out the consequences.

By the time of *The Headless Men* (June 1941) two new defenses are installed in the reception room. One is a magnetic field which paralyzes anyone stepping on the floor. Ham presses the appropriate inlay to torment Monk with the magnetic field. Also, an invisible flexible curtain is lowered into the room by pressing another inlay. One of the inlays, if pressed, will cause all elevators in the building to stop. Its neighbor causes the stairways on the eighty-sixth floor to be flooded with a gas which puts a person into a sleep even if the gas has only come into contact with the skin pores.

An adjacent inlay causes a light in the lobby to flash and so warns Doc's armed elevator starters that something is up. Pressing yet another inlay releases a chemical film on the corridor floor just outside the door. This impregnates the shoes of anyone there, and his trail may be followed by observing the traces of the stuff on the floor or ground through infrared glasses. A concealed alarm in the table buzzes, accompanied by several flashing red lights disguised as inlays, if an unauthorized person is in the private elevator. Anesthetic gas can then be released into the elevator by pressing another inlay, and two other inlays control the stopping or starting of the elevator.

On the inlaid table is an inkstand with pens and wells with red and black ink. Beside these is a box which holds cigars in individual vacuum containers. These cigars, costing at least ten dollars apiece, take the wind out of the big phony, Judborn Tugg, in *The Czar of Fear*. At one end of the table is an intercom box.

Near the inlaid table is a huge, very comfortable, stuffed leather chair (5). This is equipped with Doc's new lie detector by the time of the events of *The Freckled Shark* and probably before then. The detector is concealed inside the chair and apparently is operated by means of an inductive field. Its indicators are in a niche in the library wall (21). A large bookcase which can be swung aside conceals Doc in his chair as he watches on the instruments the reactions of Rhoda Haven to Johnny's questions. This chair is completely burned by the chief villain's gadget in *The Headless Men*, but apparently it is replaced a short time later.

The visitor will notice that the reception room windows are closed. He probably attributes this to the demands of the air conditioning. He won't know that the window glass is composed of Doc's own invention, a one-way bulletproof "health" glass. In fact, Doc has two factories going full-blast producing this much-in-demand commodity. These windows are first mentioned in *The Derrick Devil* (February 1937). He may have had them installed much earlier, since the attempt of the Mayan sniper in the first recorded supersaga should have made him aware of their necessity. However, in *The Terror in the Navy* (April 1937) crooks are watching Doc through the windows from a balloon. A few pages later, all of a sudden, the windows have one-way glass. The only explanation I can offer for this discrepancy is that Doc deliberately opened the windows so that the crooks could observe him.

The ceiling of the reception room (*Mystery Under the Sea*) is "decorated in modernistic fashion, with trim triangles and discs of shiny metals and colored glass." What seems to be an ordinary glass plate in it is actually the lens of a movie camera recessed into the ceiling. This camera takes pictures of the beautiful Diamond Eve Post, her companion, Seaworthy, and Captain Flamingo, who kicked the unconscious Ham and Monk in the ribs so hard. A flashing red light in the ceiling indicates that someone is coming down the hall. By the time of *The Terrible Stork* (June 1945) the ceiling needs repainting. If it was redone, Dent doesn't mention it.

Against the wall, near a corner, is a forty-year-old safe (6) which had belonged to the elder Savage. It is as high as Doc's shoulders, which makes it at least six feet high. It is of laminated construction with materials that can stand any conventional melting devices. Its interior is heavily insulated with lead and coated with a special rubberlike composition. One of the largest amounts of radium in the world in the possession of a private individual is kept here for experiments. Behind the safe is a niche containing a rack for the supermachine pistols.

Near the safe is a file cabinet (7). On the wall beside it is a huge stuffed fish (8) which contains a peephole through which Doc examines the reception room while hiding in a wall passage behind it.

Next is a concealed clothes locker (9), and a little farther south is a visible locker for clothes (10).

Just south of the door (D) to the library are two pneumatic tubes (11). One receives mail directly from the central P.O. on Thirty-second and Eighth. The other delivers newspapers from the stand in the ground-floor lobby. Signals flash when these are operated.

The old walnut desk (12) holds on its top a televisiphone. Its glass top is the screen for an interoffice TV communicator. One of its drawers contains a mass of phones and indicators. This old desk, however, is blasted apart in *The Headless Men* by the villains.

Around the corner from it is a niche concealing another televisiphone (13). Beside it is a blank plate on the wall which is the screen of a TV receiver (14). This shows X-ray photos of visitors in the corridor if they carry any metal object larger than a small suit button. After the X-ray quits operating, the screen shows normal films of the visitors.

A picture of Doc's father (15) hangs on the wall on the other side of the door. Dent, in *The Land of Terror*, says that its resemblance to Doc was marked. Sammy Wales, however, in *No Light to Die By*, states that Doc does *not* resemble his father very much. Such observations are, of course, strongly influenced by subjective factors. We do know from Doctor Watson's description of Doc's father in Watson's *The Adventure of the Priory School* that he was small and had blue eyes and mobile features. His hair probably was not bronze, though it may have been a vivid red, like his father's, the sixth duke's.

Next to the picture is an alarm indicator (AI) which gives visual and audible warnings of intruders in the subbasement garage or in the eighty-sixth-floor rooms. These AI are on the walls of every room and in such numbers and locations that an occupant can see them no matter what direction he faces.

Against the south part of the western wall is a teletype machine (16) connected to the police circuits.

Set in the one-way windows are huge specially constructed windows (SCW). These can be opened wide for firing of the giant wheeled ray-repeller machine (50). One of the SCW in the east or south laboratory walls is used in *The Flying Goblin* (July 1940). It does its work well, and then, apparently, is never fired again. If it had failed, Doc and Ham and Monk would have been blown apart, along with most of the eighty-sixth floor.

In the northwest corner is a cabinet (17) holding a stereopticon and some supermachine pistols.

The uninitiated, passing through the door into the enormous library, might travel directly toward the laboratory door. He will do so within an aisle (20) formed by great bookcases. If he does not progress in a certain way—unspecified by Dent—he will suddenly find himself in a glass cage dropped out of the ceiling.

The visitor, if he pauses just after passing through the door and then turns north, sees near the northwest corner a large chart case (18). In the northeast corner is a big cabinet (19) holding rifles and other weapons.

The place inside the wall (21) has been noted. But Doc could do more than watch the lie-detector indicators in the easy chair in the reception room. Through peepholes he could observe the reception room, the corridor outside it, or the library.

Near the concealed place is an easy chair (22) which snaps out steel bands to restrain a prisoner. It also contains a capacity alarm so that Doc will know if the person in the chair has suddenly left it. Like the reception room easy chair, it hides an inductive-field lie detector.

Near the chair is a desk containing some binoculars (23), which Doc always seemed to be using. Across the room from it is a table (24) with a battery of telephones. This figures quite often in the Savage supersagas. Near it is the case (25) holding the ossified body of a young pterodactyl. To its south is the mounted African lion (26) which O. W. Bittman had stuffed after shooting it to save the life of Doc's father (*The Land of Terror*). Bittman, however, tried to kill the son.

In the southeast corner is a bookcase (27). It conceals a wall niche in which are telephone robots and a loudspeaker switch.

Near the library's south wall is the display case (28) noted by Sammy Wales in *No Light to Die By*. It holds, among other decorations, the Congressional Medal of Honor and four Purple Hearts. Sammy thinks that these are Doc's. But he could not have won them for his exploits in World War II. Though a brigadier general in the Army Reserve, he was never activated. He did see action during World War II—actually, more than most soldiers. But it was always as a civilian, even though the U. S. Government sent him on most of his missions.

Doc must have won the medals for his services in World War I. The Purple Hearts would have been given him sometime after 1932. It was then that President Hoover reactivated the honor, which had been originated by George Washington but had been neglected after three were given to Revolutionary War veterans. Hoover's action made the honor retroactive.

Continuing clockwise around the library, the visitor passes another bookcase (29). He does not know that it conceals another niche, or that it also hides dials and styli connected to the easy-chair lie detectors.

The visitor then goes through the door into the laboratory. Hidden controls can cause a blue flame barrier to spurt across the doorway. This is used in *Murder Mirage* to keep the villains from leaving the laboratory.

The laboratory is a vast white-enameled room which Monk, in *The Yellow Cloud*, calls "the Wizard's Den." It occupies two thirds of the floor space, according to most accounts. It is crammed with supplies and apparatus. Not even the great Federal Department of Justice laboratory can equal it. It is the second most complete laboratory in the world, exceeded in equipment only by Doc's laboratory in his Fortress of Solitude. Some pieces of apparatus, most of them Doc's own invention, are as ponderous as trucks.

Doc, of course, has every facility needed for making models in his laboratory. But Doc is often too busy to do this himself, and so he gives much of this type of work to Tolliver Jonas. Jonas (in *The Terrible Stork*) has a model shop on the eighty-second floor of the ESB. He shares his place of business with a patent attorney, J. B. Fowler. Jonas is a young man with a wooden leg. He can do the very exacting and difficult work required by Doc in a very short time and on sudden notice. But his bills are not small.

In all descriptions which include the number of walls, the laboratory is said to have three walls of windows. The south wall is apparently solid, except, of course, for the specially constructed windows. No doubt Dent was thinking of these when he wrote in *The Monsters* that there were windows on all four sides. In *Murder Mirage* the trapped Bedouin runs over to the laboratory wall to look for a window through which to escape. He finds none. This would seem to contradict all other accounts of the windows. But this supersaga was written by Laurence Donovan. Donovan either threw in the part about there being no windows or he failed to specify that it was the south wall to which the Bedouin ran. Dent, it must be remembered, was the only writer of the "Robeson" group who was familiar with the eighty-sixth-floor setup. Even he made errors, which he did not have time to correct even if he had wished to do so.

The laboratory floor is of brick, with here and there some rubber composition mats. The unwary intruder will never guess—until it is too late—that a trap (30) lies in his path not too far from the door. This is a wolf trap designed for men—or human wolves. The brick floor will suddenly turn out to be of steel, and two sections will spring out and clamp the intruder's leg.

In the northwestern corner is an apparatus (31) for making distilled water. This has been installed after some enemies of Doc's tap the water supply to the eighty-sixth floor and pour poison into it.

Beside the still is a huge X-ray machine (32).

A long way down the laboratory, near the north windows, are several machines (33). One is a TV transmitter used to send finger-prints to the Department of Justice in Washington. Beside it is a teletype machine and a telephone robot with a loudspeaker switch.

A number of TV receivers (34) are nearby. One is for watching the corridor outside the reception room. The second screen shows the interior of Doc's private elevator. The others are for viewing the interiors of Doc's vehicles. All have been put to much good use over the years.

Also included under (34) are the extremely powerful short-wave radio transceivers used in so many supersagas. These, like the TV receivers, are enclosed in glass booths. Their antennas are up on the roof, running along the mooring mast.

The photographic darkroom (35) is often used by Doc or Monk. It contains equipment that will turn the scientists of Eastman Kodak pale with envy if they should learn of it.

Around the corner are the living quarters (36). Originally, this area seems to have been an open room. Doc later encloses it. Here he takes his refrigerated showers, changes his clothes, sleeps on the foldup bed, and occasionally cooks meals. The room holds a bathtub, but its use has gone unrecorded. It is this room that Monk uses in *Bequest of Evil* to put on the clothes Ham had picked for him after Monk inherited the earldom of Chester, Essex, and Cornwall. (Or thought he had.) It is into this room that Monk retires, cussing a blue streak, to study the book Ham has urged on him: *Ten Thousand Correct Sayings for Every Occasion*. Georgiana Lee, in *The Magic Forest*, stays here. Dent calls it, "a private room in Doc's skyscraper apartment," which indicates that the cubicle had definitely been made into an enclosed room.

On the inner wall, near the door into the laboratory, is a panel (37) with six levers. Each lever bears the name of one of the group. Depressing Renny's lever, for instance, causes transmission of a radio wave of a certain frequency. This heats up a receiving device in a ring on Renny's finger. On feeling the heat, Renny knows that he is wanted at HQ.

Near the "heat wave" panel is a niche (38) with a chair in which a hidden person can rest comfortably. It is concealed by a big piece of apparatus (39) the nature of which is not described. The table (40) has an illuminated top. Doc often uses this to clarify details in maps or manuscripts.

Just east of the table is a cabinet (41) with a televisiphone.

In the center of the eighty-sixth floor is a massive pillar (42). This contains the shaft for the mooring-mast (observation tower) elevator. The four main columns of the mooring mast are carried down through the building thirty-three feet below the surface to the bedrock. This anchoring is necessary to keep the horizontal pull of a moored dirigible from being transmitted to the upper parts of the building. Instead, the tugging will be transmitted to the massive concrete foundations. The moorings are not strong enough to keep the mast from being knocked off by the villains' repeller-ray gun during the distressing events of *Repel* (October 1937; retitled *The Deadly Dwarf*, Bantam reprint).

Doc has seen to it that the mast pillar is larger than it needs to be. He has built a false wall around it, and in the space between the two walls made not only a secret passage but a stairway (43). This leads up to a wall passage inside the mooring mast itself.

On the west-central part of the laboratory floor is a great pile of metal cases (44) containing supplies and metals.

Northeast of the big pillar is something that always catches the visitor's attention: a gigantic fishbowl (45) which holds many dangerous-looking fish, all teeth or all sharp spines or both. There are two signs on the bowl. One (in *The Men Who Smiled No More*) simply warns: POISON FISH. The other (in *Spook Hole*) reads: THESE FISH ARE POISONOUS SPECIES. KEEP AWAY!

The base of the fishbowl rests on the floor. Its top, chest-high to Doc, must be about six feet from the floor. In the bottom, on one side, is an aquarium castle. In the first-named supersaga above, Doc hides a photographic plate in the castle. In *Spook Hole*, Doc uses the bowl as a secret exit. A touch on a valve causes the water level of the bowl to sink about six inches. This exposes a circular glass tube over three feet in diameter which extends upwards in the center of the bowl. The optical design of the bowl makes it almost impossible for the tube to be seen when the water level is at its height. Doc jumps to the rim (who else can do this?), balances himself, then squats down and leans way out to remove the glass cover from the tube. Having done this, he steps over to the edge of the tube, balances himself, and then goes down into the tube. After replacing the glass cover, he lowers himself below the floor level on a ladder in a metal shaft. Dent does not say so, but doubtless Doc turns a lever inside the shaft so that the water level in the bowl will rise again.

The hole at the floor level inside the tube is invisible to observers because of the placement of mirrors in the bowl.

The ladder in the shaft leads to a tiny elevator just big enough for Doc (or two ordinary-sized men). The cage goes down into the building and deep under the ground. Doc steps out of the cage into a narrow tunnel. This leads directly into a big tool locker in the Broadway subway. Here Doc changes into grimy work clothes and emerges from the locker disguised as a subway worker.

Doc has a number of secret exits, horizontal and vertical. As Figure 2 shows, he can ease through secret wall panels (SWP) from any one room into the next or from any room into a corridor. One of the wall passages has a shaft down which he can go to a lower floor. From there he takes a regular elevator down to the lobby.

Laboratory test equipment is everywhere, of course, including big electric furnaces and a workbench (46). Ham often sits at the latter sharpening the point of his sword cane. Near this is a giant test chamber (47), and farther south is a large chest (48) which holds the cylinders Doc uses in *The Man Who Shook the Earth* to trace criminals. The cylinders are thrown out of all the windows, including the SCW in the south wall. Renny worries that the heavy cylinders might hit people on the sidewalks below, but they all blow up in green flames while still in the air. A gray vapor succeeds the flames, and the streets around the ESB are soon filled with a gray cloud. The villains escape in a touring car, though the vapor has settled on them before they do this. Doc then uses an ultraviolet device to locate them. Under its light, the touring car and the villains fluoresce greenly.

In the southeast corner of the laboratory is a table (49) with a typewriter which Doc uses in *The Pink Lady* (May 1941). No doubt, every room has a number of typewriters. Otherwise, Doc will have to walk half a city block every time he wants to type out a letter or a report. But this is the only time when one of the eighty-sixth-floor typewriters is mentioned.

Around the corner is the giant wheeled ray-repeller machine (50) described in *The Flying Goblin* and noted earlier in this chapter. The "flying goblin," by the way, is located by Doc's private radar set. He developed radar long before World War II but has found no personal use for it until now. Doc has, however, been a consultant on the Signal Corps development of the long-range radar first used in 1939.

Near the corner where the ray machine is kept is another niche (51) with a couch. This niche, like the others, is air conditioned and holds Doc and his aides when they have to hide and, at least once, Doc's prisoners.

Halfway along the south wall is the storeroom (52). It is as large as the living room of many mansions, though it looks small compared to the vast room housing it. It contains many supplies, including Doc's specially prepared cases and chests. These bear numbers to indicate their contents. The numbers are raised so that they can be identified in the dark by feel alone.

Inside the storeroom, accessible through a secret wall panel, is the terminus of the giant pneumatic tube (53) to the Hidalgo Trading Company warehouse on the Hudson River. The tiny car in it—Monk's "go-devil" or "angel wagon"—can hold just four passengers.

The car is bullet-shaped and has a thickly padded interior. No seats or seat belts are ever mentioned, but the occupants have straps to hang on to. Once all are aboard, the hatches are closed and the operator pulls a lever. A shock, a whining noise, and a great vibration follow. The passengers are jammed against the lower end as compressed air cushions it to a stop. Then the click of holding devices is heard, and a red light signals that the trip is over.

Doc does not fail to have medical facilities on the eighty-sixth floor. In addition to first-aid supplies stored in several places in each room, he has a completely equipped operating room (54) in the laboratory. Doc uses this in *The Green Death* when he is trying to determine the nature of the horrible Matto Grosso disease which has struck down Frick. He also used it on several other occasions to perform autopsies on visitors—wanted or unwanted—who have come to bad, and usually peculiar, ends at Doc's HQ.

The Green Death contains a puzzling reference which it would be nice to be able to ignore. It states that Doc took Frick's corpse deeper into his suite of offices. What suite? It's obvious from the majority of stories that the eighty-sixth floor is occupied by Doc only. Moreover, only three major rooms are ever described (except in one story). The three rooms are the reception room, the adjoining library, and the laboratory beyond the library.

But this use of "suite of offices" can be explained. Dent sometimes thought of the rooms as "offices," though his use of this is rather idiosyncratic. Thus, in the first story, *The Man of Bronze*, Dent refers to the great library as "another office adjoining." And he refers also to Doc's suite of offices.

Dent does not, however, explain the situation in the fifth published supersaga, *Pirate of the Pacific*. Chapter 6 of that book states that a suite of offices adjoins Doc's office. It is unoccupied because rents are so high and times so tough. An Oriental villain forces open the door of the adjoining suite and cuts a hole in the wall into Doc's office. This office, evidently, is what most of the other stories call the reception room.

Pirate of the Pacific poses a hard problem. It is the only story which even suggests that there were offices open for rent on the eighty-sixth floor.

There is only one way to deal with this. That is to regard the unrented suite of offices as fictional. It may be that Dent was never informed about the exact manner in which the Oriental got into Doc's reception room to steal the window with the invisible writing. Dent rattled out a scene to explain this without pausing to remember that the eighty-sixth floor had only one renter or ever would have (up to 1949, anyway).

Thus, we can be sure that the villain from the East did get into Doc's office. But just how he did it is something that perhaps only the Oriental knew. He does not live long enough after the deed to explain how he did it. Caught in the act, he starts to throw a knife at Renny, but Long Tom shoots him between the eyes.

The business of renting offices brings in another seeming contradiction. *The Metal Master* (March 1936) notes that Doc has also rented the eighty-fifth floor. He has done this to keep it unoccupied and so prevent crooks from trying to get into the eighty-sixth floor from the one below. Later, he must have decided that this was too expensive. *The Midas Man* (August 1936) tells of four men up to no good who rent some offices on the eighty-fifth and do just what Doc fears.*

By the time of *The Green Eagle* (July 1941), and probably long before that, Doc is renting the eighty-fifth floor again for his sole use. At least, he's renting some offices in it. Renny and Johnny use these to extend a net device in which to catch a crook Doc has thrown out of an eighty-sixth-floor window. Doc does this to frighten the crook's buddies into thinking he'll heave them out to a bloody death, too, if they don't talk.

Near the southwest corner of the laboratory is another secret wall panel. Doc goes through this in *The Laugh of Death* (October 1942). He then runs across the hall, opens an apparently solid pillar (55) and steps into a small elevator which he has recently installed.

In *The Laugh of Death* we learn that Doc has a secret hideout, in a not-too-respectable office building in Times Square, where he keeps supplies and disguises.

Though the eighty-sixth floor is used to the last, Doc has quit living in it by the time of the third-from-last story, *The Green Master*. He is residing in a hotel on Fifty-eighth Street not far from Madison. For some time, he's been changing his residence frequently as "a commonplace precaution." Why he doesn't continue to live on the eighty-sixth floor, where he would be best guarded, is not explained. We may, however, be sure that Doc has good reasons.

It is also near the end of his career that Doc seems to have lost much of his money, though this again is not explained. He can't afford to buy a yacht, a big comedown for a man who once purchased a newspaper publishing company as an item in a plot to catch a villain.

The big fleet of fabulous armed-and-armored vehicles in the subbasement garage is reduced to two. The others have been given to the government during the war. Those left no longer carry the distinctive license plates: DOC 1, DOC 2, or DS 1, DS 2. This may be because he is no longer so highly regarded by the authorities. He's been charged too many times with murder, kidnaping, jailbreak, flight to avoid arrest, flight to escape giving testimony, car stealing, piracy, malpractice, illegal use of drugs, illegal use of a hotel room,

---

* *According to Will Murray, the contradiction about Doc renting and then not renting the 85th floor is not a contradiction. The two stories,* The Midas Man *and* The Metal Master, *were published out of order. Doc probably rented the 85th floor as a direct result of the earlier incident.—WSE*

and a host of other misdemeanors and felonies. Even though Doc has cleared himself of these charges (though guilty of some), the police believe that where there's smoke there's fire.

Doc's wealth, and his image, have been getting steadily less and more tarnished since the war years.

7

THE HIDALGO TRADING
COMPANY AND ITS CRAFT

IN THE beginning, Doc keeps his airplanes in a hangar at a North Beach airport just outside New York City. He flies an autogyro out of there in the first supersaga, *The Man of Bronze*. Apparently, at this time no one but himself knows he is using this port. Otherwise, how account for Ham having to ask him where the gyro is kept?

An autogyro is more often spelled "autogiro," from its trademark *Autogiro*. It was a rotary-wing aircraft which used a propeller for forward motion and, instead of wings, a freely rotating rotor (like a horizontal propeller) for lift. The autogyro was a predecessor of the helicopter but, unlike the helicopter, could not hover in the air or make a vertical descent. And I feel even older because I have to explain what an autogyro is.

The first reference to the place where Doc keeps his amphibian planes is in *The Lost Oasis* (September 1933). This is a boathouse located on the Hudson River side of Manhattan Island.

Later, Doc stores his amphibian planes and boats in a huge building disguised as a warehouse. It isn't until about the time of *The Czar of Fear* (November 1933) that Doc puts up a sign on the front of the building. The sign: HIDALGO TRADING COMPANY.

The name is suggested by the tiny Central American nation in which Doc has a number of adventures and which supplies the gold for his charities and his fight against crime. The name evokes far-off vistas and exotic perfumes and hidden treasures. Many a person who went by the building must have wondered just what the company traded in and, for a minute or two, the more imaginative may have constructed in their minds all sorts of fabulous adventures. But none of the fantasies could have matched the realities that were launched from the Hidalgo Trading Company.

Adventure and excitement are the only commodities dealt with by the Hidalgo Trading Company. The company does not even have an official existence; it is not listed in the world's books; it does not have an unlisted telephone number. Doc and his five aides are the company, accountable to no one except themselves and their consciences. Their imports and exports are themselves and their varied craft.

Except for gold. This does come into the warehouse in the dead of night. Every once in a while the Mayan gold is shipped in, and Doc and his gang have to be on hand to take care of the precious metal themselves. We don't know who makes the regular runs from Blanco Grande, Hidalgo's capital and seaport, to the Hidalgo Trading Company. Probably the captain of the ship is one of the graduates of Doc's upstate New York "college." We do know that his cousin Patricia is employed on at least one occasion to bring in the gold (*Poison Island,* September 1939). Doc has to go after her and the gold, but that's another story. Patricia takes aboard the gold in her own yacht, *Patricia,* which is a converted Nova Scotia fisherman, a schooner with three masts, a clipper-type bow, and a good freeboard. When Pat isn't using the ship, she keeps it inside the company's building. It is docked alongside Doc's own yacht, *Seven Seas.* No dimensions or tonnage are given for it, but we know she is made of steel and is propelled by powerful diesel motors. Pat, Monk, and Ham are on her when she is wrecked on a reef off one of the Galapagos Islands about five hundred miles west of Ecuador (*The Fantastic Island*).

Although Doc has reconstructed the interior of the building itself, its exterior is that of an old, smoke-stained warehouse built of red bricks and having one huge corrugated metal door. Or its walls are of concrete or wood. *The Mystery on the Snow* (May 1934) says the walls are concrete. *The Headless Men* (June 1941) says they are wood. The latter was written by Alan Hathway, who obviously was not referring to his notes when he wrote this supersaga. Since most of the stories stipulate red bricks, red bricks are what we'll settle for. It's likely that there was thick concrete behind the bricks, since the building was proof against anything but a blockbuster or a cannon shell. Indeed, it must have been the concrete reinforcing that Dent was thinking about when he said the walls were concrete in *The Mystery on the Snow*. Dent also stated in this story that the walls were reinforced with stout steel beams and that the building had no windows.

Half of the building extends on a pier out over the water. The walls were built downward from the structure on the pier so that they plunge into the riverbed itself. Inside, at the river end, a concrete apron into the river permits the amphibian planes to climb into or out of the hangar. Inside are almost a dozen planes, from a gigantic trimotored plane which can go almost three hundred miles per hour to a pair of "true gyros." By "true gyro" Dent meant a prehelicopter, an aircraft that could fly perpendicular to the ground if need be. One of these gyros is so tiny that it can land on a tabletop, though the size of the table is not specified. Later, the trimotor is replaced by a two-motored plane, and after the war a speedy jet amphibian replaces that.

At first, the interior is divided into two sections. One holds aircraft; the other, boats and ships. The latter range all the way from the *Helldiver*, the polar-going submarine which Doc, in a sense, stole, to a rowboat. Later, in *Land of Always-Night*, a third section, higher than the others, is added. Its river end is fitted with enormous doors through which Doc's new dirigible leaves its hangar. This was the most advanced lighter-than-air craft in the world then, and, for that matter, now. It is very streamlined, having the control gondola completely enclosed in the hull and so cutting down air resistance considerably. Dent does not say so, but the motors must have been in the hull, too, with only the propellers and their gearing housing and struts sticking out into the air. Doc has developed the lightweight alloys of which the motors are made and certain modifications which make the motors the most powerful for their size and weight in the world. Doc and Monk worked together to synthesize a nonflammable gas with lifting powers greater than those of hydrogen or helium. This sounds incredible, since hydrogen seems to be the lightest element possible. The building block of the universe, it consists of a nucleus with one unit of positive charge and an electron, one unit of negative charge, which "orbits" the nucleus. So far as scientists know, a stable atom with a half nucleus and a half electron could not exist. Perhaps Dent imagined the gas in order to give Doc even greater stature as a genius.

My own theory is that Doc might have used hydrogen but had some means of suppressing its high flammability. On the other hand, he may have invented some kind of "gas" composed of ions only. Still, the electrical charge resulting from the quantity of ionic gas needed to levitate the craft would make the situation very dangerous. The airship carries the equivalent of several lightning strokes in its ballonets. Perhaps it was this that caused Doc to give up the use of the unconventional "gas." In any event, by the time of *The Green Death* (November 1938) his dirigible is lifted with helium. The one used in the earlier supersaga, *Ost* (August 1937), seems to be the same as that in *The Green Death*. Doc has probably reverted to helium after the destruction of the new stratospheric dirigible of *The South Pole Terror* (October 1936).

Nine of the supersagas involve Doc and his pals with the great gasbags. Their first experience is in *The Lost Oasis* (September 1933), the seventh published story. The dirigible, however, is not Doc's. The Zeppelin ZX 03, named the *Aëromunde*, has disappeared about 1920 in a flight over the Mediterranean. The body of its commander is found floating in the sea. Doc and gang, after a series of horrifying narrow escapes with "the squeaking death" of the villains, stow away on the ZX 03. Later, in the Sahara, they hijack the hijackers and get away to Cairo with the Zeppelin. But Doc returns it to the German Government, though probably not until he has got a good salvage fee for it. Doc always turns over such money to reputable charities or builds hospitals with it.

The dirigible of *Land of Always-Night* is blown up by a bomb and burned in *Murder Mirage* (January 1936).

Doc's third adventure in a dirigible occurs in *The Seven Agate Devils* (May 1936). This ship is, again, not Doc's but a European world-girdling airship on which Doc took passage from New York to Los Angeles.

The new stratospheric dirigible of *The South Pole Terror* (October 1936) comes to a bad end during that adventure. It is stolen by Velma Crale, rich, beautiful, and spoiled-rotten world-famed aviatrix, and later it is blown up by some very nasty characters.

The speedy little demountable ship of *Ost* (August 1937) is stolen by pretty Kit Merrimore, recovered near the fantastic jungle city of the blue men, and then abandoned when its lifting gas escaped.

Twice, a good-looking woman steals Doc's dirigible. Since the great rigid inflated vessels are well-known phallic symbols, it is inevitable that Freudians will make something of this double rape. But Doc gets his dirigibles back, though not always in the condition they were in before he lost them. In fact, since his airships are all deflated, and since he eventually quits using them, he should furnish the Freudians with a field day.

Doc's sixth involvement with a dirigible is in *The Motion Menace* (May 1938). The dirigible is not his property but that of some Balkan nation. Doc, Ham, Monk, and the pets, Habeas Corpus and Chemistry, stow away in it while Long Tom, in disguise, becomes the *Munchen*'s radio operator. Doc successfully completes this particular crusade, but the airship is wrecked.

Apparently, Doc returns to the jungle island to levitate the dirigible abandoned in *Ost*. A craft so similar that it must be the same is Doc's chief vehicle in *The Green Death*. After this, Doc gives up on the gasbags. The last dirigible appears in *The Headless Men* (June 1941). He has lost three, and each one has cost him more than the national debt of some European nations. Even Doc can't stand such expense.

The roof of the building is originally a solid unit. A few years after the sign is hung up on its front, the roof is rebuilt so that it can open to let out the dirigible or the autogyros.

The doors to the Hidalgo Trading Company are, in the early days, opened by ultraviolet or radio signals. In *Terror Takes 7* (September 1945) a piece of radioactive material in Doc's shoe heel does the trick.

A bulletproof glass wall which could be dropped from above is installed. This saves Doc and his aides when they are fired on at point-blank range by the Green Bells. Another wall, dropped behind the invaders, cuts off their escape from the building.

A capacity alarm system in the warehouse is connected to an electric sign on a building a few blocks away. Actuation of the alarm by intruders causes this sign to be illuminated.

A periscope is installed so that Doc can look through it and see what is going on in front of the building.

While Doc is away, automatic cameras take pictures, once every second, of the interior, and the film is automatically developed in a minute by one of Doc's processes. (He anticipated the Polaroid camera by ten or more years.)

The lighting system inside is shadowless, set up by Doc himself.

A large machine shop is installed in the building, and later (*The Men Vanished*) a small, completely enclosed compartment is erected for Doc to work in. This is soundproofed and dustproofed and holds, among other things, a desk and a telephone. Doc does not seem to use this office much.

As early as *Mystery Under the Sea* (February 1936), an "iron doctor," a decompression chamber for deep-sea divers, is installed. Doc puts an unknown man suffering from the "bends" in it, but the man dies. Not, however, from the excess of nitrogen in his blood but from acid burns and slashed wrists.

The pneumatic-tube "flea run" is first used in *The Midas Man* (August 1936). As noted in Chapter 5, work on it is started at the same time the foundations of the Empire State Building are being completed. But the flea run itself is not finished in all its aspects until the time of *The Red Terrors* (September 1938). It is possible, of course, that its use before this time had gone unrecorded. In this supersaga, we first discover that the tube has three terminuses. One is inside a large concrete block in the Hidalgo Trading Company. One is on the eighty-sixth floor in a secret compartment. The third, revealed in the last-named story, is in the subbasement garage of the ESB. Doc must have designed an ingenious arrangement for shunting the passenger car or "go-devil" to the garage or the eighty-sixth floor. This involves remote control of the great valves at the fork of the tube. But such was not beyond Doc's ability to make.

Most of the time, the Hidalgo Trading Company seems to be guarded only by electromechanical devices. It has a watchman in *The Black Spot* (July 1936). Perhaps Doc tried human guards for a while. But he had great difficulty hiring them. Word had got around about how dangerous it was to be near the Hidalgo Trading Company.

The South Pole Terror (the forty-fourth published story and the third story after *The Black Spot*) contains a curious incident. I quote a paragraph from page 65:

"The message to the Hidalgo Trading Co. was about to be

delivered. The messenger boy entered a ramshackle building on Thirty-fourth Street and mounted stairs to a musty door bearing the legend: 'Hidalgo Trading Co.' The messenger entered."

He is greeted by an elderly man in shirtsleeves and wearing a green eyeshade. The old man signs for the radiogram, puts on his hat, takes his umbrella, which never leaves him, rain or shine, and hooks it over his left arm so that he can reach inside with his right hand and remove the revolver concealed there if he needs it. Fifteen minutes later, he is handing the radiogram to Doc, who is in a hotel room.

The old man does nothing but stay in the Hidalgo Trading Company and do a few simple jobs.

The Black Spot and *The South Pole Terror* are the only ones of the 181 supersagas that mention a watchman.

But how is the outside entrance to an upstairs office in the building explained? And how explain the sign that hangs over an inside office and not on the front of the building itself?

It seems obvious to me that the old man who received the radiogram did not have his office in the Hidalgo Trading Company building. His office was in an ancient ramshackle building on Thirty-fourth Street, near the site of the company. The old man's office is in a building which contains many offices of different kinds of business. His office is the one designated as the Hidalgo Trading Company in the city directory and the telephone book. The old man's chief function is to take messages from Doc or his aides and transfer them to wherever the recipient should be.

Doc has never registered the company with the board of trade or sold stock in it; he has simply purchased the building and hung a sign in front of it. The phone company is not aware of its existence. Presumably, the utility companies know of its existence, though it is possible that Doc had installed his own electric generators and water system. The police are too aware of the place, since so many shootouts, fires, and explosions occur there.

Twice, the building is partly burned down. This does not bother Doc, who takes advantage of the reconstruction to install additions and improvements. He may be upset by losing so many expensive airplanes and ships by fires and blasts, but he can afford these losses. Besides, he has to be ready to pay a high price for the place. It is the launching platform for his many dashes around the globe and is of great service to him in other ways.

The Hidalgo Trading Company is last heard of (after not being mentioned for a long time) in *Terror Takes 7* (September 1945). At this late date it has "boarded-over windows and an air of uselessness." The latter is understandable, but "boarded-over windows"? *The Mystery on the Snow* states that the building has no windows, and a number of other stories repeat this. Moreover, a virtually bombproof structure housing so many expensive craft, a structure so often attacked by criminals, would not have windows. Doc would see to that. So we can discount this phrase as a slip of memory on Dent's part. It is also a desire to add atmosphere, since he is trying to create an impression of neglect and decay.

The letters of the sign, for instance, are barely readable. The interior, once crowded with a splendid dirigible, a four-motored giant amphibian, the fastest pursuit plane in the world, several yachts, and a submarine, now has large empty spaces. The craft are few: a seaplane, a helicopter (alas for the autogyros, extinct as dinosaurs!), a speedboat, and a somewhat larger express cruiser. Pat's yacht, the schooner *Patricia*, is not docked here, and chances are that Pat sold it long ago.

"The collection gave the place a... spidery look."

Dust and cobwebs and a sense of the forlorn.

That may have been the reality. In my mind, however, it remains clean and bright. I was always fond of the Hidalgo Trading Company. It is one of the most evocative names I know. To hear it, to see it, is to think of fluid golden images, to be enveloped in an aureate glow. It is one of the great fantastic businesses or semibusiness organizations that never fail to pull the trigger of the wonderful. It is one with the Red-Headed League, the Suicide Club, the Cosmodemonic Telegraph Company, the Universal Baseball Association, the Clyde Burke Clipping Bureau, the White Company, and Peleg & Bildad.

But don't look for it in the Manhattan telephone directory. It is like the island of Kokovoko. "It is not down in any map; true places never are."

8

THE CRIME COLLEGE

TRUMAN CAPOTE'S *In Cold Blood* (Random House, 1965) tells, among other things, of the trial for murder of Hickock and Smith in a small Kansas town. During the trial, a Reverend Post joins in a conversation about the defendants. He shows the others a photograph of a drawing of Jesus by Smith. And he says that anyone who could do such a portrait cannot be one hundred per cent evil. The reverend then continues:

"All the same it's hard to know what to do. Capital punishment is no answer: it doesn't give the sinner time enough to come to God. Sometimes I despair." A jovial fellow with gold-filled teeth and a silvery widow's peak, he jovially repeated, "Sometimes I despair. Sometimes I think old Doc Savage had the right idea." The Doc Savage to whom he referred was a fictional hero popular among adolescent readers of pulp magazines a generation ago. "If you boys remember, Doc Savage was a kind of superman. He'd made himself proficient in every field—medicine, science, philosophy, art. There wasn't much old Doc didn't know or couldn't do. One of his projects was, he decided to rid the world of criminals. First he bought a big island out in the ocean. Then he and his assistants—he had an army of trained assistants—kidnaped all the world's criminals and brought them to the island. And Doc Savage operated on their brains. He removed the part that holds the wicked thoughts. And when they recovered they were all decent citizens. They *couldn't* commit crimes because that part of their brain was out. Now it strikes me that surgery of this nature might really be the answer to—"

A bell, the signal that the jury was returning, interrupted him.

The Reverend Post was depending on his memory when he related the "facts" about Doc Savage. It is no wonder that it partially failed him. He did not have Doc's total recall. In the first place, Doc had only vowed to fight crime. He had not set himself the impossible Augean labor of ridding the world of all criminals. Nor did he buy a big island out in the ocean, kidnap all the world's criminals, and transport them to his institution.

He did operate on those criminals who made the mistake of attacking him. He did not remove the part that held their wicked thoughts. It is true that the operatees did become decent citizens. It is not true that *all* of them did.

The institution where Doc sent the captured criminals is first mentioned in the second published supersaga, *The Land of Terror* (April 1933). In this story Doc captures some of the gang of the fiendish Kar. He does not turn them over to the police. Doc never gives his prisoners to the authorities unless the police happen to be on the scene of the capture. And this seldom happens.

In *The Land of Terror* Doc ships his prisoners to a private sanitarium located in the mountains of upstate New York. The place is owned and operated by Doc for one purpose—to cure the criminals of criminality. The cure is based on the principle that criminals are mentally unbalanced. Otherwise, they wouldn't be criminals. But no definition of "criminal" is given. Would Doc classify as criminal a man who stole food to keep from starving? Hardly, and especially in Depression times. Doc would see that the man got a job, and if anybody had the influence to do this, Doc did. But what about a black militant? How would he be classified? How would Doc categorize a militant of any color who preached violent overthrow of the government or justified violence in taking from the Haves?

No problem. Doc would do nothing to anybody who just shot off his mouth. But when action was taken, when bombs wounded and killed innocent people, mere bystanders, just for the purpose of making a terroristic point, then Doc would not hesitate.

Doc, however, never went out of his way to fight criminals. He was against crime in the abstract, but he only attacked criminals, not crime. And that was only when they had attacked him. The whole battle against evil was a highly personal one for Doc.

According to *The Land of Terror*, a famous psychologist had been hired by Doc to treat the prisoners. The treatment might take many years, but it would eventually result in a cure.

The Land of Terror says nothing about Doc's brain operations on criminals.

In *Quest of the Spider*, Doc ships off to the institution some criminals whom he's put to sleep with drugs. *Quest* contains the first mention of brain surgery.

The fourth published adventure, *The Polar Treasure*, reveals for the first time that "a delicate brain operation" will "wipe out all knowledge of their past." This will cause the criminals to revert to a childlike state, and then they will be re-educated. The ideals of honesty and good citizenship will be drummed into them. They will be taught a vocation before being released. They will know they were criminals at one time, but they'll have no memory of their precollege life.

The surgeons and psychologists who run the place are famous in their professions, extremely well paid, and have been trained for their work by Doc himself.

Why is there a discrepancy between the first two stories and the third? Why is the impression given in the first two that only conventional psychological methods are used to rehabilitate the criminals?

The explanation is simple enough. Dent got most of his information about Doc and his activities from Doc or his aides. Occasionally, he learned about some new exploit of Doc's in the newspapers. Most of his information consisted of short outlines of the particular adventure with brief comments by Doc or his pals. These were dictated by them and probably typed out by one of the secretaries of the agency that did detective work for Doc. Lea Aster, Monk's pippin of a secretary, did the typing in the early years.

Dent may have talked to Doc face to face now and then, though there is no record of such a meeting.

Apparently, Doc had felt in the beginning that the brain surgery might be too shocking to readers of *Doc Savage* magazine. Later, he changed his mind. If the violence and killing in the first two issues of the magazine did not upset them, then the forcible seizure and surgery of men who deserved it was not going to cause a controversy.

It was, we may be sure, not a matter of Doc suddenly deciding to use a new method. From *The Purple Dragon* (September 1940) we know that the college doctors had been operating on criminals since at least 1929. Mavrik (Shalleck) had been shipped to Doc's place in that year for the surgical treatment. Thus, the discrepancy in the first two accounts of the college is due to Doc's hesitation about revealing to Dent just what was really going on there.

The term "the college," by the way, is first used in the twenty-second published story, *The Annihilist* (December 1934). This is one of the most interesting of the supersagas. In it we learn of the weird disease which causes its victims' eyes to pop out before they die. We find that the college has been run for Doc by Robert Lorrey, "a scientific surgeon of fabulous skill." He's been trained by Doc himself. His chief assistant is Leander Court. Court does not last long after the events of *The Annihilist* begin. He is murdered in cold blood, shot down in the reception room of that peculiar institution called the Association of Physical Health. Lorrey had taken the Hippocratic oath, as had Doc, but he is bothered no more than Doc by the ethics of what he is doing at the college. He is breaking the laws of the United States and New York State every time he accepts a criminal for treatment. But he is doing it in a good cause.

Doc and everybody associated with operating the college could have been brought up on charges of kidnaping, forcible drugging, infringing on civil rights, transportation across the state line, and malpractice. The total number of years for these charges could have kept Doc in the penitentiary for life. Indeed, if the jury and judge had so decided, Doc could have been sent to the chair. The "Lindbergh law" made his activities a federal offense, punishable by death.

Never mind. Doc is endangering himself for the greatest benefit of the majority. And though he is himself acting criminally—from a legal viewpoint—his actions can easily be justified. It is not a case of evil means being used to achieve good ends. Although unlawful, the means themselves are not evil. If Doc turned his prisoners over to the police, he would see most of them rot in jail and some die in the execution chamber. None would go straight when they got out. Under Doc's administration, the criminals are not housed and fed at the state's expense; Doc pays for all this. Moreover, Doc's treatment guarantees—almost—that the crook will re-enter society as a useful member.

Robert Lorrey is No. 7 on Doc's payroll (which listed many thousands). He is, of course, paid more money than he could possibly have earned as a freelancer. Robert is bright, but his twin brother, Sidney, is brilliant. Sidney is an inventor who spends most of his time experimenting in his private laboratory in New York City. Sidney's chief invention is a device which generates the same emanations as radium but less expensively. The device, however, has not been developed to the point of being commercially profitable. Sidney hopes the invention will eventually become useful in treating cancer. Sidney, the idealist, is to become a prominent figure in the events of *The Annihilist*.

A strange man by the strange name of Janko Sultman also plays a large role in this story. It is from him that we first hear Doc's theory of the cause of criminal behavior. Sultman states that Savage has discovered that crime is a disease. Using infected tonsils as an analog, Sultman says these send poisons through a man's system and so affect him physically and mentally. To go a step further, glands, for instance, secrete everything from sweat to digestive acids. The brain contains many glands, and these glands are the least understood of any in the body. A certain tiny gland in the brain governs the workings of a part of the brain which, in turn, controls a man's behavior. A malfunction of this gland results in a disturbance of his ethical sense. He becomes confused about the distinction between right and wrong.

Doc corrects the malfunctioning of the gland. He also severs certain nerves so that the criminal entirely forgets his past.

The identity and exact location of the gland are not even hinted at. Since it may be presumed that, as of 1972, all glands in the human brain have been located and labeled, though all their functions haven't yet been discovered, it should be a simple matter to name the gland. So far, no scientist has come forward with this information.

However, it's doubtful that any psychologist or social scientist of today would agree with Doc's explanation of the causes of criminal behavior. These are very complex, and to go into all the theories would make this chapter into a book. Doc's explanation of the crimogenic gland may not be the true one at all. It is possible, in fact, very probable, that Doc misled Dent.

Why he would do this is not certain. But it may have been that he felt it would be dangerous even to hint at the true nature of the method used. From the sketchy description Dent could have supplied, a scientist may have got a clue which would lead him to Doc's methods.

These methods would be a two-edged sword. If they could be used for good ends, they could also be used for evil. Perhaps they could become a tool for the control of the operatee's mind. Or they could be used to make criminals out of honest men.

This latter possibility is why the master criminal Boke raids the college. He intends to force the secret of the treatment out of the college's staff. Then he will forcibly give industrialists, politicians, and statesmen the reverse of the treatment and make criminals of them. (He overlooks the fact that many industrialists and politicians are already criminals). These will then be his partners in crime.

The college is situated in very wild and rugged terrain. A single dirt road winds from the distant country highway through heavy timber. It generally follows creeks and goes through many small valleys. The road terminates at a massive gate of steel. This is the only visible entrance in a high and heavy wire fence, topped by barbed wire, which circles an area of many acres.

An observer in an airplane would think that the fence guards only a small lake and a log hunting lodge. At one side of the lake is a high craggy hill of gray stone. About a mile outside the gate, on top of a hill which commands a view of the encircled area, is a small cabin.

The institution is equipped with a number of devices for detecting intruders. In the woods outside the fence are capacity alarms. Amplifiers for sonic detectors are all over the place and are monitored by one man in the lodge.

When Boke launches his attack, the monitor hears the approaching planes and alerts the college. At that moment there are two hundred men on the grounds. Most of them are patients dressed in white. The few men in blue are the nurses, former criminals who have remained to work in the college.

On hearing the warning signal, all two hundred march into doors that have opened in the seemingly solid rock hill. In a few minutes, the doors close on them. The patients go into the many rooms inside the hill.

As the planes fly over the college, sections of dirt slide back, exposing concrete pits. These hold antiaircraft rapid-fire guns loaded by automatic machinery and remotely controlled by a staff member in a concealed place. Boke soon finds out that the place has no WELCOME sign hung out.

Doc's treatment seems to be very effective. In *The Vanisher* (December 1936) it's stated that not one of the graduates has "ever returned to the avenue of crime." But, as we'll see, this won't be true in the future.

In *The Flying Goblin* (July 1940) Doc has erected buildings inside the fenced area. Why he did this is not known. Possibly the college, like more conventional educational institutions, has expanded. The increased population not only resulted in a boom in students, it also resulted in an explosion of the criminal class. The rooms carved out in the stone hill are not enough, and there is no more space inside the hill for more rooms to be carved out.

Besides, in nine years Doc has been increasingly busy and has accumulated a large collection of crooks.

A large building now exists inside the fence. It is at least three stories high, and its windows are barred. These bars are not so close together that a small object can't be thrown between them. This is done by two crooks who've sneaked onto the grounds. (How they get past all the detectors is not explained.) The object is a device which guides in Oscar, "the flying goblin," who strikes the corner of the building, blows it open, and thus permits Birmingham Jones to escape.

Jones is the first failure of the criminal-curing operation. Apparently, a blow on Jones's head by one of Dillinger's boys, given some years before, has prevented the usual one hundred per cent cure. Jones does not remember his former life, but he still has his psychotic lust for killing.

It's worth noting that Doc does not care what crimes his captives had committed. Even mad-dog murderers—with one exception—go to the college. The only requirement for admission is violent action toward Doc. In fact, during World War II, Doc even sends to the college Germans and Japanese who've attacked him. It doesn't matter to Doc that he is breaking the Geneva Convention or that these men were motivated by patriotism, not criminal desires. They get the full treatment and are graduated with honor.

On the other hand, Doc is doing most of them a favor. Many are spies who would be executed if turned over to the U. S. Government.

The sole exception to Doc's rules is the same Birmingham Jones who's escaped from the college. Doc recaptures him, but he tells his men that Jones will probably not be returned to college. His murderous compulsions are too strong.

Dent does not say what happens to Jones. He writes an ambiguous statement: "All understood what the bronze man meant."

Monk, Ham, and Renny may have understood. I don't. What did Doc intend for Jones? Did he just surrender him to the police? How could he, when Jones could tell them all about the college? Or did Doc do something more sinister? The latter seems unlikely, since Doc did not believe in taking life unless it was absolutely necessary.

The next supersaga in which a graduate plays an important part is *The Purple Dragon* (September 1940). In this story the operation consists in severing certain nerves to isolate the memory of the pre-college life. The "crime" gland is not mentioned here nor in any succeeding story. Hiram Shalleck (real name: Joe Mavrik) disappears one night. He has been living in the small town of Lamar, Colorado, for ten years, but he is never seen by the citizens again after he vanishes.

The Lamar sheriff, investigating, finds a number of newspaper articles about Doc Savage in Shalleck's room. He does not, however, connect the well-known man of bronze with Shalleck. Nor does he connect Shalleck with a strange newspaper story which comes out of Chicago a few days later.

I won't reveal what happened afterwards to Shalleck/Mavrik. *The Purple Dragon* is one of the best of the supersagas, still enjoyable for anyone who likes an excellent mystery story. But it's evident that Doc had operated on the gangster, Mavrik, in 1929. Also, the villain, the Purple Dragon as he styled himself, has found means for reconnecting the neural circuits cut by Doc.

Every once in a while, a graduate pops up. One is Bob Castron, mentioned in *The Man Who Fell Up* as the operator of the newsstand and cigar counter in the south lobby of Doc's skyscraper. A number of others appear as taxi drivers or mechanics. Many are employees of a private agency which is personally directed by Doc.

(His cousin, Sherlock Holmes, had his agency, too. It's mentioned by Watson in *The Sussex Vampire*.)

Doc's organization was worldwide. Bill Lee, an ex-professional thug, runs the London agency. Another graduate heads the Capetown, South Africa, agency. Onie Morton, who lives with his sleepy redheaded wife in the Bronx, is a news condenser for Doc. He is a member of a complex organization of specialists who gather news from all over the world and condense it for Doc's perusal. Doc can go through these items and smell the ones that mean trouble just as a bloodhound smells tracks, according to Monk. It is Onie's failure to report for work one morning that initiates the chain of events in *The Time Terror* (January 1943).

(Doc's American cousin, A. Rassendyll, sometimes known as Kent Allard, Lamont Cranston, etc., has a similar setup but on a much more modest scale. The Clyde Burke Clipping Bureau is owned by him. His office, when he is the Shadow, is an unoccupied room in an old building on Twenty-third Street east of Broadway. It is on the third floor, and the door bears on its frosted glass only the legend: B. JONAS. Beneath is a mail slot with a sign: LEAVE MAIL HERE. The Shadow picks up communications from his small group of agents and sometimes plans his campaigns here. He has none of Doc's desire to reform criminals. He stops the criminals' careers by putting huge holes in them from his two .45 automatics. Doc would have deplored this attitude, and he certainly would have rebuked the killer if he had had the chance. Their paths may have crossed now and then, and it's likely that Doc knew the true profession of A. Rassendyll/Kent Allard. There was not much that Doc did not know.)

All in all, the college is a great success. It's too bad that the legislators and the social workers and social scientists in this country are still resistant to Doc's advanced ideas. The adoption of his techniques would cut down the problem of repeats by law offenders to almost zero. Of course, society would still turn out new criminals every year. Doc had no ideas for striking at the sources of crime. But, then, who does, except for a few largely ignored proponents of an economy of abundance?

Of course, it would be necessary to get the convict's permission for the operation, and many might refuse. Doc, as a private individual, did not ask the criminals for their consent. Why should he? He saw what needed to be done, and he did it.

9

THE FORTRESS OF SOLITUDE

THE FORTRESS OF SOLITUDE exists from the beginning. The first story, *The Man of Bronze*, says that it was Doc's father who thought of setting it up. Doc followed his recommendation and build it "on a rocky island deep in the arctic regions." Here he "retired periodically to brush up on the newest developments in science, psychology, medicine, engineering. This was the secret of his universal knowledge, for his periods of concentration were long and intense... And no one on earth knew the location of the retreat. Once there, nothing would interrupt Doc's studies and experiments."

In the first supersaga, Doc has just returned from the Fortress to discover from the newspapers that his father has died of a weird disease.

Jerome Coffern, in *The Land of Terror*, says, "At intervals, Savage vanishes... as completely as though he had left the earth. And when he returns, he nearly always has one or more new and incredible discoveries to give to the world... Any scientific man would give half a lifetime to inspect that laboratory, so remarkable must it be."

In the third published story, *Quest of the Spider*, Ham takes offense at beautiful Edna Danielsen's criticism of Doc because he can't be found when needed. In a severe tone, Ham says, "Young lady, you do not realize that Doc Savage's benefactions to humanity extend beyond helping every Tom, Dick, and Harry, or Mary, Jane, and Anne, out of their private troubles... No doubt he has retired there, and when he appears, he will be bearing some new contribution which will save thousands of lives.

"That contribution... will be of vastly more importance than any personal misfortune you or anybody else might meet in the meantime!"

Fortunately, Doc comes back from the arctic retreat just in time to catch the man who is trying to kill Big Eric and his daughter Edna. And we're off on another great adventure.

Succeeding supersagas mention the Fortress; only occasionally is a reference to it missing. But it is not until the October 1938 issue that it is directly involved in one of Doc's exploits. This story, fittingly enough, is titled *Fortress of Solitude*.

Doc is not at the place when the action begins. Otherwise, events would have been different. A man finds the Fortress, and he is the last man on earth who should find it. He is John Sunlight, "a weird, terrible being." That he is the only villain ever to appear in two of the supersagas gives some idea of his intelligence and high survival quotient. All the other great villains were either dead or sent up to the college by the end of the particular story in which they first appeared.

John Sunlight escapes on a ship from Siberia. In the arctic fog, the ship blunders into the island on which the Fortress sits. The ship's lookout thinks it is a blue whale. But a closer inspection disproves this. "It was like nothing that should be. Its height must be all of a hundred feet, and there was a shimmering luminance to it that was eerie… it resembled the perfectly spherical half of an opaque blue crystal ball."

The island on which it stands is of smooth gray rock. The wind has swept the snow off the rock at the island's edges. Inland, the snow is piled high around the Strange Blue Dome. John Sunlight claws at the glazed blue, which feels as hard and as cold as steel. He can't see into the stuff. It is a "solid substance of a nature unknown. Not glass, and yet not metal either."

John Sunlight tries to break the dome with blows from a sledge hammer. A clear ringing results, "as if a great bell had been tapped once," and the sound carries for miles even if it is not loud. The substance is not even nicked, and more blows fail to affect it in the slightest.

The local natives tell Sunlight how to enter the seemingly impenetrable dome. The information, however, does not come from the Eskimos voluntarily. Torture can't force it from them, but Sunlight's acute observation finds the key. Sunlight enters and gets hold of some of Doc's weapons. These are so terrible that Doc's impassive face is twisted with horror when he realizes that someone has been eating his scientific porridge.

Late in this supersaga, we learn that the dome was built by the island's Eskimos under Doc's supervision. He brought the materials in himself in a huge transport plane. It took many plane trips and a long time a building. The Eskimos are, in a sense, caretakers, although they do nothing to, or for, the dome itself. They can get dehydrated food from the dome whenever they wish. The secret door opens for any of them when he gets close while wearing a white rabbitskin cape, a gift from Doc. The tiny permanent magnets sewed into the cape's lining activate a door-opening mechanism.

Near the end of the adventure, Doc tells Ham that the blue stuff is "a form of glass composition which could be welded with heat and which had strength far beyond that of true glass. The welding operation explained how the dome had been constructed without joints. The stuff... being a nonconductor... kept out the cold."

John Sunlight escapes with about twenty of Doc's "deadly scientific devices," and Doc can't sleep easily until he has found John Sunlight. But he will not do so until about three months later, when Sunlight comes looking for him. This is narrated in the strange—and near-fatal, for Doc—events of *The Devil Genghis* (December 1938).

The Fortress of Solitude is mentioned often in the following issues, though not as frequently as before. In *The Laugh of Death* Doc is at its site again. This time he is out in sixty-degrees-below-zero weather in the arctic night. He is stark naked and exercising.

"The jumping around in the snow made him sweat, and the sweat gathered between his *skins*." (Italics mine.)

This statement is one of Dent's many narrative "hooks." Doc's outer skin is actually an experimental plastic. The stuff is "almost a complete insulator against heat or cold." It is designed specifically to be used by the military. But, like many of Doc's devices, it has some disadvantages. In this case, perspiration makes the false skin crack and peel. Disgusted, Doc walks back into the dome to work on the stuff some more.

The structure of the retreat no longer resembles that seen in *Fortress of Solitude*. Doc has lately changed its appearance. Now it looks just like a great chunk of ice sticking up from the arctic ice pack. The change is necessary because so many more planes are now flying over this area. The war has brought them over the polar skies. This is not the early 1930s, when it was easy to find an isolated, unobserved place.

The Fortress now has three doors. When Doc is inside and looks up, he can see the stars. The plastic is polarized so that the light passes in only one direction. Doc listens to the daily report before going into the laboratory, but he never gets into the laboratory because of the daily report he hears.

The reports are made thus. One of his aides, or Pat, dials an unlisted number and dictates the report to a recording machine. Promptly at 12 A.M. and 12 P.M., the reports are automatically transmitted via radio beam to the Fortress.

Doc is listening to Pat's report when a sinister laughing interrupts her. "It was certainly not human, and it did not seem animal, so maybe 'laughing' was not the word for it. It was a completely unexplainable sound… It had a macabre, chilling quality."

Pat screams; a ripping sound follows. Pat is then silent, but the laughing goes on for at least ten minutes. And we're off with Doc again, but this time Doc is sweating with anxiety about Pat.

We are allowed to be present at the site of the Fortress no more. The references to it dwindle away in succeeding adventures. Of course, Doc was really too busy to go there. He had been too busy since *The Man of Bronze* to do more than make short visits. He had to work swiftly on his inventions, because he usually no sooner got there than a crisis demanded that he return to New York.

10

MONK, THE APE IN WOLF'S CLOTHING

IN *THE MAN OF BRONZE* Monk Mayfair makes his first entrance trailing behind the others. Pigeon-toed, walking with a peculiar apelike waddle, he trails the other aides. "Last came the most remarkable character of all." And this he is indeed. Lieutenant Colonel Andrew Blodgett Mayfair would be remarkable in any group.

Monk is five feet two inches tall and weighs two hundred and sixty pounds, mostly bones, guts, and muscles. He is "a hammered-down Cardiff Giant," "a dwarf edition of King Kong," "half a man tall and two men wide." He's covered with red hair as coarse as pig bristles, and his skin is brick-red. His chest is thicker than it is wide; he has no hips; his arms dangle below the knees of his bowed legs. His forehead is so low that it looks as if he has no more brains than would fill a cigarette. His ears are little and cauliflowered. The tip of one has been chewed off and the other perforated by a rifle bullet. His eyes are so surrounded by gristle from fist and club blows that they resemble pleasant little stars twinkling in pits. (No eye color is ever mentioned, but the cover illustration for *The Awful Egg* shows them as blue-gray.) When he grins, which is often, his mouth looks as big as a frog's or as if it had been widened by the knife of a villain.

Of the six adventurers, he alone bears scars. His skin looks as if a flock of chickens with gray chalk on their feet had paraded over him. He is so proud of these that he's refused to let Doc remove them. He glories in his tough looks, yet he is the only one of the five to carry a pocket mirror. Frighteningly rough as he looks and is, he gets seasick easily and suffers from claustrophobia. He once tells Doc during a voyage that the only reason he stays alive is so he can die and get the sickness over with. This is a typical Monkicism.

He has a squeaky voice which sounds like a wet stick being rubbed over a tin can or a nail being pulled out of green lumber. But when he is in a fight, he roars like a grizzly defending his territory.

Monk's technique for running in the dark is to double over, traveling anthropoidally in great bounds, using his unnaturally long arms to balance himself if he stumbles. As a runner on two feet, he lags behind Doc and Johnny but is even with the long-legged Renny. Despite his gorilloid structure, he is the most agile of the aides.

His strength is indeed apelike. He can bend pennies between thumb and forefinger and then unbend them. In *The Land of Terror* he bends a villain's revolver barrel as if it were a hairpin and hands it back to him, telling him to shoot it. Despite this, he never exercises but depends on his rigorous life to keep him fit.

When he sleeps he snores, and, peculiarly, no two snores sound alike.

He loves a fight more than anything; the worst possible thing that can happen to him is to miss one. His second love, according to what he once tells a cop, is blondes over twenty-one. Third, he loves eating, and in *The Three Wild Men* he is interrupted while devouring his third steak. Actually, his greatest love is probably tormenting Ham Brooks.

He has little tact except when chasing skirts, and often not then. In fights, though a terrible antagonist, he is not cool and calculating. He is as wild and uncontrolled as a wild bull on ice and as likely to slug one of his compatriots as the enemy. This frenzy doesn't prevent him, however, from seeing everything that is going on.

Other characteristics are a distinct sound made by his feet when he's pacing back and forth in an upset condition, and some false front teeth. When they're out, he lisps. Ham steals them in *Rock Sinister*, and so prevents Monk from going out on a date. In *The Green Master* he hides a precious green stone in the hole recently occupied by a wisdom tooth.

Monk's clothes always look as if slept in. They're as garish as those of a sideshow barker's; he thinks nothing of wearing to the most elaborate affair a $19.98 checkered suit, bright-yellow tie, bright-green shirt, loud plaid vest, and bulldog-toed shoes. His favorite hat looks as if it has been used to fight bumblebees. His tastes are low, but he dresses this way partly to offend the fastidious fashion-plate Ham.

His car is as garish as his clothes. It is "a combination of sunset and earthquake on wheels."

He carries an old-fashioned watch with a closed front which opens by pressure on the stem. This may be a family heirloom, but if it is, Dent never says so.

Of Monk's early life, little is known. He was born in Tulsa, Oklahoma, probably about 1889. When a child, he had a hound named Ponto. When Ham, in *The Freckled Shark*, says that Ham's family sprang from the best stock around Boston, Monk replies, "My family never sprang from anybody! They sprang at 'em!"

Despite this disclaimer, some of Monk's ancestors were descended from passengers on the *Mayflower*.

His parents were Blodgett Mayfair and Melissa Rutherford. Her brother was the famous, or infamous, zoologist, anthropologist, and explorer Dr. George Edward Rutherford. (Doyle calls him Challenger in the semifictional stories based on his colorful career. For details of Monk's genealogy not mentioned here, see Addenda 2 and 3 of *Tarzan Alive*.)

Monk's father probably was a professional man with good connections and from a high social class; otherwise, it's doubtful that he would have met the daughter of a British baron and married her. The evidence is strong that the Mayfairs had intermarried with the Rutherfords for several centuries. He seems to have been related to the Canadian Mayfairs, who were in line for the British earldom of "Chester, Essex, and Cornwall." (Dent used these titles to cover up the real ones of the "Mayfair" family. Chester and Cornwall are ducal titles and belong to the heir apparent of the British king. The earls of Essex are Capells.)

Mr. Mayfair was probably a chemist working for one of the American oil companies. Whatever his profession, he sent Monk to a high school which had classes specializing in ancient Greek and Roman mythology. It is doubtful that Tulsa had such a school. Possibly, Monk was sent off to attend an English institution such as Rugby. He must have had a hard time there, since he was not one to submit gracefully or quietly to the relentless hazing of the upperclass boys. How anybody with his abominable substandard speech could have been admitted to Rugby, let alone graduated, is puzzling. My theory is that Monk was well aware of correct grammatical and vocabulary niceties and could use them when the situation demanded. He adopted his low-class, highly American language to bug his schoolmates and perhaps occasionally his professors. When examination time came, he spoke and wrote with the best of them.

When he met Ham, he discovered that the elegant Harvard lawyer was irritated by his "ain'ts," double negatives, and slang. Since he was with Ham so much, the sloppiness of speech became a habit.

His parents probably had a comfortable, though not large, income. Monk, we know, drove a truck in his early years. He probably did this during the summers for one of the Tulsa oil companies. Something happened when he graduated from high school. Either his parents died and left him little, or they lost their money. Monk was forced to put himself through a New York City college by working as a messenger boy at Grand Central Station. After graduation, he got his Ph.D. in chemistry at Columbia or Fordham. He then went to Leipzig to do some postgraduate work. Dent never says anything of his doctorate, but it's safe to presume that one of the world's foremost industrial chemists would have a Ph.D.

His first love was, however, not his profession. It was fighting, and when the outbreak of World War I caught him in Italy while overlooking the setup of a new chemical factory, he at once signed up with the Italian Army. It was while battling the Austrians that he met an American volunteer ambulance driver. This man later talked to Ernest Hemingway about Monk. The description of Monk left a lasting impression on Hemingway. In later years he was to use some aspects of Monk's character, physical and emotional, for his hero Harry Morgan in *To Have and Have Not*.

Monk was severely wounded. This, plus weakening caused by malaria, led Monk to resign his Italian captaincy. He went to England to recuperate and to offer his services to the English when he recovered. He was accepted and served several months as a captain in the Royal Engineers. Sometime after the U. S. declared war on the Central Powers, Monk transferred to the American Army as a lieutenant colonel in the infantry.

He encountered Brigadier-General Theodore Marley Brooks on the front in France, and the two were thereafter inseparable. Monk didn't know French at that time, and this enabled Brooks to play the first of his tricks on Monk. He coached Monk in a number of

Gallic compliments he was to deliver to a French general during a ceremony. The phrases, however, were the most obscene and insulting to be found in a language noted for its vigor in these areas. The enraged general clapped Monk in jail, and it took several days for the U.S. authorities to get Monk out of the guardhouse.

A week later, Brooks endured a great humiliation. He was arrested for having stolen a truckload of hams. Brooks was able to prove himself innocent, though he was never able to nail Monk for the frame-up. And he was stuck with the nickname of Ham.

It was after this that Monk became an authority on hogs. He carried a manual on *Sus domesticus* in his pocket and would often read aloud from it just to tee-off Ham.

After the war, Monk resumed his profession. He seems to have traveled over the world as a consultant chemist. During this time he learned some Finnish. He also took time off for explorations, and it was while swimming naked in a South American jungle river that a naturalist mistook him for a member of an undiscovered species of ape and tried to capture him.

Ham seems to have been along on this trip, since Monk wouldn't tell this story on himself. Whenever they were both in New York, they palled around insulting each other and trying to cut each other out of the current chorine or waitress. Monk's tastes in women, according to Ham (not a reliable witness), ran to tramps. This may have been so, but Monk was always chasing the high-class heroines of the supersagas. More often than not, he won over Ham.

Doc himself thought that Monk was the world's homeliest man. Monk had once been offered fame and fortune if he would star in a series of horror films. But he had a quality that appealed to dogs, little children, old ladies, and long-legged bosomy pippins of every class. Pat Savage said he was a sucker for any female. This didn't keep him from describing the ugly Miss Bridges in *Fire and Ice* as looking "like seven miles of bad road."

Monk thinks of women even when sleeping. While escaping from the Nazis in *The Black, Black Witch*, Monk is asked by Doc why he's so cheerful. Monk tells him of his dream. He was chased by a dazzling blond witch riding, not a broomstick, but a motorcycle. He ran at first because he was so scared. When he got a good look at her, he turned around and chased her. He and the witch raced at a hundred miles an hour up and down the French country roads, and finally he was able to outrun the cycle. He doesn't tell Doc what happened thereafter, but he obviously is pleased by it. He asks Doc what he thinks of a dream like that. Doc doesn't reply, but he thinks it is a typical Monk Mayfair dream, since it had a blonde in it.

Shortly thereafter, Monk is astonished when a girl looking much like the one in his dream and owning a motorcycle appears. This is Monk's first psychic experience and probably his last, unless the insulting thought transference between him and Ham in another story is counted. This telepathic communication seems more likely to be one of Dent's inventions.

Monk says that he and Ham never fall in love with the dames they chase. They are just wolves, and that is all. Monk, as usual, is lying. Princess Gusta, rejected by Doc in *The King Maker*, falls for Monk on the rebound. Monk stays in the kingdom of Calbia for a few weeks to woo her, but the affair peters out. Monk has a passion for Doc's cousin Pat, and there are certain suggestions, explored in Chapter 16, that the two may have had more going on than either Doc or Dent suspected. In *The Roar Devil* Monk proposes to Retta Kenn but is turned down. And Monk is more in love with his secretary, the prettiest in New York, than he cares to admit. Lea, however, after the frightening episodes of *The Red Skull*, may have gone to a lower-paying but safer employment.

Monk is very serious in his proposal of marriage to Princess Amen-Amen of Egypt. His pals send her a telegram purporting to be from Monk's wife, and that is cooled off.

One of Monk's techniques for breaking the ice with a girl is to propose marriage in the first half hour of a date. The above cases are not examples of this because Monk meant it. But a blonde named Hester accepts, and Monk has to run for it. After this, he drops that particular attack.

He is, though, an incurable skirt-chaser to the last. According to Sammy Wales, he looks as if he "didn't have brains enough to run a test on anything, unless it was to run his eyes up and down a pretty leg." Rhoda Haven tells Monk he's "robin-eyed." When Monk asks what that means, she says, "Eyes that are always resting on limbs."

Monk's judgment of and memory for female legs is accurate. He exposes the identity of a disguised villainess in *The Death Lady* when he remembers having seen her legs from behind once before.

Monk has many successes in his Don Juaning, but this is because he's always trying. His failures are many, too. Often, the girl he is after rejects him for the handsome Doc. Sometimes he loses out to Ham. And every once in a while a woman is more impressed by his ugliness than the peculiar charm he radiates. Thus, in *Once Over Lightly*, he asks Miss Trunnels if she's hunting for something. And she replies, "Stuffed bison. I suppose you'll do for a substitute."

Monk doesn't care. He goes on to the next peach. And he uses another icebreaking technique. This is his pet pig, Habeas Corpus. The pig often startles young dames by addressing them with the most outlandish, but cornily poetic, compliments. After the initial shock, the beautiful broad is intrigued to find that the voice is actually Monk's. He is a superb ventriloquist, maybe better than Doc because he practices more. The pig then becomes a conversation piece and quite often leads to a piece of another kind.

Though he looks like a racetrack tout, Monk is a famous chemist. Outside of his specialty, his knowledge is not too extensive. Electronics, except for radio, is a closed field to him. He knows even less than the average layman about history, archaeology, and paleontology. He has no appreciation of fine music. He loathes orchids, a feeling which would not go down well with his cousin, Nero Wolfe. He tips generously to good-looking waitresses, of course, but he never gives a male waiter money. "Tipping undermines a man's character," he says, though failing to specify if it is the waiter's character or his own character he worries about.

His command of languages is limited and peculiar. He speaks Italian passably well, but he has somewhere sometime picked up enough Yaqui Indian speech to make out with the Yaqui girls. He is supposed to be fluent in Spanish, but in one story he doesn't know the commonly used word for ape: *mono*. In *The Black, Black Witch* he speaks German perfectly, though in a later adventure he has to brush up on it, and in *Violent Night* he understands it but can't speak it. He's been taught to speak Mayan fluently because all of Doc's group use it when they don't want anybody else to know what they're talking about. Monk "murders" it.

Aside from chemical terms, he is ignorant of, or has forgotten, Latin and Greek.

He reads the daily comic strips devotedly. He is a fanatic sports follower. He can tell you the records of the baseball and football players and the scores of the big games for the past twenty years.

He doesn't drink, though he must have tried liquor at one time. He admits that champagne tastes like vinegar to him.

In the early supersagas, he smokes cigarettes which he hand-rolls. He is so addicted that he risks his life to grab a can of tobacco before abandoning a falling plane. He gives up the habit for many adventures, but then he starts to smoke cigars. Later, he quits again, but, given his temperament, he probably takes up the habit a dozen times and quits as often.

He has a powerful fear of shotguns, since he saw a man blown apart by one in his youth. He also shares with Doc a strong fear (not irrational) of sharp penknives in the hands of murderers.

When he is hit hard on the head, he sees, not stars, but a green waterfall. And several times, coming out of unconsciousness, he mumbles about Mabel.

All of the group, Doc, Pat, and the five men, are knocked senseless many times. Monk seems to have held the record. He was whammed unconscious at least fifty-four times during the 181 supersagas. In *The Seven Agate Devils* he is knocked out three times. A rock between the eyes, a blow on the head from some unspecified weapon, and a rifle butt on the head send him down for a long count. In *Phantom City* an accidental blow on the jaw from Doc, from a gun butt, and a flying brick put him to sleep three times. In eight other stories he is knocked unconscious twice. On an average of about every three exploits, he suffers a blow which makes him senseless. These last from ten minutes to half an hour or even for hours. At least sixty times he is struck dazed or semiconscious.

These severe head traumas do not seem to have impaired his physical or mental abilities at all. This may be attributed to an atavistic bony structure much thicker than most men's. Still, it does seem reasonable to assume a certain amount of brain damage. He admits in a late tale that he isn't the man he used to be. Missing a good night's sleep weakens him. In *The Pure Evil* he describes himself as "a broken-down old chemist that has been associated with Doc for quite a while." At another time he laments that he doesn't have half of Doc's memory. He can remember faces but not names.

Still, in *No Light to Die By*, a 1947 issue, he displays a Sherlock Holmes ability of which Doc would not have been ashamed.

When we first meet Monk, he lives in a penthouse of a building some sixty stories high in lower Manhattan just off Wall Street. In fact, Monk owns the building. The penthouse is furnished with ultramodern metal and glass in a style that makes it look like "an overdone movie set." It contains Monk's apartments, a private room for his pig, and a big laboratory. Doc and the others use this lab when they're on the run from crooks or the police, which is often. Outside on the roof is a court where Monk and his secretary play tennis.

Monk's fees are high. In *Poison Island* he collects ten thousand dollars for two days' work as consultant for a large chemical plant. Despite his fees and ownership of the building, he is broke several times a year. (Doc says once a month.) To quote a phrase which would be offensive to Ham, Monk lives too high off the hog. Also, now and then, he is forced to make expensive repairs to the penthouse. In *Death in Silver* the blast that kills Paine L. Winthrop and wrecks the Seven Seas office also blows out Monk's windows, ruins his laboratory, and knocks him down.

During repairs, Monk uses a secret laboratory on the second floor of an unimpressive building in Queens. Doc and gang use this when neither Doc's nor Monk's laboratory is available, usually because the police are watching both places.

In *The Men Who Smiled No More* Monk has moved to Long Island to get the peace and solitude needed to carry out some chemical experiments. He lives in a cottage in the Shinnecock Hills, but his expenses there are higher than anticipated. He has to dig into his pocket to pay for the ducks his pet pig is killing on the neighboring farm. The only woman around is his fat housekeeper, Mrs. Malatkas. This rural retreat is only a temporary place. In the next tale he is back at the penthouse.

By the time of *The Ten Ton Snakes* (March 1945), he has left the penthouse for an apartment in a fashionable building near Radio City. The apartment is expensive but much less so than the penthouse. He is evicted from the apartment because he can't pay the rent.

Dent doesn't say where Monk went to live after this, but in *Trouble on Parade* (November 1945) his telephone number is Central 0-9000.

In *Se-Pah-Poo* (February 1946) Monk is living in a hotel on Forty-first Street which is extending him credit. Even Doc and his four buddies refuse to lend him money. The "incendiary blondes" he pursues are giving him the cold shoulder.

He is still broke in the last adventure, *Up from Earth's Center*. And no wonder. Of the five aides, he and Ham are in the great majority of exploits. They've not only spent twice what they earn, they can't earn much because they've been too busy helping Doc. When he calls, they drop whatever they're handling—test tube, lawsuit, or peroxide blonde—and rush off joyously.

Whatever is going on, Monk is in it up to his nauseating bright-green tie. And he doesn't pay much attention to Doc's orders to avoid killing enemies unless absolutely necessary. Monk is the bloodthirstiest of the lot, and his actions draw strong reprimands when Doc catches him.

In *The Red Skull* Monk deliberately allows the villainous Buttons Zortell to escape to his death. He lies, telling Doc that Zortell hit him in the left eye and thus managed to get away from him. Doc doesn't say anything this time, but Monk feels that Doc knows the eye was injured when he ran into an outcropping in a tunnel.

It is Monk who complains, at the end of *The Sea Magician*, that not "a dang soul" has been killed. (This, by the way, is the only one of the 181 supersagas that has this feature.) Monk, however, did his best to come as close to killing as he could.

In *The Majii* Monk, an accomplished thrower of knives, hurls one into a gunman's heart. This saves the lives of Long Tom and Ham, but Doc grimly accuses him of purposely breaking his rule. Doc says that Monk should have tried to cripple him. Sheepishly, Monk pleads overexcitement.

Doc is in a bad situation in *The Midas Man*. The villainous Hando Lancaster is about to throw a jug of deadly hydrocyanic acid at Doc. Doc is about fifty feet away and weaponless. He removes his shoes, holding one in each hand and hoping to hit the jug with one or the other (he's ambidextrous), and break it in midair. But Monk enters and shoots from behind Doc, so close to his ear that he deafens Doc. The jug breaks above Lancaster's head as he raises it to throw. Lancaster dies horribly. Doc asks Monk why he didn't wait until the jug was thrown, so nobody'd be hurt? Monk protests that he's no Annie Oakley. He was lucky to hit the jug while it was still in Lancaster's hands. Doc, knowing the futility of it, says no more. In my opinion, Monk was using good judgment. He could have missed the jug; under the unnerving circumstances, even a superb marksman could.

Monk, in *Poison Island*, shoots a crook in the leg. Doc praises him for his humanitarianism. What Doc doesn't know is that Monk had aimed between the man's eyes.

Monk's slickest trick is pulled off under Doc's eyes. In *The Laugh of Death* the chief villain, Mathis, escapes during a wild melee in an airplane. Wearing a parachute, he runs to the cabin door, opens it, and, laughing triumphantly, jumps out through the door. Monk has taken a long knife from a minor villain and is standing by the door. He can stop Mathis easily, but he does nothing until Mathis has launched himself. Then he sticks the knife deep into the parachute pack.

Later, Monk tells Doc, "He made quite a splash."

"Who?" Doc says.

Monk replies, "Mathis. For some reason or other, his parachute didn't open."

Monk is always the practical joker. The tricks he plays on Ham are many. Perhaps the ultimate is when he teaches his pig to chew tobacco and spit it in the pocket of anyone he's near. Monk makes sure that he's usually nearest Ham.

Monk doesn't limit his jokes to Ham. In *Danger Lies East*, he intends to ship the corpse of a murdered man in a trunk to a guy in New York City who's given him trouble over a chorus girl.

Monk's ego is large and powerful. Modesty, he says, is not one of his vices. He brags to a girl that he is one of the world's greatest chemists, though some in his profession deny this. He doesn't mind what they say; they're jealous.

He boasts of his fighting abilities with all the gusto of the nineteenth-century Mississippi flatboatman. There are, however, two fights he never mentions. One is with the ponderous Captain Ben O'Gard, who slugs him into senselessness. The second, and by far the most humiliating, is when the little, feeble-looking Butch (in *The Talking Devil*) takes him to the cleaner's. Fortunately, Ham is unconscious during both of these shameful defeats.

Despite his boasting, he readily admits that Doc is the better man by far. "Second fiddle is the instrument he plays best." And he is only "a spear-carrier for Doc."

This is true.

But Monk was the one I enjoyed and loved most among the six.

Realistically, though, he could not have taken all those massive blows to the jaw and head without becoming punch-drunk. He has to be undergoing some traumatic changes. In the last of the supersagas his final words are, "I won't argue." And that isn't the Monk of old speaking.

11

HAM, THE EAGLE WITH A CANE

BRIGADIER GENERAL Theodore Marley "Ham" Brooks is "slender, waspish, quick-moving," and "one of the ten best-dressed men in America." He is Harvard's most astute law graduate. His voice has "a deep-throated chest-driven quality" with "pear-shaped tones."

Lester Dent's notebook says he has black eyes, is five feet ten inches tall, and weighs one hundred and fifty-five pounds. One of the first-person accounts that Dent was fortunate enough to obtain, *Let's Kill Ames*, contains an eyewitness description of Ham. Miss Ames says he isn't tall. His hips are thin, but his shoulders are wide. His hair is straight and as black as anthracite. He has a large eaglelike nose and a large but mobile mouth.

To this we can add a high forehead (*The Freckled Shark*).

Ames also says he looks as if he were somewhere between forty and fifty years old. Very few men under thirty years of age were brigadier-generals in World War I, so Ham must have been born, at the latest, in 1888 or earlier. Since *Let's Kill Ames* took place in 1947, Ham would've been about sixty years old. However, as noted in Chapter 3, Doc's group was using silphium or Kavuru pills and so was not aging as swiftly as normal mortals.

Miss Ames comments in a later passage that his hair is now brown. This change in color is presumably caused by a hair dye. He was disguised as a Mr. Futch at that time.

Ham has an international reputation as a high-flying legal eagle. This must have been gained after World War I before he joined Doc for the first great adventure. From 1931 on, he had little time to practice law. When he did take a case, he must have commanded tremendous fees. In *The Man Who Shook the Earth* he lives in a top-floor six-room suite as a member of the Midas Club. The club is so ritzy that "even the bellhops are ex-dukes." To be a member, a man must have at least five million dollars in the bank. (This resembles the English club, the Blades, which James Bond visited as a guest of M. The Blades' requirement was much smaller, however, a mere one hundred thousand pounds in cash or securities.)

In addition, the money has to be earned, not inherited. Ham, like Monk, Johnny, and Long Tom, started out poor.

Ham, like Doc and Monk, has one parent born in England. Ham's doesn't seem to have come from nobility, but he has at least one distinguished ancestor. The portrait of Colonel Blackstone Brooks, a famous soldier and jurist, hangs on the wall of Ham's apartment. It's not until *The Too-Wise Owl* that we find out much about Ham's family. Because his parents wanted him to become a banker, he started college with that goal. Sometime during his early years at Harvard, he changed his mind and switched to law. Monk would have said that happened because Ham had the soul of a shyster.

Ham has an elder half-brother, Oliver Brooks, an Englishman who's always lived in South Africa. He is a professional actor, which is not surprising since the stage and the bar have much in common. He is murdered in New York City as a result of a complicated plot by the chief villain. Ham and Oliver's father is dead, and Ham's mother is dead. Oliver's insurance policy left his money to his mother, but it goes to Ham if she dies. Apparently, Ham's father, after divorcing Oliver's mother, moved from South Africa to the States. There he married a Bostonian named Marley.

Ham's favorite oath was "By Jove!"—a peculiar one for an American. He must have picked it up from his English father.

At Harvard, Ham worked to put himself through, but he found time to participate in amateur boxing, and his skill with his sword cane indicates he was an intercollegiate champion in fencing. His roommate was Carl John Grunow. He made friends with Eric Danielsen, whom he would meet again years later in *Quest of the Spider*.

In 1913 he graduated from the Harvard Law School *summa cum laude*. Instead of going into practice, he joined the French Army in 1914. Only this could have gotten him enough experience and a high enough French rank to be given a brigadier general's commission on transfer to the U. S. Army. Dent says a number of times that it was Ham's quick thinking that saved several regiments. Possibly, the regiments were French, not American.

Ham is a fop, changing his clothes according to the appropriate place and time, sometimes every two hours. Tailors follow him down the street just to enjoy the greatest in sartorial art. Whatever the occasion, he carries his long black cane with its concealed sword. The tip is coated with a drug which sends its victims into an immediate stupor. Ham, however, at least in the beginning, has no compunctions about running the blade completely through the villains.

Ham, despite his eagle beak, is handsome, so much so that Captain McCluskey, in *The Polar Treasure*, calls him "pretty boy." But in the eternal competition between himself and Monk, the ugly Monk wins most of the time. This galls Ham, and he does his best to turn the girls against Monk. The ploy most often used is to tell the girl that Monk has a wife and thirteen half-witted children.

Ham is husky enough to give most professional boxers a drubbing, according to Dent. If this is so, he is very humiliated when he encounters the pretty, but fiery, Kateen MacRoy. The first time he is knocked flat by her fist and is doubly humiliated because Monk witnesses it. The second time, Kateen knocks Ham out with a haymaker right. Another injury to his pride is when he and Long Tom, in *Fortress of Solitude*, are beaten up by two women, Titania and Gigantia. This time, Monk was not around to enjoy the sight.

Ham often flips coins with Monk to determine who is going to take a nifty dame out or get the most exciting task in an exploit. Ham almost always calls heads. Monk, finding this out after some time, makes a coin with two tails. Finally, he drops the coin through a hole in his pocket after cheating Ham for the hundredth time. Ham picks it up, looks at it, and then knocks Monk out with a monkey wrench. That he actually did this is doubtful; Dent probably inserted this for comic relief. A wrench brought down hard on the skull can result in a fracture, days of coma, subdural leakage of blood, nausea, vomiting, a reduction of intelligence, insanity, and often death. Ham may, however, have rapped Monk just hard enough to cause him a little pain.

An astonishing event occurs in *The Sea Angel*. Monk swindles Ham out of three million dollars. Evidently, Ham has lost his membership in the Midas Club, because this pauperizes him. He is so depressed that he tries to commit suicide. The grand jury fails to indict Monk, which causes the D.A. to tell the newspapers that it's an awful miscarriage of justice. Doc kicks Monk out of the group.

Is Monk defrocked? Is the great love affair between Monk and Ham over? It seems incredible. And so it is. The whole business is a setup to trap the men behind the horrendous thing known as the Sea Angel.

Ham's reactions on being knocked out are as unique as Monk's. Instead of stars, he sees curtains of colored lights. On several occasions, when awakening from unconsciousness, he mumbles about a woman named Nola. Dent fails to tell us her identity, just as he fails to tell us who Monk's Mabel was.

In the strange exploit of *The Stone Man*, Ham's position as leader of male fashion in America is threatened by Herman Locatella, a crooked lawyer. Ham is worried by this, though Locatella, in the end, is literally frozen out of the competition.

If Ham is upset by Locatella, he can at least enjoy the trick he's played on Renny and Monk. They have bet Ham that Harvard will lose its Saturday football game with Princeton. They lose and so have to submit for a week to getting down on all fours and barking like a dog whenever ordered to do so by Ham. Monk is furious. He accuses Ham of going out of his way to catch them on the street or at important meetings. He has forced Monk to act like a dog in the middle of a lecture he was giving to professors and big shots at the Chemical Institute.

Monk and Renny then discover how Ham has tricked them. He has connected a microphone in another room to a radio which is broadcasting the game. During it, he switches the mike into the circuit. Imitating the announcer's voice, he describes a game in which Harvard loses. He then walks into the room and eggs Monk and Renny into betting that Harvard will win. He doesn't seem to know that the game is over.

The two can't resist a sure thing. The bet is made, and they call up the local radio station to prove to Ham that he's lost. They're flabbergasted at the news, but they must obey the terms of the bet.

Having found out how the monkey business was arranged, they plan revenge. They will put Ham to sleep with anesthetic gas, remove his clothes, and let him wake up, dressed only in a fig leaf, on top of Columbus' statue at the corner of Central Park.

Unfortunately, they accidentally not only put Ham to sleep, they get Doc, too. And they screw up Doc's plan to catch the crooks.

No wonder Doc gets disgusted with the juvenile horseplay of his associates. It's all right playing the Rover Boys when there is time for it, but these guys never stop.

Ham, global traveler, explorer of jungles and mountains, has never been to Rockaway Beach. But, then, Ham wouldn't be caught dead in such an unfashionable place.

From the first exploit until *The Awful Egg* (June 1940), we're frequently told that Ham doesn't smoke. In this story, he is smoking cigars. At the end, he complains to Monk that the beautiful but nitwitted and gold-digging Nancy is trying to make him stop smoking.

The unsympathetic Monk says it's a good idea.

Indignantly, Ham replies he won't stop smoking until he dies.

This is too good an opening for Monk to pass up.

He says, "What makes you think you'll stop then?"

And in *Mystery Island*, Monk makes an acutely perceptive remark about Ham's near-paranoid suspiciousness.

"A guy like you would look for bones in animal crackers."

None of the group drinks until *Three Times a Corpse* (August 1946). In this supersaga, Ham asks for sherry. It may be that Dent did not consider the consumption of sherry to be "drinking."

Ham, in *No Light to Die By*, though he must be at least fifty-nine years old, is still a wolf. Doc has assigned him to shadow Miss Fenisong, which Monk says "is about as practical as posting a hound dog to watch a beefsteak."

The last supersaga finds Ham and Monk still at their old tricks. Monk has caught Ham swindling him in a card game and is about to take physical revenge when Doc interrupts with business. Doc tells them they've promised to quiet down their quarreling. Virtuously, Ham replies that they have. Not a blow has been struck for days, although the heavens are witness that Monk has provoked him enough.

Doc sighs wearily.

Good old Monk and Ham. In character: retarded youths, boys at heart, and ferocious lovers of women, of Doc, and of each other. But, in the final battle, Ham is separated from Monk. He lies unconscious until Doc and Monk return from the campaign against the forces of Hell itself.

Ham's last words, questioning a police sergeant, are, "Where'd you get that idea?"

A lawyer to the end. And, of the two, he has the last word. Monk's final speech is three paragraphs before Ham's. It's too bad that the two Gold Dust twins of the group could not have left the supersagas as they entered: insulting each other lovingly. It would have been esthetically more appropriate.

But that's life for you. No attention to art.

12

HABEAS CORPUS
AND CHEMISTRY

OF THE nine continuing characters in the supersagas, six are
men and one is a woman. Two are animals. Habeas Corpus
is Monk's pet pig, and Chemistry, an ape of some kind, is Ham
Brooks's pet.

Monk obtained the pig originally just to get Monk's goat. As
Chapter 10 says, Monk had framed Ham during World War I into
being charged with stealing hams. Ever since, Monk takes every
chance that comes along to remind Ham of ham.

In *The Phantom City*, the tenth published tale, the intrepid six
take their submarine, the *Helldiver*, on its second trip. Pursuing the
villainous Arab, Mohallet, they venture into the Red Sea and stop
off at the little town of Bustan. Monk sees a strange-looking razor-
back with legs as long as a greyhound's and with ears so large they
look like wings. (They're so handy, in fact, that Monk often carries
the pig by one ear.) Monk pays the owner one *qirsh* (four cents
American), and takes him along in the submarine.

The Arab from whom he bought it must have been a Christian.
Moslems do not keep pigs. They are tabu, ritually unclean.

Monk names him Habeas Corpus to enrage Ham and then dresses
up the pig in Ham's necktie to drive Ham into a killing frenzy.

Monk says, "Habeas Corpus likes corn. The necktie was corny
yellow, and Habeas was a bit seasick, so the tie made him work up
an appetite—"

The tie isn't the only thing corny about this scene, but as long as
Ham and Monk enjoy it, why should we object?

Renny, laughing, asks Monk where he got the missing link of the
pig race?

Monk says he found him chasing a dog big enough to fight a lion. Its owner was eager to sell it because it was killing hyenas and dragging their bodies home.

Doc doesn't say anything about this. It is just one more item of Monk's incessant tormenting of Ham, one more thing for him to endure silently from the two clowns. He has no idea that Monk will keep the pig or become so deeply attached to it. He soon becomes aware that the pig, though it looks as dumb as its master, is like him in that it conceals a highly intelligent brain behind its utter homeliness.

Monk gets his first chance to put Ham in a bad spot by the use of Habeas. The group is captured and imprisoned in the submarine by Mohallet and gang. Suddenly, the prisoners hear Mohallet's men wailing and cursing. Monk says that Habeas must be "doing his stuff." He tricks Ham into swearing that he'll kiss the one who rescues the group. He then tells Ham that he's put a very strong itching powder in the pig's bristles. One of the gang has brushed up against Habeas. When the others handle him to find out what's making him burn, they'll get the stuff on them, too. Trying to wash it off will make the burning worse, and blisters will develop.

The powder is so agonizing that the villains agree to release the prisoners if they'll prepare an antidote for them. Later, Monk tries to get Ham to fulfill his promise. The adventure ends, however, with the pig unkissed.

In *Dust of Death* the group is in South America fighting the insidious Inca in Gray. While lost in the jungle, Ham encounters a pack of monkeys. At least, Dent calls them monkeys. They are actually apes. Their hair is rust-colored, like Monk's, and they are larger than chimpanzees but smaller than gorillas. Their very presence is remarkable. Any primatologist will tell you that there have never been any apes in the Americas. However, scientists have scoffed at the reports of the gorilla, the okapi, and the pygmy hippopotamus, much to their later embarrassment—if scientists can be embarrassed.

And the late great Professor Challenger claimed to have found apes on that high Amazon hinterland plateau known as Maple White Land. There is no record that any zoologist ever put the lie to Challenger. If one had, he would have been lucky to escape with less than a broken leg and a fractured skull. (Challenger was as violent as his cousin Monk.)

I have the utmost faith in Challenger's veracity and do not doubt that there is indeed a species of native ape in South America. Nor do I doubt that those found by Ham Brooks had wandered down off the plateau into the jungle.

In any event, one of them saw in Ham a soul brother. Whether it was a compulsive or elective affinity, he attached himself to the Harvard lawyer. Ham tried to drive him away. Then, seeing its remarkable resemblance to Monk, he also saw his revenge for Monk. Very well. Monk had his Habeas Corpus. He would have his Chemistry. It would be Monk's turn to be tormented.

His decision was confirmed when hostilities broke out between the pig and ape on sight. Chemistry seized a stick and beat Habeas until the latter took off into the jungle.

The doubt about Chemistry's exact classification is never cleared up. Sometimes he's a monkey. Sometimes he's called a chimpanzee. Other times he's a baboon (which is actually a monkey). Once, he's an orangutan. Usually he's a what-is-it?

Monk's label, in *Ost*, seems the best to adopt. He calls Chemistry a "goriboon."

The same sort of zoological indecision seems to cling to Habeas. Several times, Dent says it came from Central America. Both Dent and Donovan call him an Australian bushhog in several stories. Hathway says he's a South African warthog.

None of them seem as uncertain in primate classification as H. C. McNeile, author of *Bulldog Drummond*. In one page in that book, he calls a simian a monkey, a baboon, and a gorilla.

During *Dust of Death*, Chemistry saves Habeas' life. This forces Monk to like him at the same time he hates him. Habeas shows his gratitude by biting the ape's big toe, and this puts Monk in a good humor again.

"Habeas," Ham says, "has about the same disposition as the guy who owns him."

Though the animals continue their feud, they become valuable to the group. They save the lives of Doc and his gang many times. They pitch into the battles and bite and tear the enemies. They carry messages. Monk, when captured, sometimes diverts his enemies for a saving moment by using his ventriloquism. As the villains stare in astonishment at the talking pig, Monk goes into action. Once,

Chemistry, dressed up to look like Monk, actually fools the villains and leads them on a chase.

The two pets not only accompany their masters in many exploits, they live with them. Monk's penthouse has a big marble-and-silver wallow with perfumed radioactive mud. Habeas wears a platinum collar studded with jewels. Ham dwells with Chemistry in the hoity-toity Midas Club apartments.

The two pets often go with their masters into exclusive clubs and restaurants, apparently with little objection. In those days, it must be remembered, many places that barred black humans would accept animals—if tipped heavily enough.

As the years go by, the pig and the ape participate in fewer and fewer adventures. Whether this was because they were growing old, or because Monk and Ham were increasingly in situations where the animals would only have been fatal embarrassments, Dent does not say. They make their final appearance together in *The Man Who Was Scared*.

After that, we see neither of them again, though the pig is mentioned as being in New York in *The Pharaoh's Ghost* (June 1944).*

---

* *Habeas Corpus was also mentioned in* The Red Spider, *which did not see publication until a Bantam Books edition in July 1979.—WSE*

13

RENNY, DOOR-BUSTER
AND HOLY-COWER

A FIST the size of a quart bottle of milk rams through the panels of a thick wooden door. Sometimes the door has been locked by a villain, who waits on the other side. Sometimes victims are inside, tied up by the villains and awaiting death. More often the door is busted just for fun.

Following the lightning of the knuckles is a voice "like thunder gobbling out of a barrel."

Enter Colonel John Renwick.

"Renny" is six feet four inches tall and two hundred and fifty pounds of massive bone and muscle. (Sometimes he's nearly seven feet tall, but most of the descriptions agree with the first above.) He has a head "of leonine proportions." He has dark, disapproving eyes and the facial features of a seventeenth-century English Puritan or of "an unhappy horse." He dresses well but has a habit of wearing his clothes for too long a time. His single foppish trait is smearing his dark uncontrollable hair with pomade.

He rarely smiles. When he does, he is disapproving whatever is going on. When he looks most unhappy, he is having the most fun. According to *The Thousand-Headed Man*, he has never been known to laugh. In later supersagas, he does laugh occasionally.

His favorite expletive is "Holy cow!" This, plus his huge fists, possibly the largest in the world, are his trademarks. His frequent use of this exclamation finally gets Doc, Monk, and Ham into the same habit near the end of the supersagas.

He is one of the world's most sought-after civil and mechanical engineers. In *Hex*, he is called "the greatest engineering expert alive." His books are classics, used as texts in universities all over the world.

He has built dams, tunnels, airfields, roads, railways, and submarines and ships everywhere. He has helped Doc design the Empire State Building.

When on a job, he makes a thousand dollars a day.

Renny is an accomplished boxer, though, surprisingly, he is the least effective of the five assistant archenemies of evil in a free-for-all. Still, his fists are as big as his head, and a man struck by one of them is under the impression a bank-vault door has fallen on him. As Monk says, "It takes a lot of guys to outnumber Renny."

(There is a discrepant statement in *Mystery on Happy Bones* [July 1943], that Monk and Renny are the two best of the five in a free-for-all. Perhaps, in his later exploits, Renny had improved.)

Unlike his four buddies, Renny was born wealthy, but near the end of the tales he is almost broke. He's spent too much time and money aiding Doc. Also, it must have cost him plenty to replace all those doors he busted just for fun.

Like the other aides, he prefers bachelorhood. Like them, he can, however, be strongly affected by beautiful women. He falls in love with Vida Carlaw in *The Derrick Devil*. Either she rejects him or he resists the temptation to propose marriage. We hear no more of her in the succeeding stories. In *The Three Devils*, Renny falls for Nell Grunow. These two, as far as we know, are the only ones he ever considered as lifemates.

Renny rarely smokes, though in *Pirates of the Pacific* he does smoke a cigar. Unlike Doc, he is "a skilled cook."

Renny's grammar, like Monk's and Ham's, is not that of a college graduate. This can be attributed, as in Ham's case, to a failure to report Renny's words verbatim to Dent. Dent inserted his own words with a disastrous result. Or, possibly, Monk was the one who wrote up the notes for Dent and deliberately made Ham and Renny use substandard English. It would be like him.

Renny seems to have been in the artillery or the Engineer Corps during World War I. We do know, from a comment in *Resurrection Day*, that he was at the Battle of the Marne. In postwar years he became a very skilled flier, having been instructed by Doc himself.

Next to Doc, he is the most expert of the gang in the use of firearms and is a superb machine-gunner. Despite this, he accidentally shoots Doc in *The Crimson Serpent*.

He is the slowest runner except for Ham (who's usually too worried about his clothes to run fast), but he, with Monk, is the most agile. In *The Black Spot*, he climbs up eighteen stories inside a dumbwaiter shaft to rescue Doc, Monk, Ham, and Pat.

Renny is not in many wartime (WW II) adventures. He is kept busy building roads for the U.S. military or airfields in China and elsewhere. Occasionally, he comes home for a rest, which, however, he seldom gets. In *Satan Black*, he and Monk are leaving the skyscraper and discussing the future. Renny claims that skyscraper construction will be renewed after the war. Monk says this won't be so. People will live out in the country and fly in to work. Renny silently disagrees. What will people use for money? The national debt is incredibly huge, and he sees nothing but its increase in the future. But why should he argue with Monk, who "belonged to the live-today-worry-about-tomorrow-when-it's-here school"?

About this time, two armed men try to take them for a ride. Alone, Renny wouldn't resist; he's sensible. But he knows Monk's character. Regardless of the consequences, Monk is going to tackle one of the gunmen. So Renny might as well tackle the other. Both men render the thugs *hors de combat*, but a third man with a sawed-off rifle forces them to take refuge in a doorway.

Monk's excited state amuses Renny. He tells Monk to stick his head out and see if the men will shoot at it. Monk, overstimulated by the fight, starts to stick his head out but catches himself in time. And Renny laughs.

"There was no humor in Renny's laugh. It was a kind of uncaring, desperate feeling he got when there was intense excitement. Ordinarily he was a taciturn and somewhat sour fellow, but excitement seemed to make him drunk. Afterward he would look back on the emotional binge with pleasure."

As Dent says elsewhere, excitement was the glue that held the six together.

Renny's immediate reaction, after losing the three in a chase down the subway tunnel, is to become somewhat shaky. He has time to reflect on what happened.

"Fear, like the measles, took a little time to develop."

Renny, despite his wealth in the beginning, lives simply and in no one place for long. He seems to have resided with Johnny and

Long Tom in a hotel near the Empire State Building in the early days. In *The Ten Ton Snakes* (March 1945) he lives in a sparsely furnished room adjoining his office. This is in a big old building on Fortieth Street, two blocks from Grand Central Station. The walnut furniture of the office is just short of seedy. His "office girl," Mrs. Carter, is middle-aged and seems to have absorbed the walnut hue of the furniture.

In this story Renny is visited by a man he knew in China. The man wants help. When Renny finds that it's not money he needs, he tells him that he knows nothing about women. Nor, apparently, wants anything to do with them. In this, he resembles Johnny and Long Tom.

Renny is decorated by King George VI of Great Britain for his part in converting English wartime industries to peacetime work. He must have made good money for this, but by the time of *The Exploding Lake* (September 1946), he is living in a shabby hotel on Twenty-eighth Street. He doesn't appear again until *Target for Death* (January 1947). Then he drops out of sight until *The Pure Evil* (March–April 1948), and he comes onto the scene very near the end.

A free-for-all occurs. Renny strikes down the man Monk has chosen to jump, and Monk protests, "Dammit! Pick your own!"

One man gets away. Doc orders that he be let go rather than shot.

"One left for seed?" Renny says. "That won't do!"

He goes outside with a gun, and one shot is heard. When Renny comes back in, Doc says, disapprovingly, "We didn't want to kill anyone."

Renny only says, "Didn't we?"

Doc knows it's useless to chide. Renny at least doesn't try to lie his way out, as Monk often does.

This is Renny's last action. He is seen no more, though he is mentioned in *Up from Earth's Center* as being in the area on a surveying project.[*]

---

[*] *Renny did appear in* The Red Spider, *which did not see publication until a Bantam Books edition in July 1979.—WSE*

14

NEOVERBALIST JOHNNY

WILLIAM HARPER LITTLEJOHN was "named by his mother." By this it may be inferred that his father was either dead or separated from Johnny's mother when he was born. Or, possibly, he was indifferent.

In any case, Johnny grew up in comparative poverty. No other relative of his is mentioned except for an Uncle Ned, ill at the time, in *Mystery Island*. He became an extremely skinny man, one who, according to his friends, looked like "an advance agent for a famine." He is also "a man as long as his words and only somewhat thicker than a rake handle." In the very first story, and in some later ones, he is six feet tall. Later stories describe him as being nearly seven feet tall or so tall that he has to bend when going through a doorway. He is "two men tall and half a man wide," just the opposite of Monk.

Johnny has a high forehead and brown eyes, one of which was injured in World War I. He is the only one of the six who has no military rank, yet *The Living-Fire Menace* states that he was in the Army. The implications are that he was in the intelligence department and that he did the kind of work which the government would just as soon not reveal.

If he was a spy, it seems strange that he was not shot when captured by the Germans. Probably, he was in the uniform and carrying the papers of a dead Allied soldier when taken. He must have given his captors considerable trouble; otherwise, he would never have been sent to the secret POW camp where Doc and the others were being kept.

After the war, Johnny returned to college and eventually got a Ph.D. in archaeology and perhaps another one in geology. The scarecrow young man with the bulging forehead, prematurely gray at the temples, is a striking figure. A monocle over his injured left eye added to his conspicuousness. After Doc operated on the eye (in *The Man Who Shook the Earth*), Johnny still wears the monocle. It dangles from a ribbon attached to his lapel and is used as a magnifying glass in his professional work and his detecting for Doc. The concave side of its framework is engraved: $50 REWARD FOR RETURN OF THIS TO DOC SAVAGE. It is the finding of this by a schoolboy on a New Jersey road that makes Doc aware, in *The Midas Man*, that Johnny has been kidnaped.

Johnny's favorite exclamations are, "I'll be superamalgamated!" and "Supermalagorgeous!"

These are what you'd expect from a man who continually obfuscates others with long neolatinisms synthesized on the locus.

Examples of the sort of things he casts at his victims are:

"A cabalistically obreptitious anagrammitism… An ultraeffectual colluctation… Is perlustration a potentiality?"

When he phones an airport to hire a plane, he says, "Would it be feasible to charter an aerial conveyance for an immediate peregrination?"

Johnny puzzles his colleagues with these and flabbergasts Monk. But when addressing Doc, he speaks directly and precisely in conventional English. He has too much respect to use his neoverbalisms on him. Besides, there wouldn't be any fun in it. Doc would know exactly what he was saying.

Johnny apparently did not always throw his long words around so recklessly. Until the fifteenth supersaga, he talks just as anybody else does, albeit in a little more exact and scholastic manner. Then, in *The Mystery on the Snow*, he suddenly launches his Latin-studded sesquipedalian speech. It seems likely that he does this mainly to bug his colleagues, Monk and Ham especially. These two are always irritating and angering the others of the group. Johnny invents his own irritation and applies it mercilessly.

The Awful Egg states that Johnny had started using big words early in his career, when he was a young man. He began using them to draw attention to himself; they were "his vice, his hobby and his source of secret amusement." If this is so, it seems strange that he abandoned the habit for fifteen exploits.

Once, Johnny used "superamalgamated" when he shouldn't have (in *The Man Who Fell Up*) and ruined a beautiful trick Doc was playing on the Nazi villains.

Before joining Doc in 1931, Johnny had headed the natural science department of a famous university. He had already gained recognition as one of the world's foremost authorities in the fields of archaeology and geology. Mr. Lively, in *Mystery Island*, says that Johnny is the greatest authority in stratigraphy. Doc says he's probably centuries ahead of his time. Doc has as broad a knowledge of geology as Johnny has, but Johnny's is deeper.

Dent never says what institution it was which Johnny adorned. From certain oblique references and shadowy hints, linked obscurely with vague, shuddery intimations, it seems likely that he taught at Miskatonic University, Arkham, Massachusetts. Indeed, if we can put any trust in certain cryptic authorities, he was the man who led the Miskatonic expedition into the Antarctic in 1929. His horrifying report was suppressed by the authorities, but a pulp-magazine writer named Howard Phillips Lovecraft managed to get a look at it. From what he remembered of his hasty reading, he wrote a fictional tale, *At the Mountains of Madness*, which was published in 1936 in *Astounding Science Fiction* magazine. Except for some inaccuracies of memory, and fictional names for the human characters, this story hews to reality.

The original, unexpurgated document was once believed to be locked up in the archives of Miskatonic University. However, certain elusive suggestions and guarded comments, some bordering on the blasphemous, have led me to believe that Johnny has (or had) the manuscript. If this is so, it is very doubtful that it will be available for many years, if ever. No one seems to know where, in 1972, Professor William Harper Littlejohn is.

Johnny, like Long Tom and Renny and Doc, doesn't smile much, nor does he have much to do with women. He does, however, like Pat, and he is not the bitter misogynist Long Tom is. He falls in love once, with the same beauty, Lam Benbow, for whom Long Tom had a passion. Neither seems to have pursued his suit with much vigor. They preferred losing her hand to losing their place in the Famous Five.

One of Johnny's characteristics was his appetite. The "long hank of a bone" could outeat even the gluttonous Monk; he devoured enough to keep two Doc Savages going.

Another characteristic was that he never bet on anything but a sure thing.

His endurance was second only to Doc's. He could go three days and nights without sleep or food. His peculiar metabolism, however, required more water than the average man's.

Of the five, he was also the fastest runner.

His linguistic abilities, while not equal to Doc's, are not far behind. In *The Screaming Man* he is fluent enough in Japanese to pass for a native. This supersaga (December 1945) is the last in which Johnny personally appears. Even here, he comes onto the stage only at the last. It's revealed that he has been trailing the sinister Jonas Sown for six months from Europe through China and Japan and the Philippine Islands. He is working for the U. S. Army but has no military rank.

The only reference to Johnny's residence is in *The Too-Wise Owl*. In this story, he is living in a bad neighborhood in lower Max Street. The location and reputation of this area keep visitors from interfering with his studies. He thinks no one knows where he lives, but Doc, of course, knows all about it.

Johnny is last heard as a voice over the phone in *The Devil Is Jones* (November 1946). Doc, in Jefferson City, Missouri, on a murder case, calls Johnny in New York. He asks him to check out, as quickly as possible, all the employees of Sam Karen, a private investigator killed in Jefferson City that day. Ham takes the return call from Johnny, who has efficiently dug up all vital information.

And that is the *ave atque vale* of William Harper Littlejohn.

15

LONG TOM, WIZARD OF THE JUICE AND MISOGYNIST

LESTER DENT'S notebook records that Major Thomas J. "Long Tom" Roberts is five feet four inches tall and weighs 140 pounds. He has a gold tooth in front and a tremendously bulging "Steinmetz" forehead. In fact, in his youth, this wizard of the electron, this "electricity shark," was an apprentice sorcerer for both the great Steinmetz and the great Thomas Alva Edison.

Of Doc's five aides, Long Tom is the physical weakling, though he is such only in a relative sense. His skin looks as if he'd been raised in a cellar. His too-big ears stick out like an owl's tufts and are so thin the light shines through them as if they were light bulbs. His hair is pale blond; his eyes, pale blue. In *Spook Hole* he has two huge gold teeth in front and so would seem to have lost another tooth in one of his many fracases. In *The South Pole Terror* the beautiful but spoiled-rotten Velma Crale describes him as "a pale runt." Undertakers, on seeing him, glow with happiness and rub their hands together in anticipation of imminent business.

Yet Long Tom has never been sick a day in his life, and he can lick nine out of ten men on the street without seeming fatigued. The tenth would think he'd been fighting an ocelot before it was over.

Long Tom neither drinks nor smokes, and he doesn't often swear. His temperance does not extend to his temper, which is awe-inspiring when he's aroused, so much so that even the giant Renny and the gorilloid Monk speak softly when his dander is up.

He owns a flashy racer which is equipped with every conceivable electrical device from a TV receiver to a short-wave radio set which emits bug and mosquito-killing frequencies. Generally, though, he drives a vehicle which looks as if it were on its way to the junkyard but which has under the rusty hood a liquid-cooled airplane motor.

He is a multimillionaire from his many patents but, except for a brief stay in an expensive apartment, lives in the slums of Amsterdam Avenue in a miserly room off a basement laboratory. This has a secret door for use in the battle against evil men and also when the police are looking for Doc and his gang. Despite his wealth, he is very tight-fisted. He grumbles in *The Terror in the Navy* when he has to pay a dollar for taxi fare. In *The Too-Wise Owl* he is displeased when, doing detective work for Doc, he has to pay five dollars rent for use of a peanut wagon. Not only does he dislike its whistling—he can't stand whistling of any kind—but the idea of losing five dollars irritates him.

Yet he has compassion behind his sour face and disposition. As noted in *The Golden Peril*, he can't resist giving money to beggars or to the poor.

He got his nickname during the Great War (1914-18) when he stopped a German attack in a village by loading up an old "long tom," a seventeenth-century cannon standing in the square, with scrap metal and firing it off. This would seem to indicate that he was in the artillery or perhaps the infantry. But in *Dust of Death* he visits his old buddy, Ace Jackson, while he's in South America. Long Tom hasn't seen Ace since Ace was flying a Spad in the war. Could Long Tom have been an aviator in Ace's outfit? Dent definitely states that he was in the Army, but at that time the Air Service was part of the Army.

He is described as being essentially humorless. Yet, he has his lighter moments. In *The Metal Master* he is disguised as a crook, "Punning" Parker, who shows great aptitude for puns, though their quality is not Shakespearean. And in *Devils of the Deep* he grins when he sees Habeas Corpus, Monk's pet pig, dressed up by Monk with a small cane and a top hat in imitation of foppish Ham.

Of the many gadgets Long Tom works on, his favorite is the short-wave bug killer. Perhaps this is because he hates mosquitoes, which he calls "Jersey canaries." In many of the early novels he is working on the insect-slayer, and he once lectures to a congressional commission on its potentiality for use by farmers and cotton growers. It seems, however, to have been effective only at short range. There is no record that he ever patented it or made any money on it.

He invents a sonar device far ahead of anything else in that line. This is first used on the submarine, the *Helldiver*, in *The Polar Treasure*.

In *Men of Fear* Long Tom develops two devices. One is for locating minerals by fluorescent activity. The other is based on an idea by Doc and is a paste that bursts into flames when subjected to certain frequencies from a short-wave radio set. It is Long Tom's idea during this story to set up short-wave sets at the subway exits and so identify some crooks whose clothing has been smeared with the paste. It is effective but hard on the crook, which doesn't bother Long Tom, or any of the group, one bit.

Long Tom is a misogynist and generally acts like one. However, in *The Feathered Octopus* he falls in love with the beautiful blonde Lam Benbow. The gang see him blush for the first time when Pat kids him about this. And in *The Awful Dynasty* he reveals a secret crush on Pat.

He appears fewer times in the supersagas than anyone else in the group, perhaps because he is always off on some big project halfway around the globe. This may explain why he is knocked senseless fewer times than the others. His worst injuries during the adventures are the broken right wrist and hip caused by a rifle bullet in *The Too-Wise Owl*.

One reason for his frequent absences is his disappearance during World War II. He dropped out of sight in 1942. According to Dent, he was "one of those few dozen men who had vanished mysteriously... been heard of *not at all during the whole course of the war* [italics mine], and only reappeared a few weeks ago..."

This quotation is from *Terror Wears No Shoes* (May–June 1948). Dent also states that Long Tom had been confined in various laboratories "tinkering with cathodes and making electrons say Uncle..."

But in several novels published in 1943 he is said to be in Russia and China. In *Death Had Yellow Eyes* (February 1944) he is called home from China by Doc. He is present in *The Pharaoh's Ghost* (June 1944). In *Weird Valley* (September 1944) he is back in China. Three 1945 issues state that he is still in China. *Death in Little Houses* (October 1946) says that he is "out of the country at the moment." He is in Europe in *The Devil Is Jones* (November 1946).

When he appears on the stage again, in *Terror Wears No Shoes*, he is disguised as the villainous Karl Sundwi, the real Sundwi having been eaten up in an acid bath. His experiences in chasing the man who may have caused World War II have changed him. He is twenty pounds heavier, tanned, and looking fit enough to whip a fourteen-year-old kid, which makes him look fit indeed. He says that he has never felt worse in his life, and he is not kidding. He has a stomach ulcer.

Perhaps the ulcer was even more serious than Dent indicated. This, the 176th supersaga, is the last one in which Long Tom plays a role. He is not even mentioned in the remaining five stories.[*]

---

[*] *Long Tom did appear in* The Red Spider, *which did not see publication until a Bantam Books edition in July 1979.—WSE*

16

PATRICIA SAVAGE, LADY AUXILIARY AND BRONZE KNOCKOUT

ONLY ONE woman appears more than three times. She is Patricia Savage, Doc's cousin, and she is as bronzely beautiful as he is handsome. She is a real knockout, a pip, a peach. But she doesn't just stand around and wait to be rescued, as so many heroines of fiction and the movies did and still do. She is, though in a less noisy and in a very female way, as aggressive as Monk. The first description of her notes "a wealth of bronze hair very closely in hue to that of Doc Savage." She is tall and has a fabulous physique. "Her features were as perfect as though a magazine-cover artist had designed them."

When we first see her, she is wearing high-laced boots, breeches, and a serviceable gray shirt. A cartridge belt is draped about her waist, and her holster contains an old family heirloom. This is a heavy Frontier Single-Action six-shooter revolver. Pat will use it frequently in the many battles to come, and she usually carries it in her handbag. When she first appears, she is holding, in the crook of her right arm, an automatic big-game rifle. Pat is loaded for bigger game than bear. Her father has been murdered by the mysterious "werewolf," and now she is threatened by it. But Pat doesn't scare easily. As she herself will say a number of times, she has the same "taint" in her blood as her cousin has. That "taint" is a compulsive love of adventure, excitement, and danger. She is a "metallic tigress," and her small right fist swings with the timing and precision of a trained boxer's when she hits the obstreperous Boat Face in the eye and knocks him into the lake. Her feet are small, as Doc notes when he is trailing her in the woods and sees her tracks.

Pat is not only an accomplished boxer. She has learned her fencing lessons well at the finishing school she attended. She evades the blows and kicks of a villain, a husky young man, and throttles him from behind with a strong arm. She seems to be rather modest, though. She turns her back so she won't see her Indian servant, the squaw Tiny, strip the villain of his clothes. Of course, she is young then. After she moves to New York City, she loses much of this prudery.

Pat has a strong contrary streak which manifests itself at her first encounter with Doc. She questions his orders as they flee the villains, but Doc quickly straightens her out. Then Pat, for one of the few times in her life, becomes hysterical. She has been through much for the past few days, and when she is faced with crossing a deep abyss on a thin rope, she shrieks and hits out at Doc. After Doc carries her over on his back while he tightrope-walks the line over the abyss, she becomes ashamed. But she really had little to be ashamed of. Very few could go through what she did and not have a case of jitters.

Ham and Monk, the wolves, the skirt-chasers, are bowled over when they first see Pat. Monk exclaims over her bronze hair and says, "She might almost be Doc's sister." She is, he believes, the prettiest girl he has ever seen. Ham is so struck that he breaks his long-established policy and agrees with Monk. She's a "knockout."

Notice one thing. Nothing is said in her first supersaga about her eyes. Indeed, there is no description of her eyes until her fifth adventure, *The Fantastic Island.* Suddenly she has golden eyes, eyes like Doc's.

This is strange. Golden eyes are rare and so outstanding that Dent surely would have commented on them, if she really did have them, in *Brand of the Werewolf* and the three following supersagas in which she appeared. They are not features easily ignored; a writer would seize on them immediately.

The truth is, her eyes were not of the same color as her cousin's. But Dent, while writing *The Fantastic Island,* thought it would be a good idea if they were. Golden eyes like her cousin's would make Pat more colorful.

Laurence Donovan, who wrote the sixth story in which she appeared, *Murder Mirage,* also mentions her golden eyes. Undoubtedly, Dent inserted this description in the notes he gave Donovan. Donovan, however, in writing *The Men Who Smiled No More* (Pat's seventh appearance), forgot to describe her eyes. Dent resumed with this description in the eighth appearance of Pat, *The Black Spot*. In this he notes the "golden intelligence of her eyes." And thereafter in the many stories in which she plays a role, she has eyes that greatly resemble Doc's.

There is good reason to go into such detail about the color of her eyes. If the genes for the eyes really came through Doc's father's side of the family, as Dent states, then the genes did not come to Doc through Wolf Larsen and Armand Chauvelin, as claimed in Addendum 1 of this book. These are the forefathers of Arronaxe Larsen, Doc's mother, the bearers of the yellow-eye genes.

Fortunately for this thesis, it is obvious that Pat did not have the golden eyes and that Dent only gave them to her as a fictional afterthought. Pat did, however, have Doc's bronze hair and skin, and so these must be Savage traits. (In reality, they are the traits of the Clark Wildman family, the real name of Doc's father.) The bronzeness seems to have skipped Doc's father, otherwise Watson surely would have commented on it when he described him in *The Adventure of the Priory School*. Or perhaps Watson omitted this, feeling that too exact a description might give some readers an idea of the true identity of the sixth duke of Holdernesse's illegitimate son.

Pat may also have inherited bronze hair from an additional side of the family. Her mother was May Renfrew, the sister of a rather well-known policeman in Canada. If May resembled Inspector Douglas Renfrew, she would have had a skin burned brown by the elements and bronze hair that glinted with fiery particles of copper. His eyes were large and of a sea-gray color, and so it is likely that Pat's were either gray or blue.

In her second supersaga, *Fear Cay*, Pat makes her appearance by sliding out of Doc's sedan. It's been less than a year since Monk last saw her, but he doesn't recognize her at first. She has her back turned, and not until he sees her face does he know her. Before this, he's been watching her legs and thinking that if the rest of her is like them, she has to be a knockout. It seems strange that Monk could not instantly identify her. In *The Death Lady*, Monk recognizes a villainess in disguise by her legs. He even states that he never forgets them if they're worth remembering. Monk is a liar, but in this case he would seem to be telling the truth.

However, the last time Monk has seen Pat, she had been wearing men's clothing, and this probably keeps Monk from getting a clear view of her legs. In any event, Monk is delighted to see her. Even Doc, who doesn't like girls cluttering up the landscape and hampering him, is pleased. She is the exception he's willing to make. She is a "two-fisted scrapper herself," and in her own way is almost as remarkable as Doc.

She knows how to handle Doc. Instead of flinging herself on him and kissing him, as a female relative has every right to do, she shakes Doc's hand. But warmly. Doc intends to drop her off before continuing his present investigation. He gives in to Monk's plea that she be taken along. A few moments later, crooks attack them. Pat pulls out the "enormous, much-worn single-action six-shooter." It has neither trigger nor sight, but a fanning spur is welded to the hammer. Pat bangs away with this, happy at finding danger so swiftly after encountering Doc.

A short time later, Pat is abducted along with the movie star Maureen Darling. Pat pulls a fast one and convinces the villains that she is Maureen Darling (or Kel Avery, Darling's real name). Kel is thrown out of the car, and Pat is taken away. Kel Avery says later that Pat would "go great in the movies." She's a looker and a hell of a good actress. Kel Avery describes Pat as having hair like Doc's, but she says nothing of Pat's eyes.

When Pat is slapped on the mouth by a kidnaper, Pat bites him. Pat won't take anything from anybody, even if it endangers her life. She comes very close to being killed a number of times in this supersaga, but she eagerly plunges into the next adventure, *Death in Silver*.

The attitude of Monk and Ham toward her is, in one respect, surprising. They greatly admire her beauty and her ability to handle herself in dangerous situations. But there is no hint anywhere that they try to date her. To these two wolves she is off limits. She is Doc's cousin and thus not to be chased. Doc never said anything to the two about their incessant chasing down and bedding of women, but he would have been more than upset if either had made a pass at Pat.

Pat seems to understand this. She prefers to be treated as one of the boys. Undoubtedly, though Monk and Ham suppress any sexual desire they feel for her, other men are not so constrained. Yet we get no indication anywhere of the many dates she must have had, of the many proposals of marriage and otherwise that she must have gotten. Whatever the frequency of marriage proposals, she must have turned them down. Or, if she did get married or engaged, she did not stay so very long. As for the proposals of bed without matrimony, it is difficult to imagine Pat accepting any. No matter how attractive the man, physically or mentally, he would suffer by comparison with Doc. Even without her cousin as a standard, Pat would have been difficult to please. She is so much her own "man," so realistic and self-possessed, so tough. She is a better man than nine out of ten she met.

On the other hand, she is sensitive, and she is far from lacking femininity. Nor does she give any indication that she is frigid. Would she have lived a life of self-denial, or virginity all those years? It doesn't seem likely. But if she had lovers, she certainly kept them secret. Or at least Dent was silent about them.

After the almost-fatal encounter with the weird and ancient Dan Thunden and the villainous Santorini in *Fear Cay*, Pat decides not to return to Canada. She will stay in New York City. With the money from her father's estate, she sets up a business, the Park Avenue Beautician. This occupies most of the area of a very modernistic building in the most elite part of Park Avenue. Its two doormen wear very distinctive uniforms, no doubt designed by Pat. It is into this posh place that Doc escorts Lorna Zane for safekeeping by Pat in *Death in Silver*. Here in a waiting room which is "a bewildering resplendency of chromium, enamel, and colored rugs," they are greeted by Pat's staff. These include blondes, brunettes, and redheads of superb physique dressed in the best taste. The girls are beautiful enough to pop Lorna's eyes, but their employer's beauty surpasses theirs.

Pat comments that Doc has never been here before. Dent doesn't say what Pat's expression or tone is when she made this comment, but both are probably knowing. She is aware that Doc won't visit her place unless he has to. All that gorgeous beauty, all those long-legged and big-eyed women gazing at him with "frank admiration" would upset him, no matter how little he shows it on his face. She knows that he is disturbed by their attractiveness, which in turn means that he is tempted and that he fears that he might not be able to resist the temptation. Undoubtedly, Pat likes to tease her cousin with visions of beautiful and sensual-looking women. She is aware that the visions will stimulate sexual fantasies in Doc's mind, and she might hope that the fantasies will send him into the arms of some woman. She may even wish, most probably does wish, that the woman will be herself.

Whatever is going on in her mind and Doc's, she seems to be all business. She wants to show him the gymnasium upstairs. "It's a knockout." She also has over thirty of the best beauty operators in New York City, and her clientele includes *all* of the leaders of fashion in the city. She does not know how she's going to get the fat off her more obese customers, but she'll do her damnedest. In any event, she's always paid in advance, and no refunds are ever given. Some of her customers are men, though she does not know if they come to the gym for workouts and the beauty treatments, or just to make time with her "snappy assistants."

Docs asks her if she wants to help him. She laughs and says, "Sure. Who is trying to kill you now?"

Doc, it seems, has denied her petition to become a permanent member of his group. But he will call on her many times, and many times Pat will insert herself into an adventure over his objections. She takes Lorna Zane into her protective custody and gives Lorna the full beauty treatment. This includes Pat's own invention, the very expensive Special Egyptian Gay Pack Facial. The treatment, however, is on the house, which makes Lorna unique. As Doc is to comment in other supersagas, Pat charges about twenty times what the treatments are worth, and he hints that highway robbers could take a lesson from her.

A silver-costumed villain uses her phone to call Lorna Zane into her office. Pat tricks him into making the call himself, which results in his being rendered helpless. The phone's mouthpiece, one of Doc's inventions, ejects a small spray of tear gas to the user's face if Pat secretly activates the device. Pat seizes the man's gun, but a second silver-clad man hits her on the head with a gun butt. This time Pat is only half-unconscious, but she is to be completely knocked out many times in the years to come, though the number is nowhere near Monk's record, of course.

The villains take Pat along to use as a lever against Doc. One of them asks her if Doc doesn't think a lot of her. She replies that she suspects that Doc sometimes wishes she hadn't been born. He has had to waste too much of his time rescuing her. Doc once more rescues her, but now he isn't wasting his time. He gets Pat out of the prison cell in the villain Ull's ship along with Lorna Zane, a man named Rapid Pace, Monk, and Ham. And he exposes Ull's real identity.

After she's safe, Pat looks "wan, a little exhausted by the whole grisly episode." But Pat's color returns swiftly along with her enthusiasm for getting into trouble.

In the mysterious case of *The Annihilist*, Doc goes again to Pat's establishment to ask her for help. He sees some men in the "sumptuously furnished reception room" who sigh with ecstasy and frustration as Pat walks in. Pat's reply is the same as the last time, "Well, who's trying to kill you now?" Doc sends her to Janko Sultman's Association of Physical Health to scout around for him. He tells her to use her own good judgment while she's being a detective.

Pat, wearing dowdy clothes and glasses, bribes the receptionist at the Association to let her take her place for the day. She listens in on the conversation between two villains, Doctor Nandez and "Lizzie." Lizzie is a very effeminate young man, undoubtedly a fairy, though Dent could not use this term or anything similarly suggestive to label him as a homosexual. The pulp-magazine tabus would not have permitted him to do this. (Neither would the slick-magazine tabus or even the hardcover book publishers' tabus of 1934.) Lizzie is, however, not only a fairy; he is a psychopathic killer. But Pat is no victim looking for a victimizer. She carries in her handbag one of Doc's small supermachine pistols, two extra magazines, a fountain-pen tear-gas gun, and a compact. For some reason, she does not have her six-shooter with her. When she sees Nandez leave his office, she makes a quick change of disguise, including a wig, and follows him. He lures her into a building and grabs her, and then quickly, and painfully, realizes that he has no trembling mouse in his hands. Pat's middle name is never given by Dent, but it could well have been Roughhouse. Refusing to wrestle with a man who's obviously stronger, she kicks him in the shins, slams her fist against his windpipe, tries to tear off his ear, jams her little finger into his left nostril, and lifts savagely (no pun intended). Nandez retreats in agony and confusion, allowing Pat time to get her supermachine pistol out. He kicks that out of her hand, only to get tear gas in his eyes from her fountain-pen gun. She has a chance to get away then, but the sinister Lizzie enters with an automatic pistol. With this he knocks her half-unconscious and then binds and gags her. Nandez starts to cut Pat into little pieces with a razor-sharp pocketknife— with results that surprise both him and Pat.

Later, Pat goes with Doc, Monk, and Ham to investigate Sidney Lorrey's laboratory in a river barge. There she shoots from the hip and downs a villain. This feat causes Monk to remark that she is bloodthirsty. Monk is being facetious, of course. She explains that the man is only unconscious. Doc has made up some anesthetic mercy bullets for her six-shooter.

Pat is then kidnaped by Boke and held as a hostage. Doc gets her loose, and, during the inevitable melee, Pat rabbit-punches a gangster, setting him up for Ham's uppercut to the chin.

Pat is tough, but even the deaths of criminals upsets her. When a large group of them are wiped out by the Crime Annihilist's weapon, she is horrified.

Pat enters her fifth supersaga, *Spook Hole*, holding a supermachine pistol. She threatens the two thugs, Braske and Ropes, with it. She is "tall and exquisitely beautiful." She has "hair of a certain remarkable bronze hue." Apparently, her eyes are not so remarkable. At least, no mention is made of them. And she is "too calm for their ease of mind."

She does lose her poise, however, when Doc dismisses her from the case. He had used her to pretend to be Nancy Law because he couldn't imitate a woman's voice very well. Pat flares up and walks out of the room. She returns in a better mood after Braske and Ropes are spirited away by Captain Wapp. She thinks she'll now be permitted to rejoin the fun.

Despite her arguments, Doc drops her off at her beauty establishment. But she beats him to the eighty-sixth floor HQ and forces him to include her in this adventure. She has information he needs very much, and if he won't take her along, she'll jump into the action on her own. Doc knows she's capable of this, so he reluctantly signs her up. And he admits to himself, "In the final analysis, Pat was handy to have around." Indeed she was, as he will have to concede time and again.

Pat goes with Doc to far-off Patagonia at the southern end of South America and almost loses her life there. But she is in on the revealing of Hezemiah Law's secret: his sick whales and the precious stuff they carry in their bodies.

In *Murder Mirage* (written by Laurence Donovan) Doc gets his cousin to pose as Lady Sathyra Fotheran. Pat does so successfully, but she lames herself for a while by not using one of Doc's devices properly. He had put a chemical mixture in the heel of one of her shoes. If the heel is rubbed against something, it will explode with a blinding light. Pat can't take the shoe off before her abduction and so has to rub one heel against the other. The resultant light and loud bang causes the car's driver to wreck it, and Pat gets away. She complains to Doc about his device, saying that he would certainly regret it the next time he puts a torpedo in her heel. Her whole shoe has been blown off; she can hardly walk.

"And this," she says, "was supposed to be a quiet little job of playing chaperone. And I shot a man."

A moment later, she is objecting because Doc is going to send her home. She does not go, of course, and a little while afterward, she is in Doc's dirigible on its way to the Syrian Desert. She is dressed only in a filmy, thorn-torn negligee and one shoe, but there isn't time for her to go home to change. Doc, however, has clothes for her on the dirigible. Obviously, he expects her to be with them on one caper or another, and Doc is always prepared.

It's in this story that we find that Pat is one of the few who ever question Doc's decisions. Usually, only women do that.

Pat has been abducted in previous supersagas, but in this one she is involuntarily carried off on three separate occasions. Each time, Mr. Kassan is the culprit. Pat tells Monk, just as he is about to tear the man apart, "Mr. Kassan's been about the only fun I've had." Mr. Kassan acknowledges that she always seems to be around when he's in "a kidnaping mood."

Pat's last words in this story, spoken hopefully, are, "Oh, perhaps I shall be kidnaped again!"

As we shall see, and as Doc must have known, there will be no "perhaps."

Pat joins Doc and his merry men for her eighth supersaga in *The Men Who Smiled No More*. In this story Donovan forgot that she was supposed to have golden eyes. Ham is angry at Monk, as usual, but he has to suppress his desire to swear, because Pat is present. It's doubtful that Pat would've been offended, but Ham's reticence does show his respect for her.

Pat Savage, it is said in this adventure, has one great asset. Like the others in Doc's gang, she has no fear. However, this is an exaggeration. Before this caper, during it, and many times thereafter, she is afraid. In later stories, Dent reveals that Doc and his men can be afraid. What all of the group possessed, including Pat, was courage. They can be afraid, but they conquer their fear and advance on whatever fearful enemy opposes them at the moment.

Pat narrowly escapes being crushed to death by the giant piston machine of Dr. Madren in *The Men Who Smiled No More*. Her cousin, as usual, carries her off in time.

In *The Black Spot* Pat is a guest at the tragic party given by the tycoon Andrew Podrey Vandersleeve. She phones Doc to tell him of Vandersleeve's death and the "black spot." A man grabs her from behind and cuts off her call (as in *The Laugh of Death*). He finds out he's got hold of a tornado in silk and high heels. She is mad enough to begin with, but when he calls her redheaded, she gets furious. Pat's hair is a dark reddish-bronze (in most of the stories) and definitely not red. She tangles with the man, both fall down the steps into the basement, and she fires a blank cartridge in his face. So much for the dangers of imprecise description.

Monk enters the HQ and listens to Pat's chopped-off message. He mutters that someday she's going to get into a jam she can't get out of. This is unfair of Monk, since Pat was not interfering in the group's affairs at that time. Monk is not really disgusted; he's alarmed. He quickly calls up Ham to come help him go after Pat.

Later, Pat ignores Doc's command and messes things up so badly that she almost gets a punch in the face from her cousin. This is not because Doc intended to hit her; he thought she was somebody else. He recognizes her just in time to keep from ruining that beautiful "kisser" and instead knocks her back down the stairs. Doc tells her to go home and adds insult to injury by telling her her face is dirty.

"Pat's happiest moments were when her face was dirty. This usually happened when she became involved in Doc's adventures."

In *The Terror in the Navy*, Pat, as usual, makes a striking entrance.

Male hearts beat faster; male hormones surge through bloodstreams. Pat, though, in this as in so many supersagas, commands attention with more than her beauty. She points her old-fashioned revolver at the villains; its barrel is so huge that any of them could easily put his little finger down it. Not that any desire to try. Pat looks as if she is capable of blowing the finger off with no hesitation.

The villainous Fuzzy asks her who she is. She replies that she's Doc Savage's cousin. And she also says that she operates an uptown beauty parlor where she charges outrageous prices and makes her clientele love it.

Coming up from behind again (Pat seems to have an innate unguarded behind), a man knocks her half-senseless. Fuzzy then uses Pat's own gun to knock her completely out. Anybody in Doc's group was bound to get hit over the head, not once but many times. Young ladies were no exception.

In fact, in this caper Pat is struck unconscious twice. She gloomily admits to Doc that he might be right. Perhaps the little parties he gives are too rough for women.

By the time of her next adventure, Pat is thoroughly recovered and raring to go. She's even ready to give away her very profitable business to the first person she meets if Doc should invite her to permanently join his group and make that the requisite for her admission. Doc only wants her to be Ann Garvin's companion-guard.

In this caper, *He Could Stop the World*, Pat's hair is golden blond. Perhaps she's dyed it. Her eyes are not described.

Pat happily receives the news that something very sinister is occurring. If a world catastrophe is coming, she hopes she'll be able to get in on it. The initial adventures are so horrendous that she declines to join Doc in solving the mystery of the burning snow, Johnny's disappearance in a new stratospheric ship, and the vapor death. She wants to go home. This, however, is not the real Pat talking. Like Long Tom, she is under the mind-bending influence of the villain's gadget.

Pat does not enter the amazing exploit of *The Feathered Octopus* until it is half over. She enters on her own in order to find Doc and get him out of a particularly sticky mess. She has what no other member of his group possesses: female beauty. She uses this to get information from a stockbroker which should lead her to the right trail. The broker is bowled over; his toes curl at her smile. She is "the kind of girl who causes men to bump into telephone poles and fall over fire hydrants when she walks down the street."

She finds a communication from Doc in invisible chalk and tells the others they should go at once and rescue Doc. Renny tells her to go back to the "mud packs and rowing machines and electric vibrators." Pat agrees to do so. Not, however, she adds, until the Sphinx turns handsprings. Renny puts her to sleep with anesthetic gas and sends her home unconscious in a taxi. To make things worse, Renny tells the taxi driver she's dead-drunk. On wakening in her beauty establishment, she is ready to blow her pretty lid.

(In this story, by the way, her business is said to be, not on Park Avenue, but on a side street just off Park. It may be that Dent slipped up here and inadvertently gave the correct location.)

Pat tells Renny off over the phone and rushes in a cab toward the HQ. You not only can't keep a good man down, you can't keep a good woman down either. But this time she's anesthetized by the villains and held hostage by them for the return of Lo Lar, the Eurasian villainess. Doc offers a reward of $25,000 for any information leading him to Pat's whereabouts.

We know from this story that Pat's shoes are expensive custom-mades. Renny finds one of her slippers in an abandoned farmhouse. Inside is a label: MADE EXPRESSLY FOR PATRICIA SAVAGE.

In *Devil on the Moon* Pat is disguised and helping Doc fight another band of villains. When Doc is through with her, he tells her to go home. Doc just never seems to learn. She flatly refuses, and Doc permits himself to be buffaloed.

Pat informs a heroine, Lin Pretti, that there are two ways of curing hysteria. One is the doctors'; the other, hers. And she slaps Lin so hard on the face that she dazes her. A little while later, it's Pat's turn to look foolish. She falls for a trick that any of the veterans of the group would see through at once. Renny gets his revenge by telling her that perhaps now she'll understand why Doc doesn't want women mucking around in his business.

Doc is more gentle with her. When she, Doc, and the Famous Five are prisoners on the moon (or told they are), she tells Doc to chew her out for her mess-up. He only gives her a sweet and encouraging smile.

In her fourteenth supersaga, *The Motion Menace*, Pat is taking a vacation in Shanghai. She is disguised as a Miss Enola Emmel. Spelled backwards, this comes out: Lemme Alone. Which is how Pat feels at this time. She's fed up with the beauty business. But not with Doc. She phones him in Manhattan because she suspects that someone is out to kill her. Doc tells her that he knows she's trying to find a certain Captain Wizer. The captain had been in New York a few months ago and had interested her in a device which electrically "cured" blackheads. It was this interest which led her, along with Doc, to become involved with some peculiar old men known as The Elders.

In her fifteenth adventure, *The Yellow Cloud*, Pat forces Doc to take her along. She sneaks into the Hidalgo Trading Company building and locks the exit of the pneumatic tube from the eighty-sixth floor to the Hudson River-front structure. When Doc's gang arrives in the little car, they're trapped. She tells Doc she'll let him out if she can join in the quest for Renny. Resignedly, Doc agrees. Monk reproaches her, only to be reminded of the dirty trick he once played on her. He had given her a package and told her to take it to the mountains and there guard it with her life. After a week she got suspicious and opened the package. Inside was a picture of a goat.

Monk replies that it kept her out of danger.

By this time, Pat has changed the name of her establishment to PATRICIA, INCORPORATED. (It's back on Park Avenue now.) The latest addition to her business is Florenso, a political refugee and plastic surgeon from Vienna, Austria. His office is on the seventh floor of her establishment. No mention is ever made of the exact number of stories, but seven floors is very impressive for a "beauty parlor."

Florenso's hair stands on end as if he were full of static electricity. He furthers this impression by his insulting manner, that is, he gives his customers a lot of static. This overbearing attitude, far from hurting him, endears him to his rich patrons. Florenso is so good at his profession, however, that Monk goes to him to have his face changed into something beautiful.

Shortly after this, Pat is kidnaped again. She does not get taken easily. The female Japanese jujitsu artists she employs have taught her much. As has happened before, despite her wildcat battling, she is knocked over the head with a revolver and carried out unconscious.

During the course of this supersaga, we learn that Pat has acquired a knowledge of the deaf-and-dumb sign language. Knowing that she may be watched by Doc over the secret TV transmitter in the plane in which she is a prisoner, she sends a message with her fingers four times. Because of this, Doc knows that his stolen plane is heading for a landing field twenty miles west of Caracas, Venezuela. Neither she nor Doc has any way of knowing, of course, that they are being fooled.

In *Poison Island* Pat is captain, not just owner, of her three-masted schooner named (what else?) *Patricia*. She becomes involved with Herb March and a sinister Hindu while she is picking up a shipload of gold for her cousin in the harbor of the only seaport of the little Central American nation of Hidalgo. Herb March is very much attracted to Pat and notes especially her bronze hair. Dent says nothing of March's noticing her golden eyes.

March finds out that, though Pat is a woman, discipline aboard the schooner leaves nothing to be desired. Pat is chaperoned, or at least accompanied, by a French maid and a huge dark-skinned woman who could have got a job as a bouncer in any seaport beer hall. Pat spends some time during the voyage by popping fifty Portuguese men-o'-war with fifty shots from her family heirloom. Amazed, March asks her if she has ever missed. She admits that she did once three years ago, which is why she's practicing so hard now.

That evening, Herb March dines with Pat. The dinner is delicious, cooked by a Frenchman who is probably the maid's husband. The wine is excellent. And Pat's quarters are very comfortable, spacious, and air conditioned. Pat loves adventure and excitement, but she travels in style if it's at all possible.

The *Patricia* does not provide her captain with comfort for very long. Like another Nova Scotia-built ship, the *Mary Celeste*, she would be found sailing along without a soul aboard.

Pat appears next in *Hex*, though rather late in the story. Doc calls for Pat to help him, and she flies into Boston with some truth serum he needs. She does it so quickly that she has to wait for Doc to show up. As usual, Doc thanks her and then tries to send her home. As usual, Pat doesn't go.

There is a curious incident in *Hex*. This hints that Dent might not have told us all that is going on between Pat and Monk. Pat finds Monk holding the lovely June Knight in his long hairy arms. Pat kids Monk about this and Monk, very flustered, tries to explain. Why should a well-known wolf, the acknowledged stud of the group, be so taken aback merely because he's embracing a girl? Is it because Pat and Monk have been having more than just a friendly relationship? And do Pat's seemingly jesting words conceal a bitterness or some trace of jealousy?

We'll never know. Dent never tells us.

In *The Spotted Men* we learn that Pat is an aviator. Unknown to Doc, his aides have taught her to fly. She is a whiz at the stick. This is to be expected, since Pat has many talents and since her instructors are among the world's best fliers.

Pat doesn't enter *The Awful Dynasty* until the ninth day of this supersaga. Dent describes her bronze hair but says nothing about her eyes. Here he reiterates that she is Doc's only living relative. This statement would seem to invalidate some I've made about the bronze man's family tree. However, Dent not only did not reveal everything about Doc, he often made certain distortions of the truth. Doc himself, in a memorandum to Dent (see *No Light to Die By*), stated this. In the case of the relatives, however, Dent was under orders to reveal only those family affiliations which were pertinent to his story. If he had disobeyed these orders, and his editors had let certain information slip by, the publishing firm of Street and Smith would have been sued by Doc. That Dent did follow his orders is proved by the undeniable fact that Doc never sued Street and Smith. (Not to my knowledge, anyway.)

The truth is that Pat was far from being Doc's only living relative. As I have demonstrated in *Tarzan Alive* (Doubleday, 1972), Doc had a number of famous, and even infamous, cousins. Monk was one. Three more were operating in New York City at the same time as Doc. One was the great (in many senses) detective Nero Wolfe. He lived on West Thirty-fifth Street, not very far from Doc's HQ. Wolfe's address is variously given as in the 500, 600, or 900 block. In any event, since the Empire State Building is in the 100 block on East Thirty-fourth Street, it's a short walk north one block and only five, six, or nine blocks west. Too far for the hippopotamoid

Mycroftesque Wolfe to go on foot. But no doubt he has been disturbed many times by the underground rumblings of the pneumatic-tube "flea run" as Doc and pals shoot from the eighty-sixth floor and deep under Thirty-fourth Street to the Hidalgo Trading Company.

The second relative operating in New York City, mostly at night, is (or was) Richard Wentworth. He was that great crime fighter, the Spider, and probably the world's best pilot. (Once he landed an airplane on a penthouse.) The third was of course the Shadow.

It is during a tense and perilous moment in *The Awful Dynasty* that Dent shows us Long Tom's deep feelings for Pat. Long Tom is a misogynist, or pretends to be, but when he thinks that something "might happen to the lovely Pat," he almost has a heart attack. Though the group seems to have treated her, on the surface, as a kid sister, all of them may have been secretly in love with her. As for Monk, we can assume he was in love with Pat, since he always falls in love with any "pip" he meets. Pat, however, is not a Snow White taking care of the house for the Seven Dwarfs. She wouldn't have fallen for the old poisoned-apple trick, and she would have slugged the evil stepmother.

In her twentieth supersaga, *The Men Vanished*, we get a deeper glimpse into Pat's character. Pat distrusts the beautiful Junith Stage. She has no solid reason to do so. It is just that she has "an inner impulse to distrust all women."

We are not told why she has this compulsion. Nothing is said in any of the supersagas about her mother or her childhood. Her mother died before her father, but we do not know if it was shortly before or years before.

Perhaps she distrusted all women because she distrusted herself.

In this adventure Pat, facing death, says that if she can get out of the mess at this very moment, she'll take a vow never to be involved in another adventure with Doc.

And then she adds, "Maybe."

Pat undoubtedly did not believe herself, though it was a long time before she got back into action. Her next caper is *Birds of Death*. Once again she shows that she respects Doc but will take his orders only when it suits her.

By her twenty-second adventure, *The Invisible-Box Murders*, Pat has learned to lip-read. It is this ability that Ham uses as feeble excuse to employ her, even though Doc has forbidden her to get involved. Doc is too busy escaping the police and proving he's not a murderer to do anything about Pat.

In her twenty-fourth supersaga, Pat has evidently been deprived of her key to the eighty-sixth floor. Doc, phoning in, is surprised when Pat answers. He asks her how she got in, and she says that she stole Monk's key out of his pocket. She tells Doc that the others are planning a birthday party for him. Doc, who has a photographic memory, has completely forgotten it's his birthday. It makes no difference. He's deeply entangled in a desperate case, and he needs his aides at once. Forget the party. Everybody come galloping. Except Pat. She's to go home.

Pat laughs scornfully and says that he should know her better than that. And so he should.

Pat disables one man with jujitsu techniques in *Men of Fear* and then breaks the chief villain's arm. Pat almost always pulled her own weight.

In *Men of Fear* Pat shrewdly observes that Doc has been fooled a number of times by a pretty girl. Apparently, she has analyzed her cousin's character and knows that his appearance of stoicism is just that—appearance.

The Man Who Fell Up, Pat's twenty-fifth adventure, is a story of a strange green fog in New York City and of men pulled up by the sky to some unknown doom. In this we find that, though Pat distrusts women, she does have female friends. One is Susan Glaspell, who lives in Westchester and has a maid.

Pat surprises Doc with her suddenly acquired ability to speak Mayan in this caper. She admits that she talked Monk into teaching her the language. Monk is embarrassed, though whether it is because he disobeyed Doc or he is remembering how she got him to teach her, Dent does not say.

It is disclosed in this supersaga that Pat is very hard to wake up once she's asleep. Renny says that she'd sleep through the end of the world. We also learn that, though Pat loves adventure, she hates parachute jumping. And it is Pat who gives Monk's new chemical invention a name. She calls it Compound Monk because both the compound and Monk chase movement and warmth. Both have a compulsive affinity for "hot numbers."

In *The Fiery Menace* Pat owns an undistinguished-looking dark coupe which she calls Clarence; two cars named, respectively, Tarzan and Adolf Hitler; and a truck, Churchill.

Pat also has a new experience in this story, which is an old one to Doc and Long Tom. She is arrested on suspicion of murder.

The Laugh of Death is the first supersaga to tell us her exact height. She is five feet seven inches, tall for a woman born in 1914.

In *The Time Terror* Monk announces that the circus is in town. None of the group ask him what he means by that. Only Doc comments, monosyllabically, "Pat."

In this story, Dent slipped up and stated that Pat was "one of Doc's *few* living blood kin." (Italics are mine.)

Pat is at the HQ at two in the morning because a policeman friend had told her that Doc was offering a five-hundred-dollar reward for a certain skinny man in a gray suit. When Pat refuses to leave, she is locked in the library by Doc. Doc should have known better. Pat picks the lock and gets to the reception room just in time to witness its door being blown open. The skinny guy in the gray suit enters, and Pat is deep in the affair, whether or not Doc likes it. At the moment, Pat does not like it. She is scared.

In *Waves of Death* Johnny, Renny, and Long Tom are just about to dash out to investigate the tidal-wave mysteries in Lake Michigan. Johnny hears a noise and looks into the reception room. He mutters, "Guess who?" Long Tom gestures, indicating such events as Judgment Day, the earth blowing up, and the like. Renny says, "Right. Miss Patricia Savage in person."

Pat addresses Renny and Long Tom as Grumpy and Grouchy. This is probably not for the first or the last time. Renny has his own label for her: excitopsychic. It means that she has some sixth sense tuned in to the possibility of adventure.

Pat takes off in her own plane, which she keeps in an airport north of Westchester County. She disguises it by painting on it: Norpen Lumber Company. This, unfortunately, is the only reference we get to this new concern. It is not destined to become as famous as the Hidalgo Trading Company.

It is in *Waves of Death* that we learn that Doc is not the only gadgeteer in the Savage family. Pat has designed and had installed on her plane an arrangement of vanes which intercepts the slipstream from the muffler. This alters the sound so that it resembles that of a car speeding on the highway at some distance. She uses it to fool some crooks.

Pat is tough, but she faints for the first, and the last, time when she learns that Doc is not really dead.

Pat is not in *The Black, Black Witch* until near the end. But she's in it long enough for us to find out she's added to her list of skills. She can quack like a flying duck.

The Mental Monster contains something puzzling about Pat. Doc calls Pat over the short-wave radio she keeps tuned to the frequency Doc uses to communicate with his aides. He can't get a reply from any of them, so he uses several other frequencies. His group shifts the frequencies at certain times of the day to keep Pat from hearing the messages. Doc needs Pat now, so he calls her on the frequency she uses. There is no answer. Thinking that perhaps (or most probably) Pat is on to their trick and has changed her frequency to match theirs, he calls her on several different wave lengths. She does not reply. Nor does she ever answer in this supersaga or even make an appearance. We never learn what she was doing or why she wasn't around to answer. Yet she must have been in town. She wouldn't leave without notifying Doc. So what had kept her away from this adventure?

In *Hell Below* Pat gets mixed up with Nazis and submarines. She displays a new skill, signaling with a flashlight in Morse but using the Mayan language.

Pat is a modern young lady, but in *The Secret of the Su* we learn that she does not smoke.

Pat is mentioned in *Weird Valley* but only because she has "the family characteristic," flake-gold eyes.

Pat, according to *Violent Night*, was born in Canada. She is Doc's third or fourth cousin. More details are given about her six-shooter. It weighs more than four pounds and has large ivory grips. It was made before Jesse James's day, and her grandfather fought Indians with it.

She tells Barney Cuadrado that she was raised in the Wild West except when she was being "educated to the eyebrows." Pat is in Lisbon, having tracked Doc there. She had been in London as a war correspondent. She got angry when she wasn't allowed to go to the front, told off the authorities, and had her correspondent's clearance voided. Her old six-shooter becomes a pivotal part of the adventure, with the Nazis desperately trying to get hold of it for some unknown reason. Pat is in at the end, in Switzerland, when Adolf Hitler is prevented from escaping from dying Germany.

Or was he really Der Fuehrer?

In this caper, Pat understands German very well but can't speak it fluently.

She does not enter *Terror Takes 7* until it's two thirds over. She does so then only because Doc is on the run and has no one else to turn to. Pat comes through magnificently. She reminds Doc of the little man with the green suit. Doc is puzzled, then remembers the day he was out walking with Pat and she threw a snowball at a man in an atrocious green suit because she thought he was Monk. This was near the corner of Forty-eighth Street and Ninth Avenue. This reminder by Pat tells him where they'll meet, thus puzzling anyone listening in on the tapped phone.

Pat drives a panel delivery truck with the legend: JOE'S DIAPER SERVICE. She's borrowed the truck, she says, leaving Doc, Monk, and Ham to wonder if she really did or if she stole it. She is capable of doing anything if it'll help them, and they're not worried about the ethical implications of the theft. They've broken the law a thousand times in their battle against evil. They hide inside the truck, and she drives them to a hideout. This is the apartment of a friend, Thelia Van Zeltin, who is vacationing at Lake Placid. Pat says she won't mind them using her place. But it's probable that Thelia will never know what's happening at her apartment.

Pat also has another friend, Paula Argus, much involved in this supersaga. Pat, despite her stated distrust of women, seems not to lack female friends.

In this story we learn that Pat speaks fluent French.

Pat, it is stated in *Death Is a Round Black Spot*, is a bronzy-blonde in her twenties. But this is 1945 and definitely after World War II. Pat must be about thirty-one years old. She is oval-faced and trim. She has light-brown eyes that, when not blanked by horror (which is often), are more golden than brown.

Pat is horror-stricken because she has seen a young man die terribly. In a few minutes she is knocked over the head so hard—twice, in fact—that she becomes unconscious. Pat has been knocked out often since her meeting with Doc and pals. Her total is nowhere near Monk's, but, then, she has a much thinner skull. The next adventure for Pat is in *Target for Death*, written by William G. Bogart. Lieutenant Sally Treat, looking for help in finding her fiancé, sees a familiar name in the Honolulu newspaper.

PAT SAVAGE VISITS CITY
Patricia Savage, lovely cousin of Clark Savage, Jr., famous international figure known as Doc Savage, the Man of Bronze, is now visiting in Honolulu...

Treat remembers meeting Pat in a Manila hospital. Perhaps Pat has some of her cousin's abilities and can help her find Rick Randall. Pat does help and is very busy in the dangerous affair until Doc tricks her into going to New York so he can get her out of the way. Pat fires off a telegram to him and his aides, who are in a little town in Ohio.

I THINK YOU'RE A BUNCH OF STINKERS
LOVE
PAT

Pat is out of the rest of the adventure. Doc, Ham, Monk, and Renny finish it up on a remote Philippine islet.

I Died Yesterday, Pat's thirty-seventh supersaga, appeared in the January–February, 1948, issue of *Doc Savage Science Detective* magazine. This is the 174th supersaga. Of the 181, Pat has appeared in a little more than a fifth of them. It is thus fitting, a sort of grand finale, that Pat herself narrates her last exploit.

This begins when a long-faced, sack-suited young man enters Pat's establishment. He tells Miss Colfax, Pat's aide-de-camp, that he wants the entire beauty treatment, the whole works. Pat overhears him but walks away. Miss Colfax will straighten him out and send him on his way. Nobody, not even the extremely wealthy fat dowagers of New York City's "aristocracy," barged appointmentless into Pat's place. Certain ceremonies had to be gone through first.

But Miss Colfax, who could with a few words freeze a battleship, admiral included, has to ask Pat to take over for her. Miss Colfax can do nothing with the stubborn young man, and she is eager to see how her boss handles him. She and the other ladies of the staff want very much to see if Pat lives up to her reputation.

Pat herself wonders if she'll be able to do it. It's been a long time since she's been in any dangerous situation other than crossing a New York City street at rush hour.

The young man is very complimentary, telling her she shines with more than startling loveliness, that she has an electric quality, a vibrating force. He thinks that dating her would be about as unsettling as carrying a lighted candle through a gasoline refinery.

Pat asks him if he'd like to be thrown out—by her—head or feet first. She is one hundred per cent able to carry out her threat, since she is an expert judo fighter. The young man ignores this, and, after a few more compliments, asks her if she'd mind going to the entrance and finding out if *they* have come in yet to finish killing him.

It is then that Pat discovers that a snapped-off knife or icepick is buried in the young man's back. And she is launched into her last recorded supersaga.

In this autobiographical story, Pat tells much about both herself and her cousin. Her attitude toward money is different from Doc's. In the first place, she has very little of it, compared to him. She "doesn't mind chipping it off those who were heavily plated with it." But the big cause of trouble between her and Doc is this business of adventure. She is affected by danger in an abnormal manner—just as she is sure Doc is affected. It's in the Savage blood. But Doc just won't let her take part in all his adventures. He often won't let her know when he's in the city, because he fears—justly—that she'll bull her way in.

Now the situation is reversed. Pat is in the case long before Doc. She initiates it, in a sense, and she comes close to being killed a few minutes after meeting the young man with the icepick in his back. Only the best of surgeons can extract the pick without killing the patient, and who is better than Doc? Farrar, the doctor who X-rays the young man, Thayer, hesitates about asking Pat if Doc'll take the case. He's heard that she and Doc are not on very good terms. Pat replies that this isn't so. They fight a lot, but they're very good friends. As for getting Doc in on this, don't worry. She can outfox him any day.

She uses Doc's unlisted number to bypass the private detective screening agency. Monk answers the phone. Monk, according to Pat, isn't as dumb as he looks. He has "the manners and dignity of a fourteen-year-old hooligan from the wrong side of the tracks." Monk tells her she's "the kitten who drags the big, terrible rats into our parlor." He won't let her speak to Doc. Doc and his pals are "in the process of unofficially disowning you."

Pat tells him that Thayer is going to die if Doc doesn't do the surgery. She lays it on heavily with Monk. He's a sucker for any story told him by a woman.

Doc cuts in on the phone and tells her it's been a long time "since you came skipping in on us with a little case of trouble that would scare a normal person green. I knew it was too good to last."

Doc then says that he thinks she's being used by somebody to get him involved. In any event, Pat is to stay out of this from now on. She is to "return to the practice of that refined piracy you call a beauty salon."

Pat ignores this, of course. And she uses some of Doc's trick gadgets with great effectiveness during the course of *I Died Yesterday*. Doc has quit relying on gadgets, but Pat has collected a small museum of them. She has become, unofficially, the curator of his devices. She has several hundred of them, most of them acquired through the secret aid of Monk. A special room next to her office is jammed with them.

Wearing some of the gadgets under her clothes, Pat sallies forth. She expects the villains to attack her at once or at least to shadow her. But nothing much happens for a while. And here she gives an analysis of the Savage character. One of its strong and enduring traits is impatience. Both she and Doc are cursed with it. Her father was impatient, and so was her grandfather. The latter, she tells us, did not wait for the Indians to attack him in his log cabin. He went out looking for them. He was a "grand old guy. There were villages named for him all over the northwest."

(A study of a map of western Canada fails to find any villages or towns named Savage or Wildman, Doc's real name. But the grandfather could have been her mother's father.)

Pat soon gets into trouble. She and her car are ingeniously forced into a huge truck and carried off. Pat uses her gadgets to get out of the locked truck. She discovers it's Monk who's kidnaped her. Doc has told him to do it so he can get her out of his hair. Pat ties Monk up and threatens to put him to sleep for a week unless he'll take her into the case. Monk agrees. And they're both off on a rousing, near-fatal supersaga.

Any reader who's regretted that Doc hasn't been using his gadgets lately will find great satisfaction in this story. Pat fires them off at every opportunity. But she does get scared in this story. At the end, she wonders if she isn't cured forever. Perhaps Doc has worked the miracle, and she'll keep out of his affairs from now on.

Pat's last words are, "It could be so destined, as Lucia would say." (Lucia is a would-be psychic in this case.)

Nobody who knows Pat really believes this. Yet, she appears in no more supersagas. For me, this was, and is, sad. I fell in love with Pat when I was just sixteen. Rereading these stories at the age of fifty-four, I'm still in love with her. But all things—good or bad—come to an end. So it's good-by to tall, lovely, bronze-haired, vivacious, stunning, deadly, courageous, exciting Pat Savage. You'll be fifty-eight years old this year of 1972, Pat. I wonder if you're still living in Manhattan? I can't see you as continuing unmarried, though it'd be difficult to find men who could equal Monk, Ham, Renny, Long Tom, or Johnny and, of course, impossible to find anybody the equal of your cousin (excepting Lord Greystoke, but he's married).

But among your many suitors must have been at least a few of heroic stature. And perhaps you said yes to one and settled down and became a good wife and all that. Perhaps. But do you drive downtown now and then and look up at the Empire State Building, or drive along the Hudson River and look at an old warehouse-type building and sigh for things that shall be no more?

I wonder.

17

DOC THE GADGETEER

DOC WAS the Man of Tomorrow, according to Dent. He was the Scientific Man. In his day, however, the faith in science as our savior was strong. Today, which was Dent's tomorrow, the faith is considerably weakened. Not science, but man using science and compassion can be our only possible savior. Doc himself came to realize this in his later career and so tended to use his devices less and less. In the first phases of his battle against evil, he did rely heavily on his gadgets. He was, in a sense, an aggressive Great Wizard of Oz and Glinda the Good rolled into one.

One reason for his popularity in America was the confusion deep in the subconscious between magic and science. A physical scientist knows he's working within the limits of the natural universe; the layman still tends to think as his Old Stone Age ancestors did. The control of the natural universe depends on involving the supernatural. And the supernatural can't be separated from the natural.

Thus, the bronze knight on the running board was more than just a man equipped with the devices of science. He was Merlin waging war on evil wizards. His magic was white; theirs, the blackest. The forces of Mordor might prevail for a time, but the Gandalf of the eighty-sixth floor will come to the rescue with his gnome king, Monk, and the four hobbits. And he will be able to do this because of his sorcerer's weapons: the gadgets.

This chapter gives an account of a few of the gadgets unmentioned elsewhere. Some of these are not used in his campaigns but are the wizard's gifts to mankind.

In *Quest of the Spider* Doc is the developer of a "marvelous quick-growing timber tree" which will revolutionize the lumber industry.

In *The Polar Treasure* Doc spreads some chemical compound resembling pale molasses on the floor outside the reception room. When the blind Victor Vail is kidnaped, he and his captors step on the sticky stuff. Doc then sprays a vaporous substance on the stickiness, and the result is an odor which would startle a skunk. Doc and Renny drive uptown and shoot the vapor into each subway exit. At the eighth exit, they detect the telltale stink, and they follow the odorous trail to its end.

In this same adventure, Doc reveals his collapsible canoe. This can also be reshaped to form the framework of a tent. Web paddles are attached to rifle barrels to propel the canoe. The silk waterproof sack in which the canoe is folded becomes the skin of the canoe or the tent fabric.

In *The Red Skull* Doc has a tiny apparatus which can instantly detect any poison gas. He uses it to make sure that Bandy Stevens has not died of poison gas.

During this crusade, Monk escapes from his abductors by using one of Doc's gadgets. Moistened with saliva, deposits of a chemical mixture under his fingernails release a powerful tear gas. Monk sticks his fingers under the eyes of his two guards and then dives out of the car.

Doc always carries firecrackers. With them, he can arrange to have a gunshot seem to occur at one place while he's busy at another.

Sometimes, lacking a particular gadget, Doc improvises a pseudo gadget. During a chase in an Arizona desert, Doc throws his watch behind him. The villains, having come to expect the glass-ball anesthetic-gas grenades, and too far from the watch to see its true nature, think he's thrown a grenade. They wait for the supposed gas to evaporate, and Doc is long gone.

Doc often hoists the villains with their own gadgets. Yuttal and Hadi-Mot, in *The Lost Oasis*, have trained large vampire bats to attack on signal. When they release the bats against Doc and cronies, they take refuge in their rattan cages, only to find too late that Doc has weakened the bindings with an acid. The acid, of course, comes from one of the many vials in his vest.

Doc literally tosses an earthquake back at its maker, The First Little White Brother. Doc has discovered that the White Brother's device uses the peculiar strata of quartz under the west coast of South

America to effect his quakes. The piezoelectric phenomenon takes place in certain types of quartz when a certain electrical current is applied to them. They bend. With the current off, the quartz unbends. And the earth shakes with the two curvings of the quartz strata.

To get his electrical power, the White Brother taps into a high-tension power line. Two machines are used. These beam high-frequency waves at the intersection of which the underlying quartz reacts. Doc makes a high-frequency wave-beam projector, puts it in a plane, and turns it on the hill where the villain's projectors are. His beam intersects one of the White Brother's and sets up oscillations in the quartz under the hill. The villain perishes in the resultant quake.

It isn't easy to outsmart Doc, as several thousands of evil men find out.

Dent does not say so, but if Doc had power equivalent to that in a high-tension power line, he must have been carrying a big generator in the plane.

The King Maker has a villain who invents a flying torpedo, a 1934 anticipation of Hitler's V-1. It finds its target with a heat detector. Doc and pals and sundry others are trapped in a house which is set afire by the villains so the flying torpedo can zero in on it. Doc has figured out the villains' gadget and has secretly hidden in the tail of the villains' plane one of his own gadgets. It emits an "atomic stream" which goes through solid matter. The ordinary senses of human beings can't detect it, but it offers a much "hotter" target than the flaming house. And so the evil ones are blown up by their own gadget.

When Doc and others are in the Mystic Mullah's prison, Doc tries to wrench out bars almost an inch thick and deeply socketed in stone. Even his Samsonian strength can't get them loose. He then takes off his necktie and tears open the large end. He removes the yellowish stuff lining the tie and rips off some buttons from his coat. He grinds the buttons into a brownish powder which he puts into the lining before rolling the lining up. After tearing the now cylindrical tie into four pieces, he binds them around the lower and upper ends of two bars. A match applied to the yellow rolls results in a loud hiss, a blinding light, and a great heat.

The necktie lining is impregnated with aluminum powder, and the buttons are iron oxide. Some other chemicals are mixed with the stuff to make it burn even more efficiently. And so the thermite burns the bars apart.

The device of thermite disguised as pieces of clothing has been much used in James Bond-type movies and on TV, especially in *The Man from U.N.C.L.E.* series. But it was first used in the Doc Savage stories in the early 1930s.

A piece of wood ripped from a bench to make a handle and Doc's and Long Tom's belt buckles, tipped with tiny diamonds, make an ingenious drill in *Dust of Death*. With these, Doc cuts out the lock of the dungeon door and the two escape.

In *Murder Mirage* (by Laurence Donovan, not Dent) Doc and Renny rescue a shadow so they can identify its owner. They do so by cutting it out of a plate-glass window on the front of a music store. A woman has fallen victim to the villain's gadget, which emits a greenish light that seems to disintegrate the woman. But her shadow, its arm upraised in horrified protest, is preserved on the glass. The silhouette is guarded by policemen until gangsters get rid of them and start to cut the shadow out. Doc and Renny, masked, appear and blind the crooks with a new gas Doc's invented.

The gas comes from sulphides combined with liquefied selenium. This, Donovan says, is the first time selenium has been liquefied in a usable form. Chalk one more up for Doc.

In the same story Doc's car emits a smokescreen the gummy particles of which stick to the pursuing car's headlights. The crooks have to clean them off before they can continue the chase.

Doc and gang land in their amphibian plane on a Norwegian fjord in *Haunted Ocean*. Three enemy planes bomb the plane to smithereens. Before their craft is hit, Doc's group crowds into a tiny submarine the plane carries. It's driven by compressed air and isn't big enough to hold submerging tanks. It can't expel water to gain buoyancy for a rise to the surface. There is space between the outer and inner skins of the cylindrical vessel. This is occupied by a vacuum, if a vacuum can "occupy" anything. Doc fills the space with air generated chemically, and the sub floats to the surface after the villains have left.

Dent must have misunderstood the notes Doc gave him about the buoyancy mechanism. If the space between the skins was empty of air, the sub had all the buoyancy it needed. More, in fact, because it would never had submerged. Releasing air into the vacuum would have made the sub less buoyant.

In *The Midas Man* Doc opens the locked door of Monk's car without a key or, seemingly, anything. He does this with an electro-magnet, hidden in the palm of his hand, that pulls out a tiny iron bolt connected to a spring.

Doc deliberately lets a minor villain escape in *The Mental Wizard*. He's given the man a large yellow pill to swallow. A few days later, the pill will cause the man to have an attack which seems to be appendicitis. By then, the man has led them to other villains and served his purpose. Undoubtedly, the crook will go to the hospital where the police, warned by Doc, will pick him up.

In *Land of Fear* Doc escapes the "skeleton death" by covering his body with a paste he's invented. This prevents the instantaneous dehy-dration usually affected by the villain's gadget. Once again Doc triumphs, and the villains, as often happens, are caught in their own trap.

Doc, Ham, and Monk are captured and bound with cloth strips in *The Flying Goblin*. Doc, soaked with what looks like sweat, waits until his enemies have left. Then he tears the strips apart with a surge of arms and legs. Monk and Ham think the strips act as if eaten by acid. And they have been. Doc has broken a vial which he always carries in his coat pocket. It contains a fluid which "eats into anything except human flesh" and "spreads like kerosene." What Dent failed to mention in this episode is that the stuff would also have eaten Doc's clothes, gadgets, rings and wristwatch.

All of Doc's rings were either communication sets or containers of spring-released knives. The watch, in addition to a calendar and other things, had a small compass.

Doc could get along without these, but the acid would have re-leased so many different terrors in various vials and glass balls that Doc, Monk, and Ham would have been disintegrated and perhaps taken a whole city block with them.

That this didn't happen indicates that the acid must have worked faster on cloth than on glass and metal. Or Doc had perhaps coated these with an especially acid-resistant paste.

Still, Doc must have often speculated on what would happen if a bullet made a lucky hit on one of the explosive gadgets in his vest or coat pocket. It may have been a continuing uneasiness, an aware-ness that the odds against him were increasing in every encounter, that made him decide to give up most of the gadgets.

There are about three hundred and fifty devices that Doc and his pals used in the supersagas. The reader should have some idea of their nature by now, so we'll go on to the final chapter.

18

SOME OF THE GREAT VILLAINS AND THEIR WORLD-THREATENING GADGETS

IF THERE is a heaven for villains, or a special place in hell for only the most elite of villains, then surely Doc's chief enemies are there. And in the center of this exclusive suburb must be a museum displaying their world-destroying or world-threatening gadgets. Since these and their owners would be about seventy, describing them would make a chapter of almost book length. Only a few will be given here.

The curator of the museum would probably be John Sunlight. He is the only villain who ever escaped from Doc in one adventure for a return engagement. He is, like many of the villains, basically an idealist. He is using his terrible gadgets for the good of the world. To gain this good he uses evil means.

Moreover, the gadgets are not his creations. He has stolen them from Doc.

John Sunlight seems to have been put on this earth so that men could be afraid of him. Those who know his true nature, such as the Russian official Serge Mafnof, believe that it would be a great boon for mankind if Sunlight were shot at once. Don't wait for dawn.

Yet Sunlight, when he wishes to do so, can look like a gentle poet. He is very tall and thin; his hair is dark and thick; his forehead, remarkably high; his eyes burn in deep hollows in a gaunt face. His fingers are extraordinarily long and thin. The middle finger, in fact, is almost as long as the hand of the average man. Those spidery hands have a terrible power. Mafnof tells the Russian jury that Sunlight could grab a man with each hand and strangle him with no trouble at all. But the jury decides that Sunlight is only guilty of trying to advance too fast in the Soviet Army. And so he goes off to a prison camp in Siberia.

He waits patiently until he can arrange the correct setup. Then, with his brutal, oxlike lieutenant, Civan, and a number of other prisoners, he escapes on a ship. The crew are completely dominated by Sunlight. "Terror was the rope that John Sunlight kept around men's necks." He requires his people to get down on their knees when they approach him, and they do it without protest. Yet, when the food is almost gone, and there are not even any shoes to boil, Sunlight does without food for days. What little there is goes to the crew. A man dead of starvation can't be dominated, and Sunlight wants domination more than anything.

Sunlight is superbly, or perhaps sickeningly, self-controlled (as Doc was in his early career). The only emotional sound he makes is an occasional beastly growl. He utters this when he is vainly battering with a sledge hammer at the Strange Blue Dome he's found on a rocky islet.

John Sunlight is startled and frightened when an Eskimo wanders onto the scene and denies that there is a Strange Blue Dome in front of him. Perhaps he has finally gone insane. Insanity is the only thing he fears, and he fears it so intensely that his fear is itself insane.

He has one notable eccentricity. He wears only one color at a time. When he's in a purple mood, he dresses in all-purple pajamas, a purple robe, and his ring is a purple jewel. Even the chair he sits on when judging some of his gang who've failed in a mission is covered with a matching purple. In a later episode he wears a blood-red ensemble that makes him look like "a satanic alchemist."

John Sunlight is very thorough. Like Doc Savage, he knows that attention to detail ensures success in a venture. It is this characteristic, plus his mad drive and hypnotic hold on his mob, that almost give him victory over Doc. After getting inside Doc's Fortress of Solitude, he uses two of Doc's devices to get millions in an international bribery scheme.

He sells Doc's electron-stopping machine to a Balkan country for eleven million. Then he sells another machine, a projector of blinding rays, to the nation's enemy for another eleven million. He is interested in the money, however, for only one reason. It will enable him to start on the second phase of his plan: the domination of the entire world by himself.

It is not for his own pride that he wishes to rule the globe. He has the same aims as Doc Savage himself, he explains to Doc in *The Devil Genghis*. He wants to "right the greatest wrong of all"—the distinction between nationalities. National boundaries make for suspicion, greed, hate, and, eventually, wars. National languages encourage these because they make for lack of communication and for misunderstanding.

He intends to rectify this. After he conquers the world, he will do away with all national boundaries. There will then be one flag, earth's. He will destroy every firearm of any kind and forbid their possession on pain of death. "Mankind has advanced far enough that it does not need firearms."

The English language will be adopted as the primary language of everybody. Thus, mankind will be "one nation, one language, and without arms." Wars will no longer happen, because no reason for them will exist.

There is silence for a moment after he explains to Doc his intentions. Then Doc tells him that many men have had this dream. But it isn't realistic. Moreover, to attain this end he must kill millions. And violence can't accomplish anything worthwhile and enduring. Look at World War I. It solved nothing and settled little. The countries that suffered and bled so much are regaining their strength, and the world is headed toward another global conflict.

John Sunlight asks him if he insists on not helping the world.

Doc replies that he will help the world but only to the extent of eliminating John Sunlight. Sunlight runs, bleating with terror of the only man he fears, and Doc, pursuing, is almost killed by one of Sunlight's traps, an exploding, shrapnel-packed mattress.

In *Fortress of Solitude* Sunlight uses Doc's stolen device to pay off his old debt to Serge Mafnof. It projects a beam which causes Mafnof to turn black and then to disappear in black smoke. The gadget creates a "magnetic field of superlative intensity." This stops all orbital motion of the electrons in the target body. Doc had invented it while experimenting in the Fortress, but he had no intention of letting the world know about it The second gadget causes men to go temporarily blind by paralyzing the operations of the rods and cones of the eyes.

Actually, Sunlight had cheated Prince Karl when he sold him the electron stopper. It doesn't work beyond a range of twenty feet

Mo-Gwei, the villain of *Meteor Menace*, titters and cackles insanely. His face is covered with a purple mask, and he wears purple gloves and yellow robes. His headquarters are in the Tibetan Himalayas, but he directs a worldwide organization. In fact, his agents are in Antofagasta, Chile, when they encounter Doc and his assistant archenemies of evil. Doc is there to dedicate the new hospital he'd founded in *The Man Who Shook the Earth*.

Mad Mo-Gwei's gadget is an aerial device that robs men of their minds. Usually, it is summoned in the night and to a certain location by a Very light. Then the sky takes on a weird, faintly blue color, similar to that emitted by the arc of an electric welding torch. The radiance becomes brighter and, finally, blinding. Then a distant and weak whistling is heard. Like the blue light, it increases in intensity. It gains an eerie piping quality. Soon it becomes so high and loud that it cuts the eardrums with "razor sharpness." The hearer's head aches. The shrieking becomes louder and louder. The victim cannot look at the light without going blind nor can he hear his own voice. Then the glow fades and the shrieking dies. The meteor menace disappears in the opposite direction from which it came. Behind it, it leaves men and women in a vegetable state or with a homicidal or suicidal mania.

The mind-freezing radiation comes from a meteorite, or slices of one, Doc finds out. But the accompanying phenomenon is the work of Mo-Gwei. The device responsible for the sound and light is quite possible for the science of 1972. (*Meteor Menace* is in the March 1934 issue.) The true identity of Mo-Gwei is revealed near the end of the exploit. He is not the typical Oriental villain of the pulp magazines but is a Caucasian masquerading as such. Perhaps he got the idea of his disguise from the pulps. In any event, he is quite mad.

Fear Cay has two competing chief villains. The gadget is not electromechanical but biological, and it seems to be only beneficial in its effects. It is silphium, an herb which was grown by the ancient Cyrenes of North Africa. The tea prepared from it gave people a long life. The plant apparently perished with the Cyrenes, but Doc and pals find out that it still grows on a West Indian islet. A Roman galley with a cargo of silphium was driven by storms into the western Atlantic and was shipwrecked on Fear Cay. Cyrene was a city which was part of a larger group called Cyrenaica and was founded by

Greek colonists. It was later incorporated into the Roman Empire. Since it was in present-day Libya, next to Egypt, I wonder what the Roman galley was doing out of the Mediterranean. Perhaps it was carrying silphium to the province of Britain, which would account for its presence in the Atlantic.

One of the villains, Santini, is a typical gangster. The other, Dan Thunden, is far more colorful. He is one hundred and thirty-one years old, has a youthful physique, a thatch of white hair, and a long white beard. He is the fastest man Doc has ever encountered. He even eludes Doc for a while in a grab-and-duck chase and then leaps headfirst through a glass window. Doc has to go out a side door after him because he is too big to get through the window frame. On the straightaway, Doc overhauls old Thunden, but Thunden pulls a gun and gets away.

There is a mysterious menace on Fear Cay, a sinister thing which devours its victims alive, stripping them to the bone. It is, however, no monster created in the laboratory but a horde of flesh-eating ants.

The main gadget, the silphium, is the real menace to earth. What if it were released for public usage? What would happen then? The silphium not only prolongs life, it keeps its users healthy and vigorous. Women and men would not cease to be fertile as they aged, nor would their sexual drives diminish. They would continue to have children, and the death rate would be lowered.

If silphium had been made available in 1934, we would today have a population twice as large as the present. Doc knew what he was doing when he suppressed it. He could not keep news of it from leaking out, but he made sure that everybody would think it was just another overrated medicinal herb.

As for villainous old Thunden, he came to a bad end, betrayed by his own doublecrossing, eaten by his own trap.

The Mystic Mullah tells of pale-green shape-changing phantoms which float in the air. Their touch is painful and usually fatal. Bullets and knives pass through them without stopping them. They are directed by "the green soul" of the Mystic Mullah, who is master of all souls and has infinite power. When he kills with the green things, which are souls, he adds the souls of the murdered to the ranks. The Mystic Mullah has died a million years before time began, and, even now, though he moves and talks and kills, he is not really living.

Like most of the weird phenomena in the supersagas, the Mullah's green ghosts have a rational explanation. I will admit, however, that I could find no mention of "the neotropical rattlesnake" in zoology books.

The villain of *Spook Legion*, Telegraph Edmunds, has a gadget which makes his gang invisible. He robs and murders until all of New York City is in a panic. It's tough living in New York City nowadays, but it must've been far worse in the 1930s and 1940s. Doc tangled with one world-wrecker after another while the Gothamites ran around like blind mice. King Kong panicked Manhattan. The Shadow and the Spider ran up against scores of great villains with hellish machines and diseases which threatened to wipe out New York. The wonder is that anybody but the great heroes and the great villains elected to remain in the city. However, your New York City aborigine has a not-too-secret belief that life is not worth living outside his birthplace. He'd rather die than leave it, and if present conditions continue, he will.

The Fantastic Island is a tale which could have inspired the James Bond novel *Doctor No*. The sinister Count Ramadanoff admits, "The mortality rate among my guests has been regrettably high." And when he sits down to play the piano, no one laughs. It is "always a prelude of unpleasantness for somebody." He says, "I am impelled to unspeakable decisions when my fingers wander over the keys." His favorite method of killing is "the thumbhole death."

Doctor Madren, in *The Men Who Smiled No More*, gives Doc the toughest moments of his life. Doc himself admits this, although at that time he had not yet met John Sunlight. Who would have guessed that this pudgy little bald psychiatrist, a pillar of the community, was the inventor of the device that turned men into robots subject to Madren's slightest, and often fatal, whim?

In *Haunted Ocean* New York City at eight o'clock in the morning comes to a standstill. All electricity ceases to flow. Again, the man responsible for this is an idealist. He wants to stop all wars. And a competing fiend in human form is trying to get his hands on the gadget for his personal profit and glory. The situation is so serious that the authorities, mystified and helpless, call in Doc. Franklin Delano Roosevelt himself asks Doc to investigate. This is one of the wisest things Roosevelt ever did. Only a man of Doc's caliber could track down the Man of Peace and the villain who is after him. And who else, having got his hands on the electricity stopper, could be trusted not to use it for selfish purposes?

It would be tedious for any but the most zealous Savageologists to describe even an eighth of the villains and their gadgets. But time after time, month after month, often week after week, Doc and his group collided with, rebounded from, were captured by, almost killed by, but finally crushed, villains with the most amazing and horrifying machines and monsters.

During World War II these seemed to have been thinned out. Either the Depression years had been a sort of renaissance, a time of fruition of great villains and gadgets, or else Doc had liquidated so many that the others had decided not to try their luck against him. Or they may have felt they could not compete with the master villain, Hitler.

Whatever the reasons, though there were some fabulous devices used by wicked men during World War II and after, the villains seem pale compared to those who went before them. Except for a few, Doc's enemies lack true apocalyptic stature.

But in the last recorded supersaga, *Up from Earth's Center*, Doc may have run into somebody, or something, even he could not win out against. He did escape from his antagonists, but the implications are that they had powers which did not depend upon gadgets and which no gadgets could successfully combat in the long run.

Up from Earth's Center is a very strange tale.

Doc, Ham, and Monk are the only ones to play an active role. No mention is made of Long Tom, Johnny, or Pat. Renny is in the area but never appears on stage. Ham is knocked senseless and so doesn't accompany Doc and Monk into the deep, enormous caverns in the Maine mountains. With the two intrepids are Doctor Karl Linningen, an eminent psychiatrist, a Mr. Wail, and a Mr. Williams. The last two are devils. At least, they're inhabitants of the underground, and they claim to have been, at one time, living human beings.

Neither Williams nor Wail have horns or tails or hooves; they look quite *Homo sapiens*. Wail is an admitted escapee from Hell. He doesn't like it at all. In fact, he died in 1781, went to Hell (or the caverns), rose to the rank of assistant devil, and was sent outside to "take care" of Gilmore. Gilmore had accidentally found the caverns, which went to the center of the earth, and discovered that Dante and other infernologists were right. Hell is where they said it was, in earth's center. At least, its heart is, though its suburbs extend to the surface.

Williams had gone after the defecting Wail.

Over fifteen miles down but still only "in the outskirts of hades," Doc encounters something that freezes him with the worst terror he's ever known, and he's known the worst.

"The shape became a mass, formless and gibbous and evil. It had movement and body, but little else that seemed natural; it had no arms, no legs; it was headless and leathery, with a sour gray color that shed the ugly purplish-green light with a skull-like sheen. It came towards him, lurching, rolling, so that he could not actually tell how it progressed. There was some odor, not the flowery one, but the dead scent of lifelessness and emptiness."

Doc has seen the thing before but had thought that it was a boulder. Now the thing attacks, and it must be dangerous because it scares even Wail, a demon, though junior-grade. Others of its kind join in the attack. Doc escapes only by throwing an explosive grenade. This does not hurt the things but it does startle and confuse them.

Wail, replying to Doc's angry questions, says that Doc won't believe him if he tells the truth. The boulder-things are inmates. Sinners. For punishment, they've been transformed into stones, though mobile stones, and they are doomed to stay in that shape forever. The things, Wail adds, are only a "mild sample of what it's like down in the main area."

Later, Doc and Wail run into a forest of living trees. These hiss and try to catch them with springy-feeling tentacles. Doc is held helpless; a tentacle around his throat cuts off his air. If it were not for Monk's appearance on the scene, Doc would be dead in a few minutes. Monk throws a grenade. The things drop Monk and Doc and become still and stone-hard.

Perhaps Dante was not fantasizing; he may have been in a similar cave in Italy.

Explosives and flames are the only things that frighten these creatures. Indeed, earlier, Mr. Wail has shown his fear of fire, even of a lighted match. Doc, Monk, Linningen, and Wail escape. Doctor Linningen comes up with an explanation for their experience. The caverns must contain a gas that causes hallucinations. But this theory won't hold up under analysis. Mr. Wail is locked in a storeroom from which he can't possibly escape. But he does. He just disappears from it.

So we come, in the 181st supersaga, to the ultimate in villains and gadgets. The villains are nonhuman, though they were once human. The gadget is nonelectromechanical and nonbiological. It is evil itself, powered by evil itself.

Doc seems to have no intention of continuing the war. He closes the entrance to the caverns with explosives, though how this will imprison beings who can pass through solid walls is something not mentioned.

Would Doc have abandoned the fight? Would a man dedicated to probing "the mysterious, the inexplicable" be able to ignore the challenge? Would not his rational approach have forced him to discard the supernatural explanation? After all, Mr. Wail and his kind may have been extraterrestrials who were hiding out in the deep earth until *Der Tag* arrived. However, if the denizens of the deep earth were not of Hell, they had the powers of Hell. Doc, after long meditation and a firm decision and much preparation, would have led an expedition against the things. With him would have been his five aides and perhaps Pat. The expedition would have been loaded, not for bear but for the Forebear of All Evil. And it would have expended all the hundreds of gadgets in a final apocalyptic onslaught.

Perhaps Doc invented some kind of magnetic field to keep the denizens from passing by teleportation through his defenses. The disadvantage of this, of course, is that he has to turn off the field if he is going to launch his weapons at them. And what happens during the momentary vulnerability?

We can be sure that he would have used as his most formidable weapon the one thing that evil can't face: Light.

If the cavern dweller's were indeed lost souls encased in strange forms, Doc may have lost. And Hell is as strong as ever. If they were extraterrestrials, subject to natural laws, they might have lost. If they had won, it seems likely that they would have come out into the open by now in an all-out war. They haven't, so perhaps Doc won. Or perhaps they are among us as reasonable facsimiles of human beings.

Addendum 1

THE FABULOUS FAMILY TREE OF DOC SAVAGE (ANOTHER EXCURSION INTO CREATIVE MYTHOGRAPHY)

DOC SAVAGE not only has some distinguished ancestors, he has a number of famous (and infamous) cousins. His forebears and relatives on his father's side are described in Addenda 2 and 3 of my *Tarzan Alive* (Doubleday, 1972). In that book, Doc's family tree was not traced on the maternal side beyond his mother's parents, Arronaxe Land and Wolf Larsen. In the book at hand, this addendum and its accompanying genealogical chart (see pages xviii-xxi) are an extension of the addendum and end papers in the biography of Tarzan.

The genealogy of the end paper in *Tarzan Alive* is titled *The Wold Newton Family, 1795–1901*. Wold Newton is a small village in the East Riding of Yorkshire County, England. It is famous chiefly for a meteorite which struck near it in 1795, the exact location of impact being marked by a monument which tourists, or anybody else, may see now. At the moment it struck, two large coaches with fourteen passengers and four coachmen were within a few yards of it. All were exposed to the ionization accompanying meteorites. The descendants of all those in or on the coaches include an extraordinary number of great crime fighters, scientists, and explorers. So many, in fact, that the only reasonable explanation is that the meteorite radiation caused a beneficial mutation of genes in those exposed.

The mutated genes were reinforced, kept from being lost, by the inbreeding of the descendants of those present at Wold Newton. Marriages of cousins were, of course, common among the British nobility and gentry. *Burke's Peerage* records numerous instances of this. Moreover, most of the passengers came of stock which had been producing extraordinary men and women for many generations.

187

Some of their descendants were more than extraordinary; they bordered on, and in some cases attained, the status of superman.

Note that the "supermen" in this family tree were mostly battlers against evil. But every family barrel has its rotten apples, and this one produced two of the greatest evil men in history, geniuses in both science and crime: Fu Manchu and Professor James Moriarty. Of a lower quality, though still geniuses, were John Clay (also known as Colonel Clay), Doctor Caber, and Carl Peterson. Arsène Lupin is an "amphibian," operating sometimes as an outlaw and sometimes for the law. However, as was pointed out in the text of this book, and in *Tarzan Alive*, the great crime fighters of this family often paid no attention to laws. They were interested, not in legality, but in justice. To effect their goal, they often did things which would have put them in prison for years, or caused them to be executed, if they had been found out.

To trace the various trunks and branches that feed the genealogical sap—if this term is permissible—begin with the three people in the chart's upper-left corner. The careers of these three are recounted in John Barth's *The Sot Weed Factor* (Doubleday). Its protagonist, Ebenezer Cooke (1666–1732), led an adventurous life in the colony of Maryland. He was its poet laureate, creator of the well-known poem "The Sot Weed Factor" (meaning "The Tobacco Merchant") and of the unfinished epic, the "Marylandiad."

Ebenezer's twin sister, Anna, bore a child to Henry Burlingame, a descendant of a colleague of Captain John Smith. He was a bold adventurer, a learned man, and a man of many disguises. His child by Anna was Andrew Cooke III.

His descendant, Juno Cooke, married John Bumppo. John may have been descended from Natty Bumppo, the Hawkeye, the Deer-slayer, of Cooper's novels of the middle-eighteenth-century eastern-American wilderness. But of him, more later.

Skipping for the moment the first viscount Castlewood, proceed to Captain Blood (second level). His biography has been written by Raphael Sabatini in three volumes: *Captain Blood, Captain Blood Returns*, and *The Further Adventures of Captain Blood*. It's appropriate that this famous scourge of the Spanish Main and medical doctor should be Doc's forefather. Doc was a great sailor who experienced some of his most splendid supersagas on the sea or under it. And Doc, as the reader knows by now, was perhaps the most celebrated of all surgeons. It might be going too far, from a strict scientific viewpoint, to say that Doc inherited his seamanship and medical skill from Peter Blood. But these abilities were certainly not lost because of genetic dilution. Many other seamen and doctors were Doc's ancestors in other lines. Peter Blood was the son of an Irish medicus and got his *baccalaureus medicinae* at the same institution from which his father graduated, Trinity College, Dublin. His mother was English, a native of the southern county of Somersetshire. This was the main theater of the Duke of Monmouth's rebellion, and the decisive battle of Sedgemoor was fought there in 1685. The Bloody Assizes of the infamous Judge Jeffreys followed at Taunton Castle and Wells.

Blood's mother was a member of the seafaring family of Frobisher. Sabatini does not say that she was the daughter of Sir Martin Frobisher (1539?–94), the great navigator and discoverer, but she probably was his niece.

Peter Blood was arrested for treating the wounded Lord Gildoy after the battle of Sedgemoor. Gildoy escaped punishment as a rebel partly because of his high position but mostly because of his wealth. Blood had taken no part in the uprising; his only crime was obeying the Hippocratic Oath. He was held in jail along with the thousands of the lowly who had no money to buy their way out. It seemed certain that he would be one of the hundreds hung by Jeffreys. But the authorities put a stop to the waste of human-power. Why hang a man when he could be sold at a profit to West Indian plantation owners who would then work his slave to death?

And so Blood was shipped off to the island of Barbados. There he began that remarkable career which resulted in his marrying Arabella Bishop, the daughter of the governor of Barbados and himself becoming its governor.

Micah Clarke (next to Blood on the chart) was a contemporary of the captain. His autobiography has been edited by A. Conan Doyle under the title of *Micah Clarke.* Clarke was born in 1664 in the little village of Havant, Hampshire, a few miles from Portsmouth. He was the son of Mary Shepstone and "Ironside Joe" Clarke, a gray-eyed, broad-chested, rough-tempered Puritan who had served under Cromwell. Micah's father, Joseph Clarke, was the descendant of Solomon Kane (1566–?). The dour fighting Puritan was with Sir

Richard Grenville on the *Revenge* during its famous engagement of 1591. (Tennyson wrote a poem about this battle.) In a hand-to-hand fight lasting fifteen hours against fifteen Spanish ships and five thousand Spaniards, the *Revenge* and its one hundred and ninety men were defeated. Young Solomon Kane was carried off in chains to the terrors of the Inquisition in Spain. He later escaped and served for a while under the French in their war against Spain.

Like his descendant, Doc Savage, Kane traveled over the world to right wrongs. This tall rangy gray-eyed knight of the open road wandered through the Americas, Europe, and Africa. He penetrated deeper into the Dark Continent than any white man before him and there encountered many weird things and beings. Some of his exploits were even stranger than those of his remote grandsons, Tarzan and Doc Savage.

(Those interested in reading of Kane's life should go to the complete collection, *Red Shadows*, Robert E. Howard, Donald M. Grant [publisher], or the softcover versions, *The Moon of Skulls*, *The Hand of Kane*, and *Solomon Kane*, Centaur Press.)

Kane's lover, or wife, Bess, died after giving birth to another Bess. Young Bess married a Clarke, and one of her descendants was Micah Clarke. He was even larger and stronger than his father, Ironside Joe, and much better-tempered. Unlike Blood, he took an active part in the rebellion. Like Blood, he was held prisoner for a while before his so-called trial. Probably, the young yeoman saw Peter Blood in prison and perhaps even exchanged a few words with him, since Blood was busy doctoring the sick rebels. Clarke, like Blood, was saved from the gallows when he was sentenced to be transported to the West Indies as a slave.

Clarke, however, did not get there because his old friend, the mercenary soldier, Decimus Saxon, rescued him. Micah later settled down in his native village, married a woman unnamed by Doyle, had children, and then grandchildren. There is, however, a little family cemetery near Havant with a tombstone which bears the name of Micah's wife, Sarah Frobisher Clarke. She was related to Peter Blood's mother through the Frobishers. Another of her seafaring ancestors was a Raphael Hythloday (first level). The discoveries of this young Portuguese philosopher in the New World were related by him to Sir Thomas More, who wrote about them in his *Utopia*.

Utopia was a large island seemingly located off the Pacific coast of South America. Its Amerind inhabitants were in an early state of civilization comparable to that of the Olmecs of Mexico or the pre-Incans when they were conquered by men from an invading fleet. These seem to have been half-Persian and half-Greek, probably soldiers and sailors who had fled Persia after the death of Alexander the Great. The fleet had wandered through the East Indies and then sailed across the Pacific until it came to the island, then called Abraxa. Their leader, Utopus, was a philosopher who put into practice his Platonian ideals. He was wise enough to adopt the best of the aboriginal culture and of the Greco-Persian culture and thus to found a hybrid civilization the like of which the world has not seen before or since.

Unfortunately, after Hythloday's departure for the Old World, a great earthquake sank the island of Utopia, and it became one with Atlantis. The world lost an example of what men could be if they allowed humanity and reason to govern them. On the other hand, the Spanish undoubtedly would have destroyed the Utopian civilization solely because it was pagan, as they did the Central American and Incan societies. They would not have realized that the Utopians were, in effect, the only true Christian nation then (or now) existing.

Sarah Frobisher bore Micah Clarke many children, of whom we consider here Reuben, Micah, and Gervas (third level).

Reuben was the ancestor of Eliza Shawnessy, of whom more later.

Micah was the forefather of Allan Quatermain (sixth level). Quatermain was not descended from those exposed to the radiation at Wold Newton. But he is a member of that family in the sense of sharing some of its illustrious ancestors—Micah Clarke (second level), and Solomon Kane, Sir Nigel Loring, and Raphael Hythloday (first level)—and in his phenomenally adventurous life.

Allan Quatermain (1817–85) was a wiry little man with porcupine-quill hair and brown eyes. These eyes belonged to the best shot in England and Africa, and his small chest contained a large heart swelling with courage, mysticism, and compassion. Like Sir Nigel, he was no giant in size but was tall in bravery and ability. And, like Sir Nigel, he was a verray parfit gentil knight. Like Hythloday and

Kane, he roamed far, encountering exotic peoples and adventures. His main theater of action was South Africa. Here he made his living chiefly by hunting and trading with the natives, whom he knew intimately and whom he generally liked. He was the friend and companion of the great Zulu hero Umslopogaas, only surviving child of the black Napoleon, Tchaka. (See H. Rider Haggard's *Nada the Lily*, *She and Allan*, and *Allan Quatermain* for his epic story.) Quatermain discovered three unknown civilizations: Walloo, Kôr, and Zuvendis. His memoirs consist of fourteen books and four short narratives, all edited by Haggard. The two best known are *King Solomon's Mines* and *Allan Quatermain*. These have been often reprinted, but I expect a revival of interest in the other Quatermain tales when their mysticism-shot qualities become known to the younger generations.

Gervas Clarke (center, third level) married a Joan Hurdle. She was a descendant of that brawling giant, the ex-monk and soldier John of Hordle. He served under Sir Nigel Loring, and the story of both may be read in A. Conan Doyle's *Sir Nigel* and *The White Company*.

Gervas had two daughters, Tabitha and Monica. Tabitha was the mother of Sir John Clarke Wildman, who married Matthiette de Pierson. Monica had a daughter, Alice Clarke Raffles, who married Sir Percy Blakeney, the Scarlet Pimpernel.

Captain Peter Blood's daughter, Arabella, married a second cousin, also named Blood. Their daughter, Mercy, married Matthew de Pierson (fourth level). He was the son of Lorna Esmond, a descendant of the first viscount of Castlewood. (For the story of the Esmond family, read William Makepeace Thackeray's *Henry Esmond* and *The Virginians*.) Lorna Esmond was the wife of Lord Tiverton, a rather sinister person beheaded for treason in 1745. His ancestry may be traced in the Lineage of Lichfield section in *The Cream of the Jest*, James Branch Cabell (Ballantine Books, 1972).

Lord Tiverton's ancestry was very distinguished, even phenomenal, though his earliest recorded forefather began as a swineherd. Manuel, however, attained the title of Count of Poictesme, a sovereign area of medieval France. Manuel had many descendants through many women, but Tiverton's line came down from Niafer, who may have been the daughter of the Soldan of Barbary.

Lord Tiverton's granddaughter, Matthiette de Pierson (fifth level), married Sir John Clarke Wildman. Sir John, on being created a baronet in 1785, added his mother's name to his father's. This coupling of paternal and maternal family names is common among the British nobility and gentry. Usually the names are hyphenated (as in Smythe-Jones), but a small number omit this typographical link.

The son of Sir John and Matthiette de Pierson, Sir Patrick Clarke Wildman, married Mavice Blakeney, the daughter of the Scarlet Pimpernel. Both Sir Patrick and his father were wealthy eccentrics, medical doctors whose hobby was alchemistry and the occult. Sir John was blown to bits in 1843, apparently while trying to transmute lead into gold. His son, Sir Patrick, seems to have attempted experiments much like those attributed to Doctor Victor Frankenstein. It is claimed in Hendrik van Helsing's *Hollow Dark Places* (Zoondt, Amsterdam, 1885) that Sir Patrick had access to Frankenstein's notes. His evidence, however, is so slight that most scholars reject this theory.

What Sir Patrick was doing in his laboratory will never be known. His laboratory and its records were burned by the villagers of Upper Fogg Shaw in Derbyshire. Sir Patrick escaped their fury but was later arrested by the police. Though obviously mad, he was sentenced to death for the murder of the local vicar and for body-stealing. Before he could be hanged, he poisoned himself. It was this well-publicized scandal which caused his daughter, Patricia, to refuse to marry the sixth duke of Greystoke, even though she bore him a son. She was afraid that the marriage would ruin his career as a statesman.

It was this stigma which drove Patricia's older brother, Alex, to migrate to Canada. After becoming a wealthy landowner in his old age, he married May Renfrew, sister to a well-known Royal Canadian Mounted Policeman. Alex's and May's daughter, Patricia Savage, was named after Alex's beloved sister.

Alexander Clarke Wildman, was the father of Patricia (Savage). Alexander's sister, Patricia, died after giving birth to Doc Savage's father. (See Chapter 3.) Alexander went to the New World, but the oldest brother, Bruce Clarke Wildman, decided to stay in England. He did, however, live very quietly there, burying himself in the more exotic sciences, notably, time travel. This gray-eyed member of the

Wold Newton family succeeded in his experiments, as the readers of H. G. Wells' *The Time Machine* know. Wells respected his desire for privacy and so refers to him only as The Time Traveller.

The family background and story of the sixth duke's illegitimate son, James Clarke Wildman, is described in Chapter 4 of the book at hand. The Greystokes are fully blazoned in Addendum 3 of *Tarzan Alive*. For those interested in heraldry, the arms of Clarke Wildman are:

ARMS—Argent, a fesse chequy gules and azure, in chief an alchemical pelican between two fleams, in base a demisavage holding on his sinister shoulder a club. *Crest*—A demihuntsman proper winding a horn gules. *Mottoes*—Free for a Blast; Inicissimus Maleficorum.

The latter motto means: The Greatest Enemy of Evildoers, a very appropriate motto for Doc Savage.

Doc's mother was Arronaxe Larsen (eighth level). She was the daughter of Arronaxe Land (seventh level) and of Wolf Larsen. Larsen, a Danish-born Norwegian, was the sinister amoral genius whose story was related by Humphrey van Weyden to Jack London. London novelized it as *The Sea Wolf*, first published in serial form in *The Century Magazine*, 1904.

Wolf Larsen was a very handsome man who could be as charming and as beguiling as Lucifer himself when he wished. His charisma was, however, of an alternating current quality. When he became angry, he was as frightening as a typhoon. He became not just a man in a fury but an elemental force. He was a human wolverine in strength and aggressiveness with a mentality which, developed in a different environment, might have equaled Darwin's or Spencer's. He was a genius who had never arrived. Though lacking even a day of formal education, he had taught himself so well that he knew as much, if not more, of philosophy than many college professors. He invented a star scale that was so simple a child could use it to navigate a ship.

The genes of this extraordinary physical and mental specimen, reinforced with the Wold Newton genes, made Doc Savage the superman he truly was.

And, time and again, Van Weyden speaks of Larsen's protean gray eyes with their *glints of gold*. Both Larsen and his wife, Arronaxe Land, bequeathed the yellow flecks to Doc.

Wolf lacked most of the finer moral qualities, except courage and ambition, and he married Arronaxe because that was the only way to get her to bed. Then he deserted her.

We may suppose that the outraged Ned Land made an extensive search for his daughter's betrayer, but that story was not written by Jules Verne, though it may be written someday by somebody else.

Immediately below Wolf Larsen is a broken line ending in *Mr. Moto?*. Mr. Moto was the little Japanese mystery-solver and champion jujitsu expert whose exploits were recorded by J. P. Marquand. The stories about him were very popular in pre-World War II days, and several movies were made with Peter Lorre in the lead role. When Pearl Harbor happened, Mr. Moto lost his appeal to American readers. His inclusion in this chart is based on speculation, not documentation. But there is an incident in *The Sea Wolf* in which Wolf and his crew abducted, raped, and abandoned a group of pretty Japanese women. Possibly, Mr. Moto was the grandson of the woman whom Wolf took for his own. His superior qualities indicate the likelihood of this.

The question mark after Philip Marlowe's name indicates that he is on the same dubious footing as Mr. Moto. This private eye had the same keen detective ability, compassion, and hard-boiled but poetical worldview as Lew Archer. (Elsewhere it has been suggested, with a more solid foundation than that prepared for Marlowe, that Archer was a member of the Wold Newton family, that he was, in fact, the grandson of Professor Challenger.) Marlowe is put forth as a candidate for relationship because of his superior qualities and because of the resemblance of his eyes to Doc's. He also had light-brown eyes with flecks of gold. (See *Trouble Is My Business* by Raymond Chandler.) This indicates a possible descent from Larsen and Arronaxe Land. In any event, it would be a shame to leave him out of the genealogy. We may suppose that Arronaxe married a Marlowe in her later years and moved to California.

Readers who feel that the quality of genealogy is strained in this surmise are free to reject it.

Arronaxe Land was the daughter of the herculean French-Canadian harpooner Ned Land (sixth level). His story has been told by Jules Verne in *Twenty Thousand Leagues Under the Sea*. Ned had married a Marie Chauvelin. His first daughter was Edwina Land.

His last child was named Arronaxe after his admired friend, the renowned natural historian Professor Pierre Aronnax, author of the two-volume *Mysteries of the Great Ocean Depths*.

Marie Chauvelin, Ned Land's wife, was the descendant of French immigrants who had settled in Quebec. Marie's father, Jules, had married his first cousin, Jeanne. Jeanne's father, Guy, was the brother of Armand Chauvelin (fourth level). Armand had been the French ambassador to the English court, but during the Revolution he was a secret agent. His life became dedicated to catching the elusive, demmed Scarlet Pimpernel. Fortunately, he failed; otherwise, Doc Savage, not to mention Tarzan and many other heroes, would never have been born.

Citizen Chauvelin's peculiar yellow eyes are often described by Baroness Orczy in her somewhat fictionalized biographies of Sir Percy Blakeney. The yellow eyes were a Chauvelin characteristic, preserved by a number of cousin-marriages. Wolf Larsen's genes strengthened the quality, and it was this double infusion which gave Doc's eyes their strange appearance.

Ned Land's other daughter, Edwina (seventh level), married a John Spade. He was a Pinkerton detective, and his father, Samuel, was a policeman. Samuel Spade's father, Joshua had been in the British naval intelligence before he resigned and moved to Indiana. Why he quit and went to the States is not known, but he seems to have been involved in some scandal with a Brigadier General Sir Harry Paget Flashman. At one time such an involvement would have been unthinkable. But in view of the recently published Flash-man papers, it becomes likely. (See *Flashman*, *Royal Flash*, *Flash for Freedom*, and *Flashman at the Charge*, George MacDonald Fraser.)

Whatever happened, Captain Joshua Spade left England under a cloud with his wife and two children. He had married in 1830 the beautiful Mary Brandon, a granddaughter of the first duke of Greystoke and daughter of Sir George Brandon, baronet, of Brandon Abbas, Devonshire. Mary was a sweet and gentle girl, but two of her collateral descendants, Sir Hector Brandon and Augustus Brandon, were thorough rotters. (For the story of this family, see Percival Christopher Wren's *Beau Geste*. And for the story of another collateral descendant, Sir Charles Brandon of Brandon Beeches, Oxfordshire, see George Bernard Shaw's *An Unsocial Socialist*.)

Joshua and Mary Spade's son, Samuel, married a Faith Shawnessy. Sam and Faith moved to San Francisco, where John Spade was born. John married Edwina Land, the daughter of Marie Chauvelin and Ned Land. John and Edwina's son was Sam Spade.

Sam followed in the footsteps of his fathers and became a detective. He was well-known in San Francisco as an exceedingly capable and occasionally flamboyant private eye. But it was not until Dashiell Hammett gave him some publicity (in *The Maltese Falcon*) that the world became aware of him.

Sam, be it noted, had yellow-gray eyes. These are what one would expect from the issue of a Clayton, whose family ran to gray eyes, and of a Chauvelin, whose family ran to yellow eyes.

Sam Spade's aunt, Mary, married an Englishman, James Jorkens. Their son was Joseph Jorkens, possessor of a genius for stumbling into the most outlandish things, people, and situations. Many of his exploits were in Africa, which seems to have had a singular attraction for so many of the ancestors and relatives of Tarzan and Doc Savage.

In his later years, Mr. Jorkens became an habitué of the Billiards Club in London. Here a fellow member, Lord Dunsany, encouraged Jorkens to recount his adventures with a steady supply of tall scotches and then recorded them in five delightful books. These are *Travel Tales of Mr. Joseph Jorkens*, *Jorkens Remembers Africa*, *Jorkens Has a Large Whiskey*, *The Fourth Book of Jorkens*, and *Jorkens Borrows Another Whiskey*.

Sam Spade's paternal grandmother was Faith Shawnessy (F.S., sixth level). Faith's younger brother was John Wickcliff Shawnessy. Johnny's poignant and tragic biography was novelized by Ross Lockridge in *Raintree County* (Houghton Mifflin, 1948). This book was a best-seller when it first came out, has been reprinted a number of times since then, and is now regarded as a minor classic which may someday become a major classic. The movie made from the book failed to capitalize on the philosophic, mythic, and dramatic qualities which, in my opinion, make the book great. Perhaps someday a director of genius will make a film that measures up to the book.

Johnny Shawnessy was born 23 April 1839 in the sphinx-haunted county of Raintree, mid-Indiana. Johnny was a poet whose head, to put it in a phrenological phrase, bore too large a bump of amativeness. He pursued truth and beauty all his life, and his quest for the legendary Golden Raintree was as zealous, and as frustrated, as Sir Lancelot's for the Holy Grail. In fact, he failed for the same reason as did his knightly predecessor. Lancelot had his Guinevere; Johnny, his Susannah Drake.

Johnny wanted to be a great writer, a great poet, a Hoosier Shakespeare. But he ended his days as an obscure schoolteacher, his epic of the American Republic was never finished, and his verse-drama *Recumbent Sphinx* was never staged.

The desire to write ran through the Shawnessy family for generations. Johnny's father, Thomas Duff Shawnessy, was a preacher and a dispenser of folk medicine. His sole claim to literary fame was his *Ode on the Evils of Tobacco,* known all over the county. Its most widely quoted line was:

> *Some do it chew and some it smoke*
> *Whilst some it up their nose do poke*

Thomas Duff had his heart in the right place, but his bump of poetry was missing. Thomas Duff had always hoped that one of his sons would inherit the writing genius of his (Thomas Duff's) father. The only one who came close was Johnny. Johnny found out who his grandfather was shortly after he thought he had made Susannah Drake pregnant. Thomas Duff confessed that he, Thomas Duff, was the illegitimate son of the great Scots author Thomas Carlyle. Carlyle was a world-famous essayist and historian who thought of himself as a moral prophet, a Celtic Moses. Author of such classics as *Sartor Resartus*; *The French Revolution*; *On Heroes, Hero-Worship, and the Heroic in History*, he also translated Goethe's *Wilhelm Meister's Apprenticeship* into English and wrote a history of Frederick the Great.

Though a fanatical and harsh moralist, Thomas Carlyle, when a young man, had tumbled Eliza Shawnessy in the hay. She was the descendant of Micah Clarke's son Reuben (third level), who had settled in Scotland after years of wandering. The son of Thomas and Eliza was born in the village of Ecclefechan. A few years later she and Thomas Duff went to the Land of Promise, America. She died in 1820, a year after the still-unknown Carlyle had quit teaching and begun studying law.

Note, however, the question mark after Thomas Carlyle. This indicates that there is some doubt about his being the father of

Thomas Duff Shawnessy. Carlyle was born in 1795; Eliza Shawnessy, in 1774. This would make her twenty-one years old when Carlyle was born. Since their illegitimate son, Thomas Duff Shawnessy, was born in 1807, Carlyle would have been only twelve when he impregnated Eliza. This is possible, but then Thomas Duff Shawnessy would have been only thirteen when he married the nineteen-year-old Ellen. We're asked to believe that both father and son were extraordinarily attractive to older women even though they were only in the beginning of pubescence. The ability to copulate among twelve and thirteen-year-old males is common, and spermatogenesis begins with puberty. Twelve-year-old males can be and have been, fertile. And mature women have seduced, or allowed themselves to be seduced by, twelve-year-old boys.

However, Carlyle himself seems to have been rather passionless, in fact, if Frank Harris is to be believed, impotent. In his *Contemporary Portraits* (Brentano's, 1920) Harris relates that Carlyle himself told him that not once during his forty years of marriage had he had intercourse with his wife, though he deeply loved her. Carlyle attributed this to his own complete lack of sexual sensuality and his puritanical attitude toward sex. Harris hints that it was actually a physical disability which caused this tragic neglect. He claimed to have talked with Mrs. Carlyle's doctor, a Sir Richard Quayne, who gave him her account of her sexual life or, rather, lack of it. Harris did not give any details; he merely suggested that the doctor's account was specific, that Carlyle was impotent, and that sometime in the future he, Harris, would write about the conversation. By the time Harris talked to Quayne both Carlyles had been long dead, and so the doctor was not being unethical in passing on confidentialities.

On the other hand, Harris often stretched the truth or downright lied for the sake of sensationalism.

Even if Harris was being truthful, Carlyle at the age of twelve might have been potent and his sperm might have been motile. Possibly, the deep melancholia which afflicted Carlyle all his adult life may have resulted from a feeling of guilt about the one time in his life when he let down his Calvinistic barriers.

We'll never know the truth. Harris did not get around to describing his conversation with Quayle, and all who may have cleared up the matter for us have been dead for over a hundred years.

Eliza Shawnessy could not have told her illegitimate son that Carlyle was his father in order to make him believe that he at least had a famous father. Carlyle was a nobody when Eliza died. I incline to the theory that Thomas Duff Shawnessy fantasized that Carlyle was his progenitor. He knew that both his mother and Carlyle had come from the same village, and so he picked out Carlyle as the one who had beget him. He either did not know or ignored the discrepancy in ages between his mother and Carlyle. But I could be wrong.

Johnny Shawnessy's second marriage was to one of his students, Esther Root. Her father, the terrible-tempered Gideon Root, had a more than fatherly love for his youngest daughter, and he bitterly opposed her marriage to the much older Johnny. Esther's mother was a silent, dark woman whose name Lockridge does not mention. However, my pokings around Raintree County (which is Lockridge's name for the actual Henry County) have turned up the tombstone of a Fern Bumppo Root (fifth level). Since Lockridge's account indicates that Mrs. Root was part-Indian, she could have been the granddaughter of Natty Bumppo. James Fenimore Cooper does not even hint in the *Leatherstocking Tales* that Natty ever gave way to any amativeness while amongst the Indians (unless it was toward Chingachgook). But Cooper would never have mentioned this if he had known about it. And if highly moral Carlyle could succumb once to the sexual passion, there is no reason to suppose that highly moral Bumppo did not fall at least once. He surely must have got tired of chasing nothing but deer.

Fern's father was John Bumppo (fourth level), and her mother was June Cooke, according to the above-mentioned grave marker. June Cooke was a descendant of Anna Cooke and Henry Burlingame.

None of Esther Root's Indian darkness came out in her daughter, Eva Alice Shawnessy. Eva had brown hair and blue eyes, the heritage of the blond Shawnessys. She also had, according to her father, a scientific bent of mind. (He must have wondered if she got it from Carlyle, who had an aptitude for mathematics.) Eva was possessed with a glowing imagination, a sense of wonder, and a great curiosity about the mysteries of life and time. It was she who got lost in the Great Swamp and who found, but lost, the Golden Raintree that her father had found but lost.

She was named after the heroine of *Uncle Tom's Cabin*, little Eva, and after the heroine of Lewis Carroll's two classics, Alice. No wonder she found the fabled Raintree.

Little Eva Alice grew up and married Leo Cabell Trout, a traveler from Salem, Virginia. Trout came of two distinguished Old Dominion families but had fallen on evil days. On his way to California to make his fortune, he was hurt in an accident on the National Road near the village of Waycross (Lockridge's name for New Castle). While convalescing, he met Eva Shawnessy and decided to stay in Raintree County. His mother's family had given two writers to the world: James Branch Cabell, author of *Figures of Earth, Jurgen, The Silver Stallion* et al., and Princess Amélie Troubetzkoy, author of *The Quick or the Dead?*, a sensation in 1888, and daughter of William Cabell Rives, U.S. senator and minister to France.

Leo Trout tried his hand as a reporter-editor for *The Free Enquirer*, but he failed. Evidently, the journalistic genes were missing in him. After wandering around for a while with his wife, he got a job with the Royal Ornithological Society on the British island of Bermuda. His son, Kilgore Trout, was born there 19 February 1907.

After the unique species of eagles he was supposed to keep safe became extinct, the Trouts went to the States. Kilgore attended Thomas Jefferson High School in Dayton, Ohio, but we may be sure that he visited his octogenarian grandfather in Raintree County. (Or, if you hardheaded realists prefer, New Castle, Henry County.) He undoubtedly read Johnny Shawnessy's unpublished epic and drama, and these may have given him a bent toward satire, irony, and pessimism in his own works.

In any event, descended from such writers as Ebenezer Cooke (collaterally), Thomas Carlyle perhaps, and John Wickcliff Shawnessy, Kilgore was almost destined to become a man of letters. He did become an author, though one who struggled all his life against poverty and the neglect of the literary world. He was one of those peculiar writers who confine themselves to science-fiction because their imaginations are too big for this world. To them, this world, the real world, is like Mother Hubbard's cupboard: bare.

Unfortunately, Trout mailed his manuscripts to publishers of pornography and so ensured that his works would not be available to the readers who would most appreciate them, the science-fiction fans. Nor was his career helped by his fly-by-night publishers and unethical agents, who cheated him or went bankrupt or both.

His prose style, according to the man who's made the closest study of him, Kurt Vonnegut, Jr., was awful. But his ideas were magnificent, and his stories were on a cosmic scale. And, like his grandfather, Johnny Shawnessy, and his great-great-great-great-uncle Ebenezer Cooke, he sought always for the beautiful and true.

Vonnegut has brought this neglected genius to the attention of the world in his *God Bless You, Mr. Rosewater* and *Slaughterhouse-Five*, and has given us more biographical details in his *Breakfast of Champions*. If some perceptive publisher of repute reprints Trout, the general public may get a chance to read such classics as *The Big Board*, *The Gutless Wonder*, *Plague on Wheels*, and *Venus on the Half-Shell*.

Indeed, since the original edition of this biography came out, Dell Publications has announced that it will reprint *Venus on the Half-Shell* in February of 1975.* *The Magazine of Fantasy & Science Fiction* will precede this with an abridged serial version in its November–December issues of 1974. Dell is also negotiating to secure reprint rights for Trout's *The Son of Jimmy Valentine*.

Eva Alice Shawnessy's older brother, Wesley, married another Alice, the daughter of a Finnish immigrant, Nehemia Jalava, and of a Breton immigrant, Lys Conan. Wesley's and Alice's daughter, Allegra, married a free-lance consulting engineer, Frank Boom Tincrowdor. One of their children, Leo Queequeg Tincrowdor, was born in New Goshen, Indiana, in 1918 while his parents were on the way to a Terre Haute hospital. Leo's middle name comes from his father's fascination with the works of Herman Melville, especially *Moby Dick*. The Polynesian harpooner was Frank's favorite character, perhaps because Frank had spent so much time in the Southwest Pacific as a young man. This was in the company of Christopher "Smoke" Bellew, who went to the South Seas after his adventures in the Yukon, which have been narrated by Jack London.

Leo has a master's degree in the History of Art, but his main support comes from the sale of his paintings and etchings. (These

---

* Venus on the Half-Shell *has seen several more editions since the Dell 1975 edition.* —WSE

have been compared favorably to the works of William Blake and Robert Blake.) In the past few years, Leo has also written some science fiction, most notable of which are *Osiris on Crutches*, *The Vaccinators from Vega*, and *The Hole in the Coolth*. At present he is working on a novel based on his great-grandfather Shawnessy's unpublished blank verse drama, *Sphinx Recumbent*. Though Leo is not now as well known as his cousin, Kilgore Trout, he has great promise as a science-fiction writer.

Part of the lineage of the third duke of Greystoke (fifth level, center of chart) is described in Addenda 2 and 3 of *Tarzan Alive*. Addendum 3 also outlines the lives of his sons, the fourth duke and Sir William Clayton, baronet. Sir William's massive three-volume memoirs, *Never Say Die*, published in Paris in 1888, tells in detail his adventurous life. In fact, the details were unacceptable to the British Victorians, who regarded his book as far too frank, indeed, obscene. But the memoirs of this world-roaming seeker after gold, glory, and love are being edited by me for publication in America, which is why I can speak with authority on his life.

Burke's Peerage notes that Sir William, though married thirteen times, had few surviving children. Burke speaks only of the legitimate unions and says nothing of the children from his numerous affairs. Yet three of these have become famous in history.

While in Southeast Asia during the Opium War (1839–42), Sir William Clayton went to Hanoi. At this time this part of the Southeast was called Annam and was an empire covering the present states of North and South Vietnam. Its ruler was killing off all native Christians he could unearth, but Sir William, as a Briton, was theoretically safe. He was, however, in a dangerous situation if he were found out, since he had been sent to investigate the disappearance of a wealthy half-Chinese merchant who was a British citizen.

Sir William succeeded in his mission, rescuing the merchant and his family, including his beautiful green-eyed daughter, Ling Ju Hai. She was, on her mother's side, descended from Manchurian mandarins; her father was part-Scotch. Sir William's memoirs detail the thrilling escape and his brief but passionate affair with Ling Ju Hai. When her father discovered that she was pregnant, he spirited her away to China and sent assassins after Sir William. He killed them all in a battle on a junk which could have been a scene from the

Douglas Fairbanks movie *The Black Pirate*.

Sir William tried to track Ling Ju Hai but gave up when he heard that she had died while giving birth. This, as it turned out, was a lie originated by the father. Sir William married the daughter of a Dutch merchant on the rebound and then was ordered to South Africa.

Later, Ling Ju Hai and her son returned with her father to Hanoi. The boy grew up to become a master criminal operating under the pseudonym of Hanoi Shan. According to H. Ashton-Wolfe in his *Warped in the Making: Crimes of Love and Hate* (Houghton Mifflin, 1928), Hanoi Shan did not begin his career as a criminal. He had been a tall, good-looking man with a kindly character who was governor of a province in Tonkin-China. While supervising the roundup of wild elephants, he was smashed against a tree by one of the beasts and almost died while in the Saigon hospital. He went to Paris hoping that the surgeons there could repair his twisted spine, but found that they could do nothing for him.

From a likable and virtuous man he changed into a bitter and evil person. He disappeared from the hospital and was not heard of again until the thieves and murderers he had organized began operating. Paris of 1906 was startled and terrified by a series of seemingly impossible homicides and thefts. These were in time traced to the machinations of Hanoi Shan, who was called by the police *l'Araignée*, the Spider.

Hanoi Shan's jobs were so brilliantly sinister and *outré* that some scholars have speculated that he may have been the real-life model for Sax Rohmer's Fu Manchu.

At the time I wrote *Tarzan Alive*, I did not know this. Thus, I am retracting my statement in its Foreword that Fu Manchu was wholly fictional (And, by the way, also my statement that Fu Manchu's great enemy, Sir Denis Nayland Smith, had little foundation in reality.) It is true that Rohmer himself claimed to have got the inspiration for Fu Manchu by a glimpse of a tall old Chinese gentleman and his beautiful young Arabian companion during a foggy Limehouse night. But it has been established that many authors have denied being influenced by, or deriving, their characters and plots from other writers. It is not beyond probability that Rohmer had read Ashton-Wolfe's popular accounts of Hanoi Shan and that an investigation on his own part turned up facts about Hanoi Shan which Ashton-Wolfe had missed. Rohmer knew far more about the tall Chinese gentleman than he let on.

For one thing, it would have been dangerous for him if Fu Manchu (or Hanoi Shan) had suspected that Rohmer had a secret source of information about him. Rohmer probably put forth the fiction about the genesis of his stories and proceeded to exaggerate and distort all his novels about the evil Oriental genius. Fu Manchu (or Hanoi Shan), reading these, must have laughed at their flamboyancy, though he must also have been flattered.

The discrepancy between Ashton-Wolfe's crippled Hanoi Shan and Rohmer's straight-backed Fu Manchu is easily explained. In the twelve years between Hanoi Shan's adventures in Paris and Fu Manchu's appearance in London, Fu Manchu had found a surgeon who could repair his shattered body. Probably, Fu Manchu himself instructed the doctor how to proceed, since this genius had studied the medical arts in the interim.

Ashton-Wolfe said that Hanoi Shan returned to the East, from which a rumor years later claimed that Hanoi Shan had died. This rumor, of course, was originated by Hanoi Shan himself.

It can't be proved that Fu Manchu (or Hanoi Shan) was indeed Sir William Clayton's son. But consider this. Sir William was six feet three inches tall and Ling Ju Hai came of a tall family. Sir William had dark-gray eyes; Ling Ju Hai, brilliant green eyes. There was no genetic bar preventing their son from having his mother's eyes, especially since some of Sir William's ancestors had green eyes, notably his mother. And two of Sir William's sons by other women, Professor Moriarty and John (Colonel) Clay, were giants in their own crooked specialties. Moriarty, like Fu Manchu, was a great scientist who misused his genius.

Readers not acquainted with Rohmer's tales (if such exist) might well ask why a man born in 1840 should be alive and fiendishly active during the twentieth century. The explanation is that Fu Manchu had invented an elixir, the Oil of Life, which considerably delayed aging.

Some scholars will object that there are hints by Rohmer that Fu Manchu was actually an ancient Egyptian pharaoh, Seti I, whose elixir had kept him alive since his supposed death in 1300 B.C.

However, Fu Manchu impressed people as being at least half-Chinese, and the ancient Egyptians were definitely Caucasians, not Mongolians. Moreover, why would he have given up his pharaohship and faked his death? Perhaps he tired of the troublesome career of reigning and went off to study science and magic in the Far East, but this does not seem likely. I think that the overimaginative Rohmer was so struck by the accidental resemblance between Seti I's face and Fu Manchu's that he concocted this fusion of identities.

That Fu Manchu was an old man in 1913 is proved by the fact (according to Rohmer) that he was the governor of the province of Honan under the Empress Dowager Tz'u-hsi (1835–1908). Honan was a very important province, covering the southwestern part of the great plain of north China. It was the main center for the spread of early Sinitic civilization over the rest of China. The empress dowager became a regent for her son in 1861, so that it seems probable that Fu Manchu did not become a governor until about the late 1870s, when he would have been over thirty.

He was also a pretender to the throne of China, since he was a member of the ruling family. This mitigates against his being Seti I, since he would have had to be born a Manchu to be recognized as a prince by right of blood.

Sir William's marriage to Lady Jane Brandon (sixth level) of Brandon Beeches, Oxfordshire, resulted in a daughter, Ultima. In 1898 she married a visiting American, John T. McGee, and went to his Ohio estate to live. Their son's first name is unknown as yet, hence, the "—M."—McGee had two sons, one of whom committed suicide. The other was Travis McGee, gray-eyed amateur detective and troublebuster. His autobiography is being edited by John D. MacDonald.

Travis McGee may be a close relative of Archie Goodwin, Nero Wolfe's Boswell and right-hand man. Archie, like McGee, was born on an Ohio farm, and they have so many physical and mental characteristics in common that they could be first cousins. This possibility, however, will have to be explored at a later date.

Brigadier Gerard (fifth level, center) appears as a minor figure in A. Conan Doyle's *Uncle Bernac* and as the major figure in Doyle's *The Exploits of Brigadier Gerard* and *The Adventures of Gerard*. This dashing soldier of Napoleon married Sybille Bernac, and one of their daughters married a French-speaking Swiss named Delacroix. A descendant, Monique Delacroix (M.D., eighth level), married a Scot from Glencoe, Andrew Bond. Their son was James Bond, immortalized in semifictional form by Ian Fleming. The mother of Andrew Bond was Angela Clayton. She was the daughter of Angela O'Shaughnessy, who was the half-Mexican, half-Irish daughter of a general. After her mother died, Angela Clayton was brought to England by Sir William and raised there.

James Bond, be it noted, could have been Sir James Bond. His rejection of a knighthood had a good precedent in Sherlock Holmes, who also turned down this honor.

At the age of thirty-three, Clayton took to wife Lorina, the daughter of Lord Dacre by Jane Carfax, daughter of Lord Rufton. Both Lord Dacre and Lord Rufton are described in a chapter from Gerard's memoirs, *How He Triumphed in England*. (Gerard was possibly the brother of the Marie Gerard who married Amand Chauvelin.) Lord Rufton was also the grandfather of a major character in one of Holmes's cases, *The Disappearance of Lady Frances Fairfax*. (See also my article, "The Two Lord Ruftons," *The Baker Street Journal*, December 1971, or *The Book of Philip José Farmer*, DAW Books, Fall 1973.)

Lord Dacre was a descendant of the barons of Greystoke, Cumberland. (See Dacre, *Burke's Dormant and Extinct Peerage*.) One of his ancestors was the Earl of Burlesdon, Robert Rassendyll, from whom Rudolf Rassendyll was also descended. (See Hope's *The Prisoner of Zenda* and *Rupert of Hentzau*).

The son of Sir William and Lorina was Phileas Fogg. Three years after he was born (in 1832), his mother divorced Sir William. She remarried the eccentric and wealthy Sir Heraclitus Fogg, baronet, of Fogg Shaw, Derbyshire. The baronet adopted young Phileas and his sister, Roxana, and gave them his name. Adopted sons of baronets can't inherit the title, but Phileas himself became a baronet in 1886 and so, in a sense, continued the line.

As almost everybody knows, Phileas Fogg, at the age of forty, made and won a famous wager. During his eighty-day dash around the world, he met the beautiful Parsee, Aouda Jejeebhoy, a relative of Sir Jamsetjee Jejeebhoy, third baronet. (See Jejeebhoy, *Burke's Peerage*.) Phileas rescued her from being cremated alive and married her. Their daughter, Suzanne, married a captain of the French Foreign Legion, Armand Jacot. He had been born *le Prince de Cadrenet* but had renounced his title.

Susanne and Armand's daughter, Jeanne Jacot, married John Drummond Clayton, the adopted son and cousin of the present Lord Greystoke. He was, as noted in the book in hand, the Flight Lieutenant Clayton whom Doc met during the Argonne operation. (See also *The Son of Tarzan* by Edgar Rice Burroughs, for the story of John Clayton and Jeanne Jacot.)

Phileas' sister, Roxana, had three daughters, Wanda, Isis, and Philea Jane.

One of Wanda's husbands was a ne'er-do-well who claimed to be descended from an illegitimate son of William Blake, the mystic, artist, and poet. This is possible, since William Blake, like Johnny Shawnessy and Sir William Clayton, had a large bump of amativeness. Wanda's husband, William Blake II, was such a rotter and liar, however, that his claim is doubtful. More likely, he was descended from Arthur Blake, one of the two English coachmen present at Wold Newton. This supposition is strengthened by the claim of William Blake that Sexton Blake, the famous detective, was his brother. But, then, William lied a lot.

We do know that William Blake's mother was Jill Fagin, a woman of great beauty but low morals. She seems to have come from a long line of London criminals. One of her great-great-grandfathers was famous for training youths to become self-supporting. The authorities, not caring for the manner in which he ran his school, or its intent, hung him.

After getting into trouble with the law many times, William Blake fled with his wife to Chicago. Their son, Robert Blake, was born there on 5 April 1917. He early exhibited his genius by learning to read at the age of four and starting his studies of Greek and Latin at the age of eight. Though he had a high intelligence, his imagination was overwild, and he lacked mental stability. Like his (supposed) great-grandfather, the poet, he once saw a great face staring through a window at him when he was five. However, where William Blake saw God, Robert Blake saw a hideous monster, a thing from outer space.

Robert's parents disappeared under strange circumstances when he was ten. There is no proof, however, that he did away with them because they had not given him a promised bicycle for Christmas. What happened to him between the ages of ten and sixteen is not known, but he seems to have supported himself by a number of activities, including street-dancing and pick-pocketing.

At the age of seventeen, he was fluent in many obscure languages, self-taught from books stolen from the public libraries and private collections. He had also published short stories in *Outré Tales* magazine, five of which are now classics in their genre. These are *The Burrower Beneath*, *The Stairs in the Crypt*, *Shaggai*, *In the Vale of Pnath*, and *The Feaster from the Stars*. His fiction and his remarkable paintings, the latter all studies of monsters and nonterrestrial landscapes, indicate his unhealthy, perhaps even perverted, interest in the sinister side of the occult.

His researches ended on a stormy night in an old abandoned church on Federal Hill in Providence, Rhode Island, on 8 August 1935. Exactly how he met his horrible fate is unknown, but his diary, ending just before he died, shows that he had a large bump of curiosity. There was not enough left of his head to establish physical evidence for this, however.

Coincidentally, the same man who had written of William Harper Littlejohn's Antarctic expedition (see Chapter 14) also recorded Robert Blake's final exploit. Blake's paintings may be viewed today by certified scholars at Miskatonic University.

Like her sisters, Isis Fogg, married an American (a rich one). Their son, Richard Benson, was another of the famous enemies of crime which so distinguishes the Wold Newton family. He was not a big man, being only five feet eight inches tall and weighing only one hundred and sixty pounds. But his muscles were of a superhuman quality, and these, with his black hair, his cold gray eyes, his unflinching courage, his desire to solve crimes, to see justice done, ensure his membership in the same genetic club as that to which Tarzan, Sherlock Holmes, Bulldog Drummond, Cordwainer Bird, and others belong.

He was an adventurer, a roving business man-engineer, until he got married. He led a quiet life with his wife and young daughter until, on a flight to Montreal, his family disappeared while he was in the lavatory. No one on the airliner admitted that his wife and child had been on it. The shock drove him temporarily insane, turned his hair white, and paralyzed his facial muscles. When Benson recovered his sanity, but not the use of his facial muscles, he swore to avenge his family. Eventually, he determined who the killers were and why they had plotted against him. While doing this, he picked up some aides, and these became part of his organization, Justice, Inc. Benson also discovered that he could mold his dead, but plastic, flesh into new faces, and he used this ability to assume a quick disguise.

Justice, Inc. continued to operate against other criminals, and Benson finally got his black hair and mobile facial features back. Like Doc, he always tried to take the crooks alive. His favorite weapons were a specially designed pistol and knife, affectionately called Mike and Ike. The gun contained four .22 cartridges, the bullets of which unerringly creased the tops of the villains' skulls just enough to knock them out.

The Avenger pulp-lit series was popular, but the paper shortage of World War II forced the end of the magazine featuring his adventures after twenty-four episodes. A few shorter pieces about him did appear in other magazines. In 1972 the reprinting of his exploits by a paperback company was begun. These proved just as popular as in 1939 and the 40's. The original stories have been followed by new stories written by Ron Goulart under the Street and Smith house name of Kenneth Robeson. (Paul Ernst wrote the originals under the same name.) Whether or not they are biographical or fictional has not yet been determined.

Roxana's third daughter, Philea Jane was born when Roxana was forty-three years old. Philea married a wealthy farmer and businessman, Park Joseph Finnegan, and moved to North Terre Haute, Indiana. Park was a handsome and charming man, but he was also a heavy drinker, a compulsive gambler, and what they called in those days a skirt chaser. After losing all his money and property, he deserted his wife and their only child, Paul Janus Finnegan. Paul, after his return from the battlefields of Europe in 1946, became a student at the University of Indiana. While there he was drawn into that series of strange adventures which I have described in my Pocket Universes or Wolff-Kickaha series. These, so far, consist of *The Maker of Universes*, *The Gates of Creation*, *A Private Cosmos*, and *Behind the Walls* *of Terra.** On one level of that ziggurat-planet in a universe next-door to ours, Paul J. Finnegan is known as Kickaha. This means The Trickster, and Kickaha has used this so long that he has almost forgotten his natal name.

Richard Hannay, secret agent and soldier, has narrated his adventures in books edited by John Buchan, Lord Tweedsmuir. These include the famous *The 39 Steps*, *Mr. Standfast*, *Greenmantle*, *The Three Hostages*, *Island of Sheep*, and *The Runagates Club*. Hannay was born in Scotland in 1874 but was taken at the age of six to South Africa. He did not return to his native island until 1914, a few months before the outbreak of World War I.

Richard Hannay's parents were Scots. His mother, Colina Drummond, had married Arthur Hannay when quite young. She was the sister of William Drummond, whose lineage may be seen on the end-paper chart of *Tarzan Alive*. William Drummond was the father of Roger Drummond, whose sons included Hugh "Bulldog" Drummond and John Drummond. The latter was adopted by Lord Greystoke and took the name of John Drummond Clayton.

Colina and William Drummond's father was John Drummond; their mother was Oread Butler, a cousin of the Rhett Butler whose exploits have been narrated by Margaret Mitchell.

John Drummond, Richard Hannay's grandfather, was a son of Sir Hugh Drummond, baronet, and Georgia Dewhurst. Georgia was the sister of Lord Antony Dewhurst, a son of the duke of Exeter and a prominent member of the League of the Scarlet Pimpernel. (The duke of Exeter is not to be confused with the marquess of Exeter, which title is in possession of the family of Cecil. See *Burke's Peerage*.)

Sir Hugh Drummond and his wife were in the group exposed to the radiation from the meteorite at Wold Newton in 1795.

Richard Hannay, having made his pile as a mining engineer, took a trip to London. He had no intention of becoming involved in criminal and intelligence work. But the events of his first adventure (*The 39 Steps*) revealed a flair for solving the unsolvable, for establishing links between things that, to others, seemed entirely unconnected.

---

* *Farmer completed the series with an additional three books:* The Lavalite World, Red Orc's Rage, *and* More Than Fire. *—WSE*

He was, like another man whose early life was molded by South Africa, Allan Quatermain, distrustful of his own abilities and continually being pushed into dirty business he would just as soon have stayed out of. Hannay had a resourcefulness and pluck which, with his reliance on his subconscious, got him through perils which killed others. It is true that he would have failed if he had not had extraordinarily capable comrades, such as "Sandy" Arbuthnot, the sixteenth Baron Clanroyden. And in this dependence he also resembled Quatermain, who would have come to grief many times if it had not been for various courageous and intelligent natives who pulled his fat from the fire. Such were the crafty and brave Hottentot Hans, and, in two of his adventures, Umslopogaas, a black combination of Achilles and Beowulf.

That Hannay's government rated him higher than he did himself is demonstrated by its making him a general and a knight. Those acquainted with British history might object that these honors are not always given to those who deserve them. But the readers of Hannay's exploits know that his services were, in fact, underrated. He should have got a peerage.

If Doc did mount an expedition back to Earth's Center (see Chapter 18), a member of the family might have volunteered, if Doc could have located him. This was Jongor (John Gordon). His father was Captain Robert Gordon, an ex-naval aviator for the United States. Robert Gordon was descended on his mother's side from the ancient Welsh families of Moore and Gronow and on his father's side from the Scots Gordons. One of his ancestors was a Macgregor, the infamous Highlands outlaw, Rob Roy. (Sir Richard Francis Burton was also descended from him.) Robert Gordon was a member of the branch of the house of Earlston, sprung from Alexander, the second son of William de Gordoune, the sixth Lord of Lochinvar. Through this line Robert Gordon was a descendant also of the youth immortalized by Sir Walter Scott. He was related to George Gordon, Lord Byron, through Byron's mother, a daughter of George Gordon of Gight, county Aberdeen, and also through the Reverend Richard Byron, the poet's great-uncle, who married a Mary Farmer.

The mother of William de Gordoune, the sixth Lord of Lochinvar, was Delhi Darcy, who was born in 1825 and married —de Gordoune, the fifth Lord of Lochinvar. Delhi's father was Fitzwilliam Bennet Darcy, and her sister was Athena Darcy.* Fitzwilliam Bennet Darcy was the son of Fitzwilliam Darcy and Elizabeth Bennet, whose circuitous courtship was novelized by Jane Austen in *Pride and Prejudice* (see *Tarzan Alive*).

Fitzwilliam Darcy and his wife Elizabeth Bennet were among those exposed to the ionization of the Wold Newton meteorite in 1795.

Jongor's mother, Elizabeth Rivers, was the daughter of Patrick Rivers and Nyad Drummond. Nyad was the daughter of John Drummond and Oread Butler (see Addendum 2 of *Tarzan Alive* for their genealogy), and the sister of Colina Drummond and William Drummond. Patrick Rivers was the uncle of Patricia Rivers, who married Sir Hector Brandon of Brandon Abbas, Devonshire. Gray eyes seem to have run in this family, if P. C. Wren's *Beau Geste* is to be trusted. As already noted, Sir Hector was a rotter but of the landed gentry.

The career of Professor Moriarty (seventh level, right-hand side) is too well known to be given in detail here. This sinister genius was born as a result of a brief liaison between a housemaid of Irish extraction, Morcar Moriarty, and Sir William Clayton. According to Clayton's memoirs, he supported Morcar and their son handsomely. Morcar had two sons by other men, who also did not marry her. One became a colonel in the Army and the other a stationmaster in the west of England. It is these three unions with different men that account for Professor James Moriarty having an older brother also named James.

Morcar may have passed on evil propensities to the professor from an ancestor, Jonathan Wild (1682?–1725). Wild, like his descendant, the professor, founded and headed a vast organization for criminal purposes. He became wealthy by having his agents steal

---

* *Phil's hand-drawn notes show Delhi Darcy as a direct descendant of Fitzwilliam Darcy and Elizabeth Bennet. Delhi would have to be a granddaughter, not a daughter, of the Darcys. Elizabeth Bennet was born in 1772 (she was not yet twenty-one during most of the events of* Pride and Prejudice, *which takes place September 1792–Late Autumn 1793). Delhi Darcy was born in 1825 and it is unlikely that a fifty-three-year-old woman could bear children in the early 19th century. —WSE*

property and then claim a commission for "recovering" it. Those thieves who refused to work for him he turned in to the police. He provided an alibi with false evidence for his agents if they were arrested, and forged evidence to convict those who would not join his organization. Despite all this, he was eventually hanged.

A sketch of his life is in the *Encyclopaedia Britannica*, and he is depicted in novels by Defoe and Fielding.

When Sherlock Holmes mentioned Jonathan Wild in *The Valley of Fear*, he was thinking not only of the similarity of Moriarty's and Wild's methods and organizations. Moriarty's descent from Wild must also have been in his mind.

Some readers may be surprised to see the name of Captain Nemo in conjunction with that of Moriarty. After all, wasn't Nemo an Asiatic Indian prince, named Dakkar? Didn't Jules Verne describe Nemo's death as an old man on a southwest Pacific island in *The Mysterious Island*? Didn't Moriarty fall to his death during his struggle with Holmes at Reichenbach Falls in Switzerland? So how could Nemo be Moriarty?

Professor H. W. Starr explains how this could be in an article, "A Submersible Subterfuge" (Livingston Publishing Company, Narberth, Pennsylvania, 1959, 1972). In a few incontrovertible words, Starr demonstrates that *The Mysterious Island* was an entirely fictional sequel to the mostly true *Twenty Thousand Leagues Under the Sea*. Readers may check out the original publication dates of these for themselves and determine that Nemo could not have died an old man in the situation and on the date Verne indicates.

In many more words, not quite as disprovable, Starr shows that Moriarty did indeed operate, in his pre-Holmesian career, under the pseudonym of Captain Nemo. This article is reprinted as an addendum to my *The Other Log of Phileas Fogg* (DAW Books, March 1973). The book itself narrates some events of which Verne was not aware when he wrote *Around the World in Eighty Days*. It also clears up the mystery of the *Mary Celeste*, shows that Holmes was not the only Englishman who could defeat Moriarty, and explains why Nemo had black eyes and Moriarty had gray.

To those who object that Nemo was a hero, not a villain, I can only assert here that they are quite mistaken and have not read Verne's account carefully.

Moriarty, when Holmes met him, was an old man, afflicted with a nervous disease which caused his head to oscillate in a repulsive reptilian fashion. Holmes says that he was unmarried, but this does not mean that he had always been. Pierre Aronnax, in *Leagues,* mentions the portrait of Nemo's wife and children hanging on a bulkhead of the *Nautilus.* And it was only natural that the author of the celebrated treatise *The Dynamics of an Asteroid* should name his daughter after the muse of astronomy, Urania.

Before considering Urania Moriarty's two sons, go to Count Cagliostro (fourth level, right-hand side). Giuseppe Balsamo, self-styled Count of Cagliostro (1743–95), was a Sicilian charlatan who gained a wide reputation in Europe. He claimed to be two thousand years old and to have magical powers. His career flourished until 1786, when his involvement in the affair of Marie Antoinette's diamond necklace caused him to be banished by Louis XVI. In Rome, his wife denounced him to the Inquisition as a conjurer of demons, a heretic, and a Freemason, and he died in prison.

If it were not for the *Memoirs of Arsène Lupin* by Maurice Leblanc, we would not be aware that Cagliostro had had a love affair with, and a child by, Josephine de Beauharnais. It was Lupin who found out why Josephine had suddenly and mysteriously fled from Fontaiuebleau. The young girl, separated from her husband, the Vicomte de Beauharnais, had been living in this city not far from Cagliostro's residence. She visited him a number of times, and, like many, fell prey to his hypnotic powers.

Cagliostro disappeared the day before he was to be arrested. The next day, Josephine left. A month later, a child named Josephine (or Josine) was born in Palermo, Cagliostro's birthplace. A birth register gives the child's name as Josephine Balsamo, daughter of Joseph Balsamo, and of a Frenchwoman, Josephine de la P. (De Beauharnais' maiden name was de la Pagerie.)

Josephine de Beauharnais later married the Emperor Napoleon. In 1798 she brought to him a young girl whom she said was her goddaughter. When Napoleon fell, this Josephine Balsamo went to Czar Alexander II's court, where she called herself the Countess Cagliostro.

Lupin's memoirs state that she still looked like a young woman in 1892. This doesn't seem likely, even though she did claim that her father's secret elixir had kept her youthful. On the other hand, if Tarzan, Doc Savage, and Fu Manchu can have such elixirs, why not Josephine Balsamo?

Whether it was the original Josephine Balsamo or her daughter, she met Sir William Clayton in his old, but very virile, old age, and had a child by him. Josephine was as likely as an alley cat to drop her progeny, and in this case left her son Paul in the care of an English couple named Finglemore. When she did not return to claim him, the Finglemores adopted him.

Paul Finglemore's brilliant if checkered criminal career is told in a very amusing novel, *An African Millionaire* (1898) by Grant Allen. In this book, Finglemore, a master of disguises and of confidence tricks, operates under many names. But he was known to the police of England and Europe as Colonel Clay.

As John Clay, he was apprehended by Sherlock Holmes (in *The Red-Headed League*). He went to prison but must have escaped to resume his career as Colonel Clay. Once more he was jailed, but the prison wasn't built then (or now) that could hold the grandson of Count Cagliostro and the son of Sir William Clayton (who escaped his captors a dozen times, according to his memoirs).

John Clay, according to Sherlock Holmes, was the grandson of a royal duke. If this were true, his great-grandfather would have been George III of Great Britain. But recent evidence indicates that George III's sons were not as irresponsible and as horny as some have made them out to be. Probably, Clay (or Finglemore) lied about this as he lied about so many things. The weight of evidence indicates that Colonel John Clay/Paul Finglemore was the son of Sir William Clayton and Josephine Balsamo.

One of Clay's beautiful young inamoratas and accomplices was Urania Moriarty. Her heredity and environment ensured that she, too, would be a master of disguise and confidence games. She and Clay (or Finglemore) had two sons who were geniuses in their own dark professions: Doctor Caber and Carl Peterson. These used their true names no more than their parents had. The doctor took the maiden name of his grandmother, Moriarty's wife, which may indicate that he was raised by her. (Some of Doctor Caber's exploits are described by Joseph Jorkens.) Like his grandfather, Caber was a scientist of genius. He outsmarted himself when he found out he could affect the moon's orbit and tried to extort money from the British Government with this threat. He was sentenced to five years in prison on another charge, but the government intended to keep him locked up until he was dead. Whether or not he escaped is not known at present.

The readers of the Bulldog Drummond series by H. C. McNeile know that Carl Peterson was the greatest villain Drummond ever encountered. Peterson was about five times as intelligent as Drummond, but he kept tripping himself up because he expected Drummond to do the sneaky and the devious. Drummond wasn't bright enough for this; he always did the obvious. Besides, they had a mutual, if unconscious, liking for each other, which may explain why they didn't kill each other when each had so many opportunities.

We readers were saddened when Carl Peterson seemed to have perished in a flaming dirigible, caught in his own trap. But Gerard Fairlie, who continued the Drummond series, revealed in the final one, *The Return of the Black Gang*, that Peterson was alive and well, though not good. Peterson failed once again to kill Drummond but escaped once again. What happened thereafter has not been recorded. But both Bulldog Drummond and Carl Peterson were getting old and tired. It may be that both just decided to retire.

Irma, Carl's wife or mistress, was every bit as villainous and innovative as Carl. It was she who kept the feud going while Carl was convalescing from the dirigible disaster or else just engaged in his rotten, but colossal, projects elsewhere. Irma seems a fit candidate for inclusion in the Wold Newton family. Carl posed as Irma's father during some of their nefarious activities, so I wouldn't be surprised if she really was his daughter. Incest certainly would not have been below them; they tackled with enthusiasm anything wicked.

Simon Templar, the Saint, seems another candidate for this family. But he, Sexton Blake, and Doctor Thorndyke will be dealt with elsewhere, along with Arsène Lupin and M. Lecoq.

In *Tarzan Alive* I speculated that Richard Wentworth (the Spider), G-8 (the famous aviator-spy of World War I), and Kent Allard (the Shadow) were not three different people. My theory was that they were actually distinct personae, personalities, of the same schizophrenic man, Richard Wentworth. So many people (letter writers and telephoners from all over the country) were so disturbed by this theory that I decided to reconsider the evidence. A minute inquiry into the chronologies of the terrible trio convinced me that my theory was invalid. Though G-8's career seems to have ended with World War I, the Shadow and the Spider operated at about the same time. Kent Allard, as the Shadow, started his career in early 1931 or, at least, this is when his deeds were first recorded. Actually, he had been fighting crime in New York at an undetermined time before this. And we know from several references he dropped to his aides that he had been an aviator and spy during World War I. He had served the Czar of All the Russias as a mercenary during the first years of the war, served so well that the Czar gave him a Romanov family heirloom, a huge girasol or fire-ring, an opal that gave out varying colors depending upon the angles at which it reflected light. This ring was one of Allard's character tags, along with the big black broad-brimmed slouch hat, long black cloak, two .45 automatics, maniacal laugh, mastery at disguise, and superstealthiness. His best known, or most frequently recurring disguise was that of Lamont Cranston, wealthy playboy. Many people believe that that was the Shadow's real name. However, there was a Lamont Cranston who spent much time abroad and who had agreed to let Allard assume his identity when he wasn't in town. Sometimes, Allard disguised himself as Cranston when Cranston was in town and so had an unbreakable alibi.

Allard, as Cranston, palled around a lot with beautiful Margo Lane (who may have been the sister of Lois Lane, *objet d'amour* of Clark Kent). In none of the Shadow stories is there even a hint that Allard was sexually interested in Margo. Or, for that matter, in any woman. If this was true, then Allard was either a homosexual, impotent, or both. Or a Roman Catholic priest. The latter suggestion can be immediately dismissed since the Shadow would have had to terminate his outlaw activities after his first confession of such. However, the writers of the Shadow's adventures (chiefly Walter Gibson) depended upon him for information, and he saw no reason to let them know what was going on between him and Margo. Moreover, the readers of the Shadow stories did not (in the main) like their heroes to have a realistic love interest, and so the writers would have deleted any such interest from their stories.

It is true that the Spider, Richard Wentworth, and his female aide, Nita Van Sloan, were in love. But there is no indication by the writers that they ever exchanged more than a few kisses.

That Margo was more to Allard than just an aide is proved by the birth of their son, Kent Lane. (See my short story, "Skinburn", in *The Book of Philip José Farmer*, and my forthcoming novel, *Why Everybody Hates Me*.) Kent Lane became a crime fighter, too, but he operated (mostly) within the requirements of the law. Apparently, Margo Lane and Kent Allard never got married, though they may have omitted getting a license because of security reasons. The Shadow wanted nothing to exist which might prove to some vengeful crook that he had more than a casual relationship with Margo.

The Spider, Richard Wentworth, had been an artillery officer during World War I. As a young man he had visited India, where he became adept in Hindu mysticism and fakiry. He became involved in battling evildoers when he helped a college professor, Brownlee, who was in deep trouble with the underworld. Once launched on his career, Wentworth adopted the device of stamping the foreheads of criminals he killed with the seal of a crimson spider. This seal was hidden within a specially built cigarette lighter. Wentworth was far more bloodthirsty than the Shadow, and he would have scorned Doc Savage's thesis that the best way to handle criminals was to capture and then rehabilitate them. The only good crook was a dead crook, according to Wentworth, and he saw to it that the streets and the backrooms of New York City were littered with good crooks.

From 1933 through 1943 he was engaged in one hundred and eighteen exploits. These kept him going night and day, and so, when one considers that, in the same length of time, the Shadow was putting in nigh twenty-four hours a day in two hundred and sixty adventures, it's demonstrable that one man with two split personalities would have had some difficulties. More than some: insuperable.

I still maintain, however, that the genealogy given for Richard Wentworth in *Tarzan Alive* is the true one. He is a direct descendant of Lord Byron through the 12th Baron of Wentworth, and his father was Lord John Roxton, the South-Americanomaniac and mighty hunter of A. C. Doyle's *The Lost World* et al.

The genealogy (see pages xviii-xxi) contains the results of my revised theory. Part of it was suggested to me by Mr. Stephen Kallis, who theorized that the Spider and the Shadow were brothers. The kill-crazy Spider was somewhat mentally unbalanced because of his jealousy of his older brother, the Shadow. This was a stimulating and somewhat valid idea, but I have adapted it to fit the facts.

Wentworth's mother was Rhoda Delagardie, great-granddaughter of Sir Percy Blakeney, the Scarlet Pimpernel. (See *Tarzan Alive* for details.) She first married, briefly, Lord John Roxton, and bore a son, Richard Wentworth. (Lord John Roxton's family name was Wentworth.) She divorced Lord John, whose main passion was hunting and exploring, and she married Ralph Rassendyll. Ralph was a cousin of Rudolf Rassendyll, the hero of *The Prisoner of Zenda* and *Rupert of Hentzau*. Both were descended from Robert, Earl of Burlesdon. (The main chart shows that the earl was also the ancestor of Lorina Dacre, mother of Phileas and Roxana Fogg.)

Some will object that Lorina, Rudolf, and Ralph could not have been descended from the earl. *The Prisoner of Zenda* makes it clear that there was a scandal in the family of 1733, when George II ruled Great Britain. Prince Rudolf of the tiny Central European state of Ruritania visited England. He and Countess Amelia, wife of the fifth Earl of Burlesdon, had an affair. The fifth earl fought a duel with Prince Rudolf and wounded him so severely that the prince withdrew from the affair and the country. Though unwounded, the earl caught a severe cold during the damp and chilly dawn in which he crossed swords with the prince. He died of complications six months later. His wife bore a boy who was unmistakably Rudolf's two months after her husband died.

This event would seem to break the Rassendyll lineage genetically, though not legally. But what Anthony Hope does not record in either of his two accounts of Rudolf Rassendyll is that Amelia was also descended from Robert, first earl of Burlesdon, seventeenth Baron Rassendyll. She was the fifth earl's second cousin, descended, like him, from the third earl.

Ralph Rassendyll took his wife and her son Richard to the States to manage the American affairs of a great British firm. While in New York Rhoda bore him Allard Kent, Bruce Hagin, and Rhonda. These, along with Richard, became American citizens after the death of Ralph. Whatever the reasons, genetics or sibling rivalry or both, all three grew up to become masters of disguise and hunters of men who deserved to be hunted.

Bruce, the only one who had a license to kill, used the code name of G-8. If Robert J. Hogan, who wrote about G-8's adventures, knew his true name, he did not reveal it.

The Shadow twice revealed to others his real name. He said that it was Kent Allard, but even then he was not being wholly truthful. Obviously, he rearranged the sequence of his first two names and dropped the third. He was not one to trust wholly anybody. Even if he had, he would not have wanted his enemies to torture his name from those who knew. As it was, though, he was supposed to have crashed years before in a Central American jungle and to have died there.

Rhonda did not engage in flamboyant outlawry, but she was a family black sheep. Despite her parents' objections, she married Jason Bird, a part-Jewish acrobat and vaudeville-night club comedian. Her father refused to see her again and, indeed, his death soon after she left home was attributed to shock and grief at her marriage.

Jason's father was Richard Cordwainer Bird, an Irish photographer. His mother was Millicent, daughter of a Dublin Jew, Leopold Bloom. (See James Joyce's *Ulysses* for a perhaps overly detailed account of Bloom. See also *Tarzan Alive* for his relationship to the Greystokes, of whom Tarzan is the most outstanding member.)

Jason and Rhonda's only child was Cordwainer Bird. Cordwainer was born in 1934 in Painesville, Ohio in a rooming house near a theater. (Not, as some maintain, in the women's room of the theater.) Cordwainer grew up in Ohio, though not very far. His growth stopped when he reached the height of four feet. Sam Minostentor, a science-fiction scholar, claims in Volume II of his massive *Reachers for the Future* that Bird's lack of physical stature accounts for Bird's demonic drive to succeed, to lift himself by the bootstraps of fame and fortune above the heads of his fellow men. "Cordwainer was extremely short, like the Nome King of the Oz tales," Minostentor writes, "but like the Nome King he had exceedingly great ambitions. He, too, sallied forth from the dark underground to conquer all, but, unlike his Ozian counterpart, he wasn't afraid of eggs. Cordwainer wasn't afraid of anything—unless it was failure. It is this drive that has caused more than one person to describe him as 'an elemental force,' 'a hurricane in hush puppies.' When TV producers and directors ruined his scripts, he punched them in the mouth and went on to write science-fiction. He has gathered together more awards,

Hugos and Nebulas, in that field than any other writer. He has won the Edgar award from the Mystery Writers of America. He plans to cap his career with the Nobel Prize for Literature, though it's doubtful that this will happen, since he's punched so many publishers in the mouth."

The above was published in 1972. Since then Cordwainer Bird has become a mainstream novelist and a militant foe of evil. Though he is nowhere near as tall as his ancestors and relatives, the Scarlet Pimpernel, Rudolf Rassendyll, the Shadow, Doc Savage, et al., he has their heroic spirit and their dedication to fighting wickedness. But, unlike these heroes of an earlier age, who fought to preserve The Establishment, he fights to destroy The Establishment. One of The Establishments, anyway.

Harlan Ellison, in "The New York Review of Bird" (see *Weird Heroes*, or The New American Pulp Hero, Byron Preiss, editor, Pyramid, 1975), writes of Bird's first campaign in this war. When Bird decided to become a mainstream writer, he found himself up against that supervillain, the New York Literary Establishment. This was dominated by writers and publishers who had made their fame and fortune by counterfeiting emotion and destroying the imagination. Their books, though best sellers, read as if written by a computer, a computer powered on hokum. Perhaps they were best sellers for this very reason.

But Bird wanted to write books with genuine emotions, genuine people, and he wanted to fire the public's imagination. Frustrated by The Establishment, balked at every turn by its subtle and sinister machinations, he became, in effect, a new pulp-age hero. He was well-equipped, despite his tiny stature, for this demanding role. He had exceptionally powerful muscles, he had learned the art of Jeet Kune Do (one of his fellow students was Bruce Lee), and he had the genius of his uncles when it came to foiling evil people. In a desire to emulate the ability of his uncle, the Shadow, to cloud men's minds, he had studied the White House statements re Watergate and the techniques of Billy Graham and Oral Roberts.

Also, he had picked up a lot of pointers from reading *The Batman* comics when he was a youth.

And so this man, only four feet high, with a face like a handsome eagle's, with straight black hair, and eyes of robin's-egg blue which radiated the charisma of a Napoleon Bonaparte, ripped off the rippers-off.

I should also mention that another science-fiction author, Jonathan Swift Somers III (whose stories are described by Kilgore Trout in his *Venus on the Half-Shell*) intends to narrate some adventures of Cordwainer Bird. Bird, after his conquest of the secret rulers of New York, fell in with Ralph von Wau Wau. Ralph was a German shepherd whose intelligence had been artificially raised in a Hamburg laboratory to the level of *Homo sapiens*. (About equal to Sherlock Holmes', in fact.) Tired of working for the Hamburg police, Ralph quit to become a private eye. And while in Venice (see "The Doge Whose Barque Was Worse Than His Bight") Ralph and Bird became good friends. Later, they moved into the same apartment in Los Angeles, and they became colleagues in the incessant war against evil.

In several of their cases Bird, because of his smallness, was able to ride Ralph out of grave peril. In one of their cases, it was vice versa.

Addendum 2

CHRONOLOGY

A REALISTIC chronology of Doc Savage's life does not correspond exactly with the sequence of the stories published in the *Doc Savage* magazines. A study of the supersagas and their interrelationships shows that Lester Dent (and his aides Donovan, Hathway, and Bogart) did not attempt to write Doc's adventures in the order in which they actually occurred. Nor were all the adventures that Doc had experienced written by Dent and aides. Doc must have engaged in a number of exploits before he teamed up with The Famous Five. We know from *The Purple Dragon* that Doc's "college" was operating before the events related in *The Man of Bronze*. Evidently, his fight against evil had started shortly after he got his M.D. This must have been as early as 1927, when Doc was only twenty-six or twenty-seven years old.

Dent seems to have had little information about the pre-1927 years. He started his detailed stories of Doc with the supersaga that began three weeks after the elder Savage's death in February 1931. Only then did Doc really get going, and he could do this because he had five near-supermen to assist him. Dent adhered to a strict chronology only in the first three supersagas: *The Man of Bronze*, *The Land of Terror*, and *Quest of the Spider*. After these, he wrote whatever supersaga struck his fancy at the moment. He wrote these from rather sparse notes sent to him by Doc, Monk, or Ham. Monk seems to have done most of the note-taking, and Monk never lacked flamboyancy. Dent was forced to fill in the large gaps from his imagination, which was considerable. Dent was also forced by the pulp-magazine requirements to pour the hot fluidity of the supersagas into certain cooling molds. Dent's high imagination plus the pulp-magazine format plus Monk's exaggerated accounts made for stories that sometimes border on the incredible, if indeed they do not sometimes step over the border.

Nor did Dent mind writing completely fictional stories about Doc. The New York World's Fair of 1939 seemed like a good place for Doc to have an adventure, so Dent wrote *The World's Fair Goblin*. This came out in the April 1939, issue. However, the World's Fair did not open until April 30, 1939.

Apparently, Doc did not object to entirely fictitious stories about him. If anything, he may have approved, since these strengthened the idea that Doc was a fictional character. We know that Doc did not altogether approve of the stories written by Dent. *No Light to Die By* (May–June 1947), contains a unique item—a memo from Doc himself. In it, he criticizes somewhat disparagingly Dent's "fictionalized versions." He felt that Dent exaggerated too much and too often. Neither he nor his aides were as supermannish as Dent had portrayed them in the earlier stories.

The editorial page of the May–June 1947, issue also quotes from Dent's old notebook. "*This thing started Nov. 12, 1932.* This brusque notation, so it happens, was made the day the writing of the first Doc Savage novel began…"

This notation would seem to be authentic. However, Dent did not have the notebook in front of him when he quoted the line to his editor. He was relying on his memory, which, while phenomenally good, was not perfect. I have seen the old notebook, and the entry reads: "This thing started December 10, 1932." Dent was actually thinking of Doc's birth date, November 12, when he told the editor about the first day of writing *The Man of Bronze*. In a sense, though, Dent was right. As a literary figure, Doc was born on December 10, 1932.

In working out the chronology of a real-life person, it's axiomatic that an event must occur before it can be written about. Thus, the events of *The Man of Bronze* had to take place before December 10, 1932. But when did they occur? *The Man of Bronze* itself contains no date for reference, and the weather data is so unspecific that it could be any time of the year except the dead of winter. It is raining, and Doc and pals don't put on heavy coats when they venture out into New York City's night air. But anyone acquainted with the vagaries of New York City weather knows that it may rain there in early or late winter. That Doc's group doesn't put on warm clothing means little. Dent often fails to describe their doing so even when he's stated that it's coldest winter.

The Land of Terror, which immediately follows the first story, takes place in spring. So *The Man of Bronze* is set either in the spring or at the very tag-end of winter. Did these two supersagas take place in early 1932 or even before then? The way to find out, the first step, is to read the supersagas, starting from *The Man of Bronze*, until you come to a definite date. The thirty-fifth story, *Murder Mirage* (January 1936), is the first to give this. It is July 4, and the events of this story start a little while before midnight of July 5. Even then, the year is not specified. But this supersaga has to have occurred in 1935. It can't have occurred after January 1936. Counting backwards for seventeen stories to *Fear Cay* (September 1934) and eighteen to *The Squeaking Goblin* (August 1934), we come to a definite date for a year. Both of these stories, from the textual evidence, had to have taken place in 1934. In *The Squeaking Goblin*, Renny comments that the publication date of a book is 1834. Doc adds that that was one hundred years ago. And in *Fear Cay*, old Dan Thunden, born in 1803, is 131 years old "to this day." Since these two stories were published in August and September, respectively, of 1934, they must have actually taken place at least three months before those dates. The issues of the magazine were usually dated a month before they appeared on the stands. It took a minimum of a month and a half to produce an issue after the manuscript was turned in.

The Squeaking Goblin starts out at Bar Harbor, Maine, a summer resort for yachtsmen. The "summer resort" of Aquatania Hall is going full-blast. All indications are that it is well into summer. These include the many boats of the "summer visitors." Yet the supersaga must have occurred before July because of the above-stated publishing restrictions. It cannot have occurred in the "summer."

How can these contradictory data be reconciled? Or at least explained? It's reasonable to postulate that *The Squeaking Goblin* actually took place in warm weather. But it must have been in very early May. The "summer visitors" must have been the early birds, the very rich who can afford to take holidays before the beaches and the hotels are spoiled by *hoi polloi*. Or, perhaps, there were not so many people around at Bar Harbor at that time. Dent may have been adding some details just to make a lively, colorful, more "authentic," background.

After reworking the chronology twelve times, it suddenly became evident that the whole month of June was, after all, open in 1934. The two stories can be slipped into early June. This leaves barely enough time for them to be reported to Dent and for him to write them. Inasmuch as he could write a complete supersaga in three or four days, there was enough time.

One of the problems is finding enough time between a story and the previous one when it's stated that Doc has been away in the interim at the Fortress of Solitude. Thus, between *The Land of Terror* and *Quest of the Spider*, Doc was at the Fortress. The most time he can be allowed for his stay there is from May 12 to May 31. His usual six-months' stay just won't fit into the allotted time. In fact, at no place in the series, except from October 1932 through April 1933, and after 1945, is there time for Doc to be absent for half a year. However, he could have been at the Fortress during the 140 days I allotted to *The Red Terrors* in the original edition of this biography. Since then, I've reclassified this preposterous tale as fictional.

According to my chronology, only one supersaga occurred during 1933. This was *Meteor Menace*. It begins with the Doc's dedication of the hospital he had decided to build in *The Man Who Shook the Earth*. The latter story was in the February 1934 issue; the former, in the March 1934 issue. The sequence of one immediately after the other gives the impression that the events of one followed the other. But obviously this could not have happened. It takes time to build a large hospital. Since *The Man Who Shook the Earth* probably occurred in December 1932, *Meteor Menace* is arbitrarily placed in July or August 1933. If this guess is correct, Doc could have been in the Fortress of Solitude from January through June 1933, and for the rest of the year after August he might have been working in his eighty-sixth-floor laboratory or undertaken some adventures which Dent failed to narrate.

The Polar Treasure was published in the June 1933 issue. It contains references to the Sharkey-Schmeling fight (June 1932), and New York City's new mayor. The latter would be John P. O'Brien, specially elected in early 1933 to fill out Walker's unexpired term. These references thus place *The Polar Treasure* after these events. The only place

The Polar Treasure can be fitted into without violating chronological requirements is the thirty-five-day period in June and July of 1932. Thus, this supersaga, though fourth in publication, was actually eighteenth in occurrence.

Pirate of the Pacific states that it begins the same day *The Polar Treasure* ends. And *The Phantom City* has to follow *Pirate of the Pacific* in actuality even if it follows *The Czar of Fear* in publication sequence.

Patricia Savage appears in both *The Fantastic Island* and *The Feathered Octopus*. Pat is first met in *Brand of the Werewolf*, so the two above have to follow this. *The Fantastic Island* was in the December 1935, issue, and *The Feathered Octopus* was in the October 1937, issue. In fitting these two into slots which agree in chronology and weather data, it's necessary to place *The Feathered Octopus* before *The Fantastic Island*. One of the datum requiring this is the reference in *The Feathered Octopus* to "occasional butterflies." This removed it from its original placement in September to a slot in early June.

The magazine versions in the early years ended with hints of the subject of the next issue and stated that the next issue was the immediate sequel in time. These are often just advertising blurbs inserted at the end of the supersagas by the editors. An examination of the chronological data of these stories indicates that this must have been the case. However, wherever possible I have accepted these blurbs.

Another problem is accounting for the time spent by members of The Famous Five when they are absent from a supersaga. Frequently, only two or three of Doc's pals are actively engaged in battling the current king of crime. The location of the others is usually referred to, however. Thus, Dent will remark that Renny is off in Africa or China building a road or dam; Long Tom is in England on a government electronic project; Johnny is in South America on an archaeological expedition. The times for these absences have to be fitted into the chronology. It is obvious that none of The Five ever see any project through from beginning to end. There just is not enough time between supersagas for them to do this. So, Renny does not actually build a railroad or a dam in foreign lands, nor does Johnny personally supervise the digging of an Inca site from the first shovelful to the last. Nor does Monk see to the entire reconstruction of a chemical plant in post-World War II Germany.

All of The Five are on these projects as consultants for special problems. Like lightning, they fly in from the dark, blaze briefly but illuminatingly, and fly back into the dark. Often they must have flown halfway around the world to look over a situation, clear up the trouble, and fly back to New York City in time for the next adventure.

I hope I have indicated enough to give the reader an idea of what is involved in constructing this chronology. The complexities of fitting 181 adventures into a span of time from 1931 through 1948 have caused me much trouble and time. The chronology you see here is the twelfth reworking. I believe I can justify every placement of a supersaga. To explain in detail would, however, take at least twenty thousand words, and only the most zealous Savageologist would care to tackle an essay of that length.

The remarks in brackets indicate some of the data I used for chronologizing. Those in quotation marks are the words of Dent or the other authors; those not in quotes are my own comments based on the work cited.

The Monsters, *Land of Always-Night*, *Land of Long Juju*, *The Red Terrors*, and *The World's Fair Goblin* are not included in this chronology. They are entirely fictional.

TABLE OF CHRONOLOGY

1901

May 18	Clark Savage, Sr., and his wife Arronaxe flee from England after the events described by Watson in his *The Adventure of the Priory School*.
July	On the way to western Canada to visit his uncle, Alex Wildman, he meets in Quebec his cousin, Edward Land, and the zoologist Hubert Robertson. The four ostensibly go looking for rare fish in the Caribbean but actually are treasure hunting.
September	They find a sunken Spanish galleon which yields each of them $50,000 after the British Government takes its cut. They look for more treasure, but if they find it they don't report it.
November 12	Clark Savage, Jr. (James Clarke Wildman, Jr.), is born on the schooner *Orion* in a cove off the northern tip of Andros Island, Bahamas, during a stormy night.

1902

Doc's mother drowns when the *Orion* sinks. Doc's father, still guilt-ridden by Heidegger's murder and the kidnaping of his young half-brother, vows to make up for these deeds. He dedicates his son to a life of battling against evil.
He settles down in New York, invests his money, and plans his son's unique education. He also enters premedical school himself.

1903

March	Savage, Jr.'s, training begins at the age of fourteen months.

1909

Savage, Sr., gets his M.D.

1911

Savage, Sr., and Hubert Robertson find the valley of gold in Central America.

1914

Savage, Jr.'s, cousin, Patricia Savage, is born.

1917

Savage, Jr., passes all entrance examinations and enters Johns Hopkins in midterm.

April 7 — Lying about his age, sixteen-year-old Savage, Jr., enlists in the Army Air service.

1918

March — Savage, Jr., is captured by the Germans after being shot down while balloon busting.

April — In German prison camp *Loki*, meets Mayfair, Brooks, Renwick, Littlejohn, and Roberts.

July — Savage, Jr., and five friends escape and rejoin their outfits.

September–November — Savage, Jr., flies during the Argonne operation. Savage, Jr., meets his cousin, Flight Lieutenant John Drummond Clayton.

1919

February — Savage, Jr., returns to college.

Summer — Savage, Jr., has a reunion with his five friends and introduces them to his father, who is now a famous surgeon and explorer.

1926

Savage, Jr., gets his M.D.

1927

Doc Savage discovers how to "cure" criminals with a brain operation.

1928

With his father's money, Doc establishes the secret upstate New York "college" for the curing and vocational education of criminals.

1929

The elder Savage, operating through figureheads, begins the building of the Empire State Building.

1930

December — The elder Savage moves into the "eighty-sixth" floor before the building is quite completed.

1932

February — The elder Savage is murdered three weeks before *The Man of Bronze* begins.

Late March–middle April (25 days) — *The Man of Bronze*

Middle April–middle May (27 days) — *The Land of Terror* ["spring"]

Last two weeks of May — Doc is at the Fortress of Solitude. [Statement in *Quest of the Spider*]

Early June (7 days) — *Quest of the Spider*

June (4 days) — *The Red Skull*

July (23 days) — *The King Maker*

August (8 days) — *The Thousand-Headed Man*

August (13 days) — *The Lost Oasis*

September (28 days) — *The Sargasso Ogre*

October (4 days) — *The Czar of Fear*

November (8 days) — *The Mystery on the Snow*

1932

March (40 days) — *The Phantom City*

1932

February– Early April (9 days)	*Brand of the Werewolf*
April 12–April 22 (11 days)	*The Feathered Octopus* ["spring"; "Tuesday"]
Early June (2 days)	*The Roar Devil* ["apple orchard... in bloom... in the mountainous section of New York State"]
June (10 days)	*Quest of Qui* ["early summer"; but also "spring"]
June–July (35 days)	*The Polar Treasure*
July–August (22 days)	*Pirate of the Pacific*
September (27 days)	*The Spook Legion*
October (2 days)	*The Secret in the Sky*
December (6 days)	*The Man Who Shook the Earth* ["In New York, it was winter"; "snow"]

1933

January–June	Doc is at the Fortress of Solitude.
July–August (50 days)	*Meteor Menace*
August–December	Unwritten adventure, or Doc Savage is working in his eighty-sixth floor laboratory.

1934

January–May	Same as above.
Early June (7 days)	*The Squeaking Goblin* ["The Life and Horrible Deeds of That Adopted Moor, Black Raymond" (published in 1834) "One hundred years ago"]
June (4 days)	*Fear Cay* [Thunden was born in 1803 and is 131 years old—"to this day."]
Middle July (2 days)	*Death in Silver*
Early August (3 days)	*The Sea Magician*
Early October (10 days)	*The Fantastic Island*

1934

Late October
(2 days)

The Annihilist ["first chilly day of fall"]

Early November
15 days)

The Mystic Mullah

Late December
(10 days)

Red Snow ["December day"]

1935

January
(7 days)

Dust of Death [It's hot summer in the southern hemisphere, so it must be winter in New York.]

March
(29 days)

The Majii

Early May
(15 days)

Spook Hole ["late spring"]

Middle May
(5 days)

Murder Melody

Latest May
(3 days)

The Men Who Smiled No More

Early June
(3 days)

The Black Spot

Early June
(2 days)

The Midas Man

Late June
(3 days)

Cold Death

July 5–July 13
(9 days)

Murder Mirage ["In... minutes... July 5th"]

September
7–October 16
(40 days)

Mystery Under the Sea [It begins the "first Saturday of September."]

Middle October
(5 days)

The Vanisher ["early fall issue of a magazine"]

Late October
(3 days)

The Metal Master ["cold"; "sleeting"]

November
4–November 8
(5 days)

The Seven Agate Devils [It begins on a "Monday."]

Middle November
(7 days)

Haunted Ocean ["winter air"]

1935

Late November– early February (1936) (82 days)	*The South Pole Terror* ["The South Pole summer was just beginning."]

1936

Late November (1935)–early February	*The South Pole Terror*
February–March (57 days)	*Resurrection Day*
Late April (6 days)	*The Derrick Devil* ["insects"; "birds"]
Late April–early May (7 days)	*The Terror in the Navy* ["green shrubbery"]
Early May (3 days)	*Mad Eyes*
Early May (5 days)	*Land of Fear*
Middle May (19 days)	*He Could Stop the World*
Late May–July (55 days)	*Ost*
Late July–middle August (38 days)	*Repel* (Bantam reprint title: *The Deadly Dwarf*)
Late August–early September (17 days)	*The Sea Angel*
September (6 days)	*The Golden Peril*
September (2 days)	*The Living-Fire Menace*
September (13 days)	*Devil on the Moon*
October (15 days)	*The Munitions Master*
October (12 days)	*The Motion Menace*

1936

Early November–early December (33 days)	*The Submarine Mystery*
December (8 days)	*The Mental Wizard* ["winter in New York"]
Late December (4 days)	*The Green Death* [It's hot in South America, so it's probably winter in New York.]

1937

February (4 days)	*The Yellow Cloud*
February (5 days)	*The Freckled Shark*
February (5 days)	*Merchants of Disaster*
March 15– March 27 (13 days)	*The Pirate's Ghost* [It begins "March 15."]
Early April (6 days)	*The Crimson Serpent*
April (3 days)	*The Spotted Men*
April (3 days)	*The Boss of Terror*
July 12–July 14 (3 days)	*The Mountain Monster* [It begins "July 12."]
Late July (4 days)	*Tunnel Terror*
August (25 days)	*Fortress of Solitude*
September (20 days)	*The Flaming Falcons*
October (18 days)	*The Devil Genghis*
Late October (3 days)	*The Evil Gnome* ["early winter"—when Doc enters the case]
First Week of November (7 days)	*The Stone Man* [Ham: "They bet me Harvard wouldn't win last Saturday."—Oct. 30, Harvard beat Princeton 34–6.]

1937

Early December through most of March (1938) (140 days)	Unwritten adventures

1938

Through late March	Same as above
April (18 days)	*The Giggling Ghosts*
April (9 days)	*The Other World*
Early June (6 days)	*Hex* ["lilac time in New England"]
June (15 days)	*The Gold Ogre*
July (5 days)	*The Angry Ghost* ["summer"]
Early July–late August (42 days)	*Mad Mesa* ["summer sun"]
September 4–October 24 (51 days)	*Poison Island* ["September 4"]
Late October– November (34 days)	*The Dagger in the Sky* ["a late fall day"]

1939

April–early May (40 days)	*The Awful Dynasty*
May (15 days)	*The Men Vanished*
June (3 days)	*The Pink Lady*
June (8 days)	*The Flying Goblin*

1939

August 1– August 3 (3 days)	*The Purple Dragon* "August 1, 1940"; this story came out in August, 1940, as the September, 1940, issue. Obviously, the quoted year must be wrong. There wasn't time for the adventure to have happened in August 1940, to have been written by Dent, and printed.
Part of July	Doc is on an unspecified mission.
Late July–August (36 days)	*Devils of the Deep*
Late August (11 days)	*The Awful Egg*
September– middle December (109 days)	*The Golden Man* [Ham and Monk are in a South American jail for fourteen weeks.]

1940

March (3 days)	*The All-White Elf*
March (2 days)	*The Mindless Monsters*
April (5 days)	*Birds of Death*
Early June (5 days)	*The Invisible-Box Murders*
Early June (4 days)	*The Devil's Playground* ["summer"]
Middle June (4 days)	*The Green Eagle*
July (3 days)	*Mystery Island*
August (10 days)	*Bequest of Evil* ["August"]
September 1–September 5 (5 days)	*The Headless Men* ["fingernail moon"—the new moon was September 1.]
November 12– November 14 (3 days)	*Peril in the North* ["a birthday party for Doc"—this is November, but there is "a lawn that needed mowing"; this indicates only that the lawn has been neglected for a long time; the weather is not hot.]

1940

Rest of November– February (1941)	Doc is busy designing airplanes for the U. S. Government.

1941

Early March– middle April (47 days)	*The Magic Forest* ["cold chill of spring"]
May 10–May 11 (2 days)	*The Rustling Death* ["May 10"]
Late June (12 days)	*The Laugh of Death* ["hot summer afternoon"]
July (12 days)	*Pirate Isle*
July (6 days)	*The Speaking Stone*
August (3 days)	*The Man Who Fell Up*
September (5 days)	*Men of Fear* ["hurricane season"]
October (11 days)	*They Died Twice* ["early fall"]
October (10 days)	*The Devil's Black Rock*
September 16– September 24 (9 days)	*The Too-Wise Owl* [Starts on "Tuesday"—the third day is the "18th."]

1942

April (7 days)	*The Talking Devil*
April (4 days)	*The Running Skeletons*
May (4 days)	*The Time Terror*
May (2 days)	*The Three Wild Men*
June (4 days)	*The Goblins*

1942

June (5 days)	*The Secret of the Su*
June (3 days)	*The Spook of Grandpa Eben*
June (3 days)	*The Fiery Menace*
July (2 days)	*Mystery on Happy Bones*
July (2 days)	*The Metal Monster*
Late July– early August (9 days)	*Hell Below*
August 12– August 14 (3 days)	*Waves of Death* ["August 12"]
October 1–October 6 (6 days)	*According to Plan of a One-Eyed Mystic* ["Thursday... first week in October"]
Late October (6 days)	*The Black, Black Witch* ["fall"; "snow"]
November (8 days)	*The King of Terror*

1943

March (8 days)	*Death Had Yellow Eyes* ["early spring"]
March (4 days)	*Weird Valley*
April (3 days)	*The Three Devils* ["spring"]
June (3 days)	*The Whisker of Hercules*
June (7 days)	*The Man Who Was Scared* ["June afternoon"]
June (9 days)	*Satan Black* ["Early summer"]
September (6 days)	*The Derelict of Skull Shoal* [Shortly after Italy's surrender.]

1943

November (6 days)	*The Pharaoh's Ghost* ["near the rainy season"]
December (5 days)	*The Shape of Terror*

1944

Early January (4 days)	*The Lost Giant* [Skiing in New York]
January (3 days)	*Violent Night*
February (5 days)	*Rock Sinister*
March (27 days)	*Jiu San* ["Just a few months ago"; referring to *The Shape of Terror*]
April (2 days)	*The Terrible Stork* ["spring"]
Between July 1 and 15 (5 days)	*King Joe Cay* ["... farmers... harvesting... oats..." —This is near Chicago and oats are harvested in northern Illinois from July 1 through 15; however, "Engraved on this case was *Patrick to Trudy, Yuletide 1944.*" *King Joe Cay* was in the July 1945 issue; which means that this exploit could not have taken place in July 1945. This discrepancy can only be accounted for by another of the many typos that a hasty writer or careless printer seemed to have made during the production of this pulp magazine.]
August (20 days)	*Cargo Unknown*
September (2 days)	*Strange Fish*
November (4 days)	*The Ten Ton Snakes* ["the war near its end"]
December (4 days)	*Measures for a Coffin* ["December"]

1945

Very early April (10 days)	*Five Fathoms Dead* ["very early April";—But the "1946" must be another typo.]
Late May or early June (3 days)	*The Wee Ones* ["hail storms"—France has been regained.]

1945

June (2 days)	*Terror Takes 7* [Johnny in "occupied Germany"]
July (2 days)	*Death in Little Houses* ["July"—but "1946" is another typo.]
July (5 days)	*Se-Pah-Poo* ["One hundred and ten degrees" in the desert]
July (16 days)	*The Screaming Man*
August (7 days)	*Terror and the Lonely Widow* ["petunias"; "geraniums"; "blistering hot day"]
August (2 days)	*Trouble on Parade* ["hot Wednesday afternoon in August"]
October (2 days)	*The Thing That Pursued*
November (12 days)	*The Exploding Lake* ["winter in New York"]
November (6 days)	*Danger Lies East* ["the one we finished a few months ago"—i.e., World War II; "rainy season"—in the Egyptian littoral]

1946

March (2 days)	*Death Is a Round Black Spot* ["gray sleet"; "waiting... for summer to come"]
April (4 days)	*Colors for Murder*
May (4 days)	*Fire and Ice*
June (2 days)	*Three Times a Corpse* [Doc is on a vacation at long last.]
July (2 days)	*The Devil Is Jones*
Late September (8 days)	*Target for Death* ["since the war"]
October (2 days)	*The Disappearing Lady* ["late October"]
November (12 days)	*The Death Lady* [It seems to be summer in South America.]

1947

February (2 days)	*No Light to Die By* ["February"]
April (2 days)	*The Monkey Suit* [Farrar implies it's after *March*.]
April (3 days)	*Let's Kill Ames* ["1947"]
June (3 days)	*Once Over Lightly* ["temperature... past a hundred..."; "Southern California"; "desert"]
July or August (1 day)	*I Died Yesterday* [It seems to be summer according to the vegetation, and Ham is on vacation, fishing in Quebec.]
November (2 days)	*The Pure Evil* ["snow"]
November (17 days)	*Terror Wears No Shoes*

1948

April (7 days)	*The Angry Canary*
April (3 days)	*Return from Cormoral* ["crisp spring morning"]
June (1 day)	*The Swooning Lady* ["June morning"]
October (6 days)	*The Green Master* ["late spring down here"—i.e., in South America, so it's late fall in North America.]
November 4– November 12 (9 days)	*Up from Earth's Center* ["early winter"—this must end November 12, Doc's birthday; it's too esthetically appropriate not to be the day to complete the recorded supersagas.]

NOTE: This chronology had been criticized, sometimes justly, sometimes unjustly, as having discrepancies. Your compiler is not pleased with it, and he is working on a revision that he hopes will please everyone. However, he knows that there is a crabbed and cracked minority that always finds fault where none exists.

Addendum 3

LIST OF DOC SAVAGE STORIES

THE *DOC SAVAGE* magazines are listed below in the order of publication. All but two of the 181 supersagas appeared under the house name of Kenneth Robeson. The first, *The Man of Bronze*, had the byline of Kenneth Roberts. Then someone pointed out that Kenneth Roberts was the name of a well-known historical novelist, author of *Oliver Wiswell, Northwest Passage, Rabble in Arms*, and others. The second story, *The Land of Terror*, appeared under the name of Kenneth Robeson, and this was used as a byline for all except *The Derelict of Skull Shoal*, March 1944 issue. An editor forgot to substitute Robeson for Dent, and Dent realized his ambition to see his name on the magazine.

Lester Dent wrote most of the Savage tales; those by others are accompanied by the abbreviations RJ, LD, HD, EC, AH, and WB. RJ stands for W. Ryerson Johnson; LD, Laurence Donovan; HD, Harold A. Davis; EC, Evelyn Coulson, AH, Alan Hathway; WB, William Bogart.* B stands for those that have been reprinted by Bantam Books as of January 1975, seventy-nine so far. Bantam intends to reprint the entire series. At the present rate it'll take eighteen years before they are all available to the public but Bantam plans to step up the publication schedule when the first Doc Savage movie is released.**

---

* *In the intervening years, the information about the original pulp authors has been further researched and updated; these updates are reflected in the current edition and can also be found in Will Murray's "The Secret Kenneth Robesons" in his collection* Writings in Bronze *(Altus Press, 2011).* —WSE

** *The "B"s have been removed, as Bantam completed reprinting the books*

As of this writing, 13 million copies of the Bantam Doc Savage novels have been sold.

Street and Smith published the magazines, but Condé Nast Publications now owns the copyrights.

1933

March	*The Man of Bronze*
April	*The Land of Terror*
May	*Quest of the Spider*
June	*The Polar Treasure*
July	*Pirate of the Pacific*
August	*The Red Skull*
September	*The Lost Oasis*
October	*The Sargasso Ogre*
November	*The Czar of Fear*
December	*The Phantom City*

1934

January	*Brand of the Werewolf*
February	*The Man Who Shook the Earth*
March	*Meteor Menace*
April	*The Monsters*
May	*The Mystery on the Snow*
June	*The King Maker* HD
July	*The Thousand-Headed Man*
August	*The Squeaking Goblin*
September	*Fear Cay*
October	*Death in Silver*
November	*The Sea Magician*

---

in 1990 with Doc Savage Omnibus #13. *As of this writing, Sanctum Books is currently reprinting the whole series in double-novel trade paperbacks, with the original pulp interior illustrations, original pulp cover illustrations (with some of the Bama covers available as variants), and historical commentary by Will Murray.* —WSE

1934

December	*The Annihilist*

1935

January	*The Mystic Mullah*
February	*Red Snow*
March	*Land of Always-Night* RJ
April	*The Spook Legion*
May	*The Secret in the Sky*
June	*The Roar Devil*
July	*Quest of Qui*
August	*Spook Hole*
September	*The Majii*
October	*Dust of Death* HD
November	*Murder Melody* LD
December	*The Fantastic Island* RJ

1936

January	*Murder Mirage* LD
February	*Mystery Under the Sea*
March	*The Metal Master*
April	*The Men Who Smiled No More* LD
May	*The Seven Agate Devils*
June	*The Haunted Ocean* LD
July	*The Black Spot* LD
August	*The Midas Man*
September	*Cold Death* LD
October	*The South Pole Terror*
November	*Resurrection Day*
December	*The Vanisher*

1937

January	*Land of Long Juju* LD
February	*The Derrick Devil*

1937

March	*The Mental Wizard*
April	*The Terror in the Navy*
May	*Mad Eyes* LD
June	*The Land of Fear* HD
July	*He Could Stop the World* LD
August	*Ost*
September	*The Feathered Octopus*
October	*Repel* (Bantam reprint title: *The Deadly Dwarf*)
November	*The Sea Angel*
December	*The Golden Peril* HD

1938

January	*The Living-Fire Menace* HD
February	*The Mountain Monster* HD
March	*Devil on the Moon*
April	*The Pirate's Ghost*
May	*The Motion Menace* RJ
June	*The Submarine Mystery*
July	*The Giggling Ghosts*
August	*The Munitions Master* HD
September	*The Red Terrors* HD
October	*Fortress of Solitude*
November	*The Green Death* HD
December	*The Devil Genghis*

1939

January	*Mad Mesa*
February	*The Yellow Cloud* EC
March	*The Freckled Shark*
April	*World's Fair Goblin* WB
May	*The Gold Ogre*
June	*The Flaming Falcons*
July	*Merchants of Disaster* HD

1939

August	The Crimson Serpent HD
September	Poison Island
October	The Stone Man
November	Hex WB
December	The Dagger in the Sky

1940

January	The Other World
February	The Angry Ghost WB
March	The Spotted Men WB
April	The Evil Gnome
May	The Boss of Terror
June	The Awful Egg
July	The Flying Goblin WB
August	Tunnel Terror WB
September	The Purple Dragon
October	Devils of the Deep HD
November	The Awful Dynasty WB
December	The Men Vanished

1941

January	The Devil's Playground AH
February	Bequest of Evil WB
March	The All-White Elf
April	The Golden Man
May	The Pink Lady
June	The Headless Men AH
July	The Green Eagle
August	Mystery Island
September	The Mindless Monsters AH
October	Birds of Death
November	The Invisible-Box Murders
December	Peril in the North

1942

January	*The Rustling Death* AH
February	*Men of Fear*
March	*The Too-Wise Owl*
April	*The Magic Forest* WB
May	*Pirate Isle*
June	*The Speaking Stone*
July	*The Man Who Fell Up*
August	*The Three Wild Men*
September	*The Fiery Menace*
October	*The Laugh of Death*
November	*They Died Twice*
December	*The Devil's Black Rock*

1943

January	*The Time Terror*
February	*Waves of Death*
March	*The Black, Black Witch*
April	*The King of Terror*
May	*The Talking Devil*
June	*The Running Skeletons*
July	*Mystery on Happy Bones*
August	*The Mental Monster*
September	*Hell Below*
October	*The Goblins*
November	*The Secret of the Su*
December	*The Spook of Grandpa Eben*

1944

January	*According to Plan of a One-Eyed Mystic*
February	*Death Had Yellow Eyes*
March	*The Derelict of Skull Shoal*
April	*The Whisker of Hercules*

1944

May	*The Three Devils*
June	*The Pharaoh's Ghost*
July	*The Man Who Was Scared*
August	*The Shape of Terror*
September	*Weird Valley*
October	*Jiu San*
November	*Satan Black*
December	*The Lost Giant*

1945

January	*Violent Night*
February	*Strange Fish*
March	*The Ten Ton Snakes*
April	*Cargo Unknown*
May	*Rock Sinister*
June	*The Terrible Stork*
July	*King Joe Cay*
August	*The Wee Ones*
September	*Terror Takes 7*
October	*The Thing That Pursued*
November	*Trouble on Parade*
December	*The Screaming Man*

1946

January	*Measures for a Coffin*
February	*Se-Pah-Poo*
March	*Terror and the Lonely Widow*
April	*Five Fathoms Dead*
May	*Death Is a Round Black Spot*
June	*Colors for Murder*
July	*Fire and Ice* WB
August	*Three Times a Corpse*
September	*The Exploding Lake* HD

1946

October	*Death in Little Houses* WB
November	*The Devil Is Jones*
December	*The Disappearing Lady* WB

1947

January	*Target for Death* WB
February	*The Death Lady* WB
March	*Danger Lies East*
May	*No Light to Die By*
July	*The Monkey Suit*
September	*Let's Kill Ames*
November	*Once Over Lightly*

1948

January	*I Died Yesterday*
March	*The Pure Evil*
May	*Terror Wears No Shoes*
July	*The Angry Canary*
September	*The Swooning Lady*

1949

Winter	*The Green Master*
Spring	*Return from Cormoral*
Summer	*Up from Earth's Center*

1979

July   *The Red Spider**

1991

August   *Escape from Loki* by Philip José Farmer

October   *Python Isle* by Will Murray & Lester Dent writing as
                       Kenneth Robeson

1992

March   *White Eyes* by Will Murray & Lester Dent writing as
                       Kenneth Robeson

July   *The Frightened Fish* by Will Murray & Lester Dent
                       writing as Kenneth Robeson

October   *The Jade Ogre* by Will Murray & Lester Dent writing as
                       Kenneth Robeson

1993

March   *Flight into Fear* by Will Murray & Lester Dent writing
                       as Kenneth Robeson

July   *The Whistling Wraith* by Will Murray & Lester Dent
                       writing as Kenneth Robeson

---

*   *Note from Philip José Farmer in the 1981 Playboy Books edition:* "The
Red Spider *was not published in the Savage magazine series. Lester Dent
wrote it in April 1948, but its existence was unknown until 1975 when the
manuscript was found by Will Murray, perhaps the foremost authority on Doc
Savage. Murray also discovered that some of the stories attributed to Dent
were actually written by others. A corrected list of authors will appear in a
future reprint of this biography."* [Mr. Farmer's list has been maintained as-
is in this edition; as noted elsewhere, updated information about the original
pulp authors can be found in Will Murray's "The Secret Kenneth Robesons"
in his collection* Writings in Bronze *(Altus Press, 2011). —WSE]*
"The addition of The Red Spider *to the sagas makes the number of Savage
novels now 182. And, as of July 1981, 106 will have been reprinted. Only
76 to go, Doc Savage lovers! Inasmuch as the novels are now appearing two
at a time, there may be only six more years and two more months to go. Or
perhaps if the second Savage movie now being planned succeeds (the first one
bombed), the rate of publication will be stepped up."*

1993

November   *The Forgotten Realm* by Will Murray & Lester Dent
                    writing as Kenneth Robeson

2009

February   *Doc Savage: The Lost Radio Scripts of Lester Dent*
                    edited by Will Murray
                    "The Red Death" (*The Man of Bronze*, Part 1)
                    "The Golden Legacy" (*The Man of Bronze*, Part 2)
                    "The Red Lake Quest"
                    "The Sniper in the Sky"
                    "The Evil Extortionists"
                    "Black-Light Magic"
                    "Radium Scramble"
                    "Death Had Blue Hands"
                    "The Sinister Sleep"
                    "The Southern Star Mystery"
                    "The Impossible Bullet"
                    "The Too-Talkative Parrot"
                    "The Blue Angel"
                    "The Green Ghost"
                    "The Box of Fear"
                    "The Phantom Terror"
                    "Mantrap Mesa"
                    "Fast Workers"
                    "Needle in a Chinese Haystack"
                    "Monk Called it Justice"
                    "The White-Haired Devil"
                    "The Oilfield Ogres"
                    "The Fainting Lady"
                    "Poison Cargo"
                    "Find Curly Morgan"
                    "The Growing Wizard"
                    "The Valley of the Vanished"
                    "The Gray Spider"
                    "The Polar Treasure"

2011

July   *The Desert Demons* by Will Murray & Lester Dent
                    writing as Kenneth Robeson

November   *Horror in Gold* by Will Murray & Lester Dent writing as
                    Kenneth Robeson

2012

May   *The Infernal Buddha* by Will Murray & Lester Dent
                    writing as Kenneth Robeson

2012

September   *Death's Dark Domain* by Will Murray & Lester Dent
writing as Kenneth Robeson

2013

March   *Skull Island* by Will Murray*

August   *The Miracle Menace* by Will Murray & Lester Dent
writing as Kenneth Robeson

---

* *This novel identifies a different paternal lineage for Doc than Farmer's,
as well as a different mother.* —WSE

PHILIP JOSÉ FARMER
(1918–2009)

PHILIP JOSÉ FARMER was born on January 26, 1918 in North Terre Haute, Indiana. He grew up in Peoria, Illinois where he spent much of his childhood reading anything and everything. From the classics by Baum, Carroll, Cervantes, Chesterton, Cooper, Defoe, Dickens, Dumas, Homer, London, Shaw, Stevenson, Swift, Thackeray, Twain, Verne, Wells, and many others, to Burroughs, Doyle, Haggard, and the pulps: *Air Wonder Stories, Science Wonder Stories, The Shadow, Doc Savage, Weird Tales, Argosy, Blue Book*... the list goes on and on. He also read the Bible and many books on mythology.

All of this prepared him well for a career as a writer. He began by writing mainstream stories, and sold "O'Brien and Obrenov" to *Adventure* magazine (March 1946) before trying his hand at science fiction. His first science fiction story, "The Lovers," published in *Startling Stories* (August, 1952), is famous for breaking the tabu on sex in science fiction, and for launching his career with the 1952 Hugo Award as the "Most Promising New Talent."

After selling several more stories to the science fiction pulps, he entered and "won" the Shasta Prize Novel Contest, which included a grand prize of four thousand dollars (a lot of money in 1953). Though married with two children, Farmer now felt confident enough to quit his job and become a full-time writer. But his career immediately hit a stumbling block when Shasta didn't pay him; instead they strung him along asking for rewrites, while investing the prize money due to him in the publication of another book, which bombed. Farmer never was paid, and by the time the truth came out, he had lost his house and had to go back to work full time.

After falling back on manual labor jobs for a few years, Farmer and his family left Peoria in 1956 and moved around the country. He worked as a technical writer for the space-defense industry, eventually ending up in Beverly Hills in 1965. All the while, he continued to write and sell science fiction short stories and novels, even winning a second Hugo Award for the story "Riders of the Purple Wage." Then, just before the moon landing in 1969, he was laid off from his technical writing job, so he decided to write fiction full time once again.

In 1970, the Farmers moved back to Peoria and his career again began to take off. His World of Tiers series was very popular and he won his third Hugo Award for the first novel in the Riverworld series, *To Your Scattered Bodies Go* (a reworking of the novel that had won the Shasta contest). However, his career then hit another obstacle: writer's block.

Although fans and publishers alike were clamoring for the next World of Tiers or Riverworld title, he seemed to be out of ideas. Unable to work in those worlds, he spent the next few years looking to his favorite literature as stimulation for his novels: *The Mad Goblin* (a Doc Savage pastiche), *Lord of the Trees* and *Lord Tyger* (both Tarzan pastiches), *The Wind Whales of Ishmael* (a science fiction sequel to *Moby Dick*), *The Other Log of Phileas Fogg* (the *true* story behind Jules Verne's *Around the World in Eighty Days*), and *Venus on the Half-Shell*, written "by" Kilgore Trout (wherein Farmer pretended he was Kurt Vonnegut Jr.'s sad-sack science fiction author).

He also wrote two biographies during this period, *Tarzan Alive: A Definitive Biography of Lord Greystoke* and *Doc Savage: His Apocalyptic Life*, revealing to the world that the "characters" known as Tarzan and Doc Savage were in fact based on real living people. These books also served to introduce the Wold Newton Family mythos, a concept that may be one of the author's most enduring creations.

By the end of the 1970s, with his writer's block vanquished, he continued the Riverworld and World of Tiers series, and went on to write many more novels, including the Dayworld series.

The next two decades also saw the fulfillment of Farmer's life-long ambitions to write an Oz book, and to pen official Doc Savage and Tarzan novels: *A Barnstormer in Oz, Escape from Loki: Doc Savage's*

First Adventure, and *The Dark Heart of Time: A Tarzan Novel*.

Farmer retired from writing after the publication of *The Dark Heart of Time* in 1999, but over the next decade he worked with an ardent fan base that continued to make his work available; this ranged from a mammoth collection of rarities (*Pearls from Peoria*, 2006) to unsold mainstream stories written at the start of Farmer's career collected alongside an unpublished novel (*Up from the Bottomless Pit and Other Stories*, 2007), to new editions of novels and new collections, to the completion of unfinished works: "Getting Ready to Write" (with Paul Spiteri), *The City Beyond Play* (with Danny Adams), *The Evil in Pemberley House* (with Win Scott Eckert), and *The Song of Kwasin* (with Christopher Paul Carey).

Philip José Farmer passed away on February 25, 2009, but his legacy endures and continues to entertain his many fans and readers. Perhaps the best testament to this is the ongoing reissuing of his varied and fantastical works, of which the book at hand is a prime example.

Bonus Addendum 1

DOC'S COAT OF ARMS

Reconstructed by Win Scott Eckert and illustrated by
Keith Howell, from notes by Philip José Farmer

"Doc's Coat of Arms" previously appeared in Farmerphile: The
Magazine of Philip José Farmer *no. 14, October 2008, and in the
Chapbook for the limited edition of* The Evil in Pemberley House *by
Philip José Farmer and Win Scott Eckert, Subterranean Press, 2009.*

FROM PHILIP JOSÉ FARMER'S "The Arms of Tarzan (The
English Nobleman whom Edgar Rice Burroughs called John
Clayton, Lord Greystoke)" * and *Tarzan Alive*, we know of his deep
and abiding interest in heraldry, and the symbolism contained
therein. While he published a lot on Greystoke's arms, less saw print
regarding the arms of Doc Savage, aka Dr. James Clarke Wildman,
Jr. In *Doc Savage: His Apocalyptic Life* (DS:HAL), Farmer described
the coat of arms of the Clarke Wildman family thusly:

> ARMS—Argent, a fesse chequy gules and azure, in chief an
> alchemical pelican between two fleams, in base a demisavage
> holding on his sinister shoulder a club. *Crest*—A demihunts-
> man proper winding a horn gules. *Mottoes*—Free for a Blast;
> Inicissimus Maleficorum.

---

* Burroughs Bulletin *No. 22, Summer 1971*. Myths for the
Modern Age: Philip José Farmer's Wold Newton Universe. *Win
Scott Eckert, ed. Austin, TX: MonkeyBrain Books, 2005. Pearls
from Peoria. *Paul Spiteri, ed. Burton, MI: Subterranean Press,
2006.* —WSE

The lower* motto means: The Greatest Enemy of Evildoers, a very appropriate motto for Doc Savage.

This description formed the basis for Keith Howell's back cover illustration, coupled with information in four pages of handwritten notes and drawings by Farmer, showing his progressive research on the Clarke Wildman arms (including a lot of non-Clarke Wildman arms scribblings, such as notes for Mayfair and Rassendyll.) On the last page Farmer writes essentially the lines from DS:HAL quoted above, demonstrating that these notes do indeed culminate in the final version. With additional research and educated guesses based on Farmer's notes, there are a few "charges" (iconic images) added to Keith's final version, which are not reflected in Farmer's quote from DS:HAL.

What does this all mean?

In heraldry, coats of arms have formal descriptions that are expressed as a blazon. Tinctures are the colors which blazon a coat of arms. Argent is the tincture of silver.

The escutcheon (also called scutcheon) is the shield in a coat of arms. A fesse is a wide horizontal band across the middle section of the escutcheon. Gules (pronounced with a hard "g") is the tincture of red. Chequy is a small alternating patterns of squares of two tinctures. A fleam is a handheld instrument used for bloodletting.

The fleams and the alchemical pelican evoke the cycle of life, blood, and rebirth. In this way, the alchemical pelican is similar to the Ouroboros. "The female pelican was believed to wound her breast with her long, curved bill, drawing blood to feed her young. For this noble act, the bird became a symbol of piety, self-sacrifice, and virtue. It also symbolizes the duties of a parent or parental love." *Somewhere in Tyme, Coat of Arms Charges* <www.familynamesonline.com/charges7.html>.

A demisavage and demihuntsman are depictions of the upper half of the body of a savage and a huntsman; the symbolism in the context of the Wildman family is clear.

---

* *The British paperback edition of* Doc Savage: His Apocalyptic Life *(Panther, 1975) says "lower," while both the U.S. paperback edition (Bantam, 1975) and the 1981 Playboy Books reprint say "latter." Both are contextually correct in this case. —WSE*

The motto "Free for a Blast" is common among the arms of Clarke and Clerk families.

With Farmer's description from DS:HAL covered, two charges were added based on Farmer's handwritten notes, which follow:

• A boar's head couped (a straight line at neck as if cut by a guillotine) sable (black), above the fesse chequy gules and azure; this is called "charging" the shield with the boar's head couped sable.

• Above the fesse chequy gules and azure, two clubs saltirized (crossed, as in an X) proper ("proper" means in their proper or natural color, in this case brown).

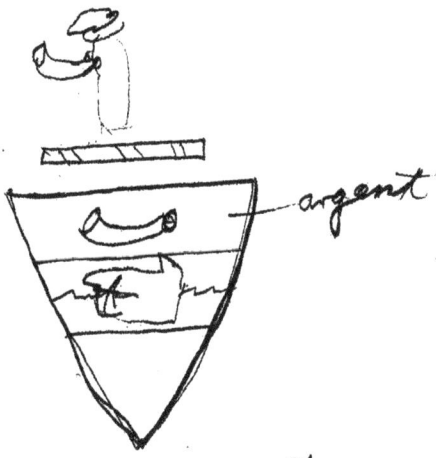

Arms –
Clarke & Wildman
arms of Sir Patrick Clarke
Wildman

argent

FREE FOR A BLAST

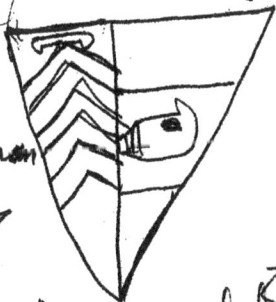

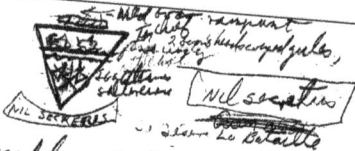

Crest: A semi-savage holding a club
on his sinister shoulder & blowing

a bugle.

Mottoes: (upper) Free For a Blast;
(lower) Imcussimus Maleficorum.

ARMS: Argent, between a fesse dancetty
gules and azure, a toad's head couped
sable and an alchemical pelican
between two fleams.

Bonus Addendum 2
LIST OF DOC SAVAGE COMICS

by Win Scott Eckert and John Allen Small

OVER THE years, the Doc Savage rights holders, Street & Smith, followed by Condé Nast, have authorized various Doc Savage comics series. These have varied greatly in quality and in their adherence to the version of Doc seen in the pulps.

In 1936, Lester Dent and pulp illustrator Paul Orban submitted a proposed *Doc Savage* comic strip to various newspaper syndicates across the country, apparently without success. The few existing panels—the storyline was loosely based on the 1933 novel *The Sargasso Ogre*—did not appear in print until Millennium Comics included them in one of their comics in 1992.

It was not until several years later that Doc Savage finally appeared in the comics. In fact, Doc appeared regularly in two separate series of comics published during the 1940s by Street & Smith: he appeared as a back-up feature in *Shadow Comics*, and starred in his own series of *Doc Savage Comics*. He also turned up as a guest star in the June 1943 issue of *Supersnipe Comics*.

Issue 5 of *Doc Savage Comics* (August1941) contained an unusual story entitled "Doc Savage & the Angry Ghost," written by comics legend by Jack Binder. In it, Doc crash lands in Tibet; there, an ancient mystic finds him and nurses him back to health. The mystic then bestows Doc with a magic blue hood, which has a sacred ruby on its forehead. This ridiculous looking cowl endows Doc with super-strength and hypnotic powers. It was apparently an attempt on the part of the comic's editors to emulate the success of the many comic book superheroes that had cropped up in the wake of Superman's successful debut in 1938; the comic book version of Doc used the hood for several years, and a short-lived 1943 Doc Savage radio program was based upon this version of the character. But following the events of "Murder Is a Business," which was published in the January 1944 issue of *The Shadow Comics*, the hood disappeared and was never seen again.

Doc Savage Comics ceased publication with the October 1943 issue. Doc's final appearance in a Street & Smith comic book came in the August 1949 issue of *The Shadow Comics*—the same year that both *Doc Savage Magazine* and *The Shadow Magazine* ceased publication. Doc's next comic book appearance came in November of 1966, when Gold Key published an adaptation of *The Thousand-Headed Man*, one of the original Savage novels. (This even utilized the same cover art that was used on the Bantam paperback edition of the novel.) This was intended to be a tie-in with a proposed film adaptation of the same novel, which never materialized.

Marvel Comics published two different series of Doc Savage comics during the 1970s. The first, a traditional four-color comic book which adapted several of the original novels, lasted a mere eight issues beginning in October of 1972. (The first two issues, a very loose adaptation of *The Man of Bronze*, were later combined into a single edition and released as a *Giant-Sized Special* in 1975, to promote both the new Doc Savage movie and Marvel's then-new black-and-white Doc Savage comic magazine.) During this same period, Doc also turned up as a guest-star in two books which (thanks to some unusual time travel storylines) teamed him up with a couple of Marvel's more popular super-heroes: he appeared with Spider-Man in *Giant-Size Spider-Man* #3 (June 1975), and later teamed with The Thing (the big orange member of The Fantastic Four) in *Marvel Two-In-One* #21 (November 1976).

Marvel's second regular Doc series was far superior to the first: a black-and-white quarterly, published in magazine format, which told all-original stories. The first issue was released in 1975, in time to publicize the release of the George Pal film; the cover art was the same painting of film star Ron Ely used on the movie posters and the back cover of Bantam's movie edition of the first novel, and an interview with George Pal appeared in the back of the magazine. Despite a strong combination of writing and artwork, and the presence of some interesting back-up articles, this magazine also lasted a mere eight issues; it was selling well, but it became a victim of Marvel's decision in 1977 to cut back on their black-and-white magazines to concentrate more on new color comic books. Those eight black-and-white issues remain one of the high-water marks for Doc Savage comics.

A decade after Marvel's second series ended, rival DC Comics obtained the rights to publish Doc Savage comics. First up was a four issue mini-series (November 1987–February 1988) which was intended to bring the Doc Savage series into the modern day. They accomplished this by teleporting a now-married Doc into an otherworldly dimension shortly after World War II (his colleagues believed he had been killed) on the very day his wife (supposedly Princess Monja, whom Doc first met in the novel *The Man of Bronze*, but for some reason she's called F'Teema in this series) gives birth to a son. In issue #2, we learn that son—Clark Savage III—is wholly unsuited to adopt his father's mantle, and he gets gunned down by a street gang in the 1960s.

Clark III's girlfriend is pregnant, however, and in issue #3 we are introduced to Doc's grandson, Chip—a mental and physical marvel like his grandfather, but a pacifist who doesn't want to get involved when one of Doc's old enemies returns to action. This paves the way for issue #4, in which Doc finally returns to our world, having not aged a single day in four decades. He teams up with his reluctant grandson to overcome the bad guys. Along the way we also learn that one of Doc's colleagues, Long Tom Roberts, had betrayed Doc back in the 1940s, thus instigating these events.

DC Comics launched an ongoing *Doc Savage* series in November 1988. The first batch of stories pick up where the mini-series ended, with a still-young Doc and his grandson at odds over Chip's pacifism. In this series, it's learned that Doc's wife is still alive after all (now called by her rightful name of Monja), and Doc's old enemy John Sunlight (from the pulp novels *Fortress of Solitude* and *The Devil Genghis*, which had ended with Sunlight's rather violent death) miraculously turns up for another rematch.

Midway through the series run, DC published *Doc Savage* Annual #1, a double-length tale which told, without authorization, Philip José Farmer's Camp Loki story of the first meeting of Doc and his aides.

Following this, the ongoing series moved to telling stories set in the 1930s, including a four-part team-up with The Shadow which carried over into two issues of DC's *The Shadow Strikes!* comic book. This redirection lasted until the final issue (October 1990), which brought readers back to the present for one final tale involving Chip Savage.

Several years later, Millennium Comics obtained the rights to do yet another *Doc Savage* comic series. Rather than one ongoing series, Millennium chose to release several self-contained mini-series of various lengths; one was an adaptation of one of the novels (*Repel*), while the others were original tales set at various times within Doc's career; one of these actually predates the events of *The Man of Bronze*, and features Doc's father in a major role. There was also a one-issue special devoted to an adventure of Doc's cousin Patricia, as well as *The Manual of Bronze*, a one-issue special which was sort of a dossier of Doc and his colleagues, in the same style as DC's successful *Who's Who* series.

Later still, in 1995, Dark Horse Comics—which had enjoyed a great deal of success with licensed comic books series based on *Star Wars*, *Indiana Jones*, *Tarzan*, and others—took over the publishing rights to the Doc Savage comics. Their first effort was a two-issue crossover mini-series entitled *The Shadow and Doc Savage: The Case of the Shrieking Skeletons*. A four-issue mini-series focusing solely on Doc (*Curse of the Fire God*) followed.

In 2009 it was announced that DC Comics had regained the comic book rights to Doc Savage and that there were plans to include the character in a series of stories set in DC's new *First Wave* universe, alongside such other characters as The Bat-Man, The Spirit, Blackhawk, Rima the Jungle Girl, and fellow pulp adventurer The Avenger. The initial incarnation of this project appeared late that year in a one-shot *Batman/Doc Savage Special* (January 2010).

Intended as a prologue to the regular *First Wave* series (set an alternate universe in which dirigibles share the skies with jets and 1930s-style gang murders are reported on 2000s-style TV news programs), the storyline was not greeted by enthusiasm by many fans who preferred Dent's original works and/or the later contributions by Philip José Farmer and Will Murray.

The six-issue *First Wave* mini-series (focusing on Doc, The Bat-Man, and The Spirit) was launched in May 2010 and was published semi-monthly. In June 2010 DC released the first issue of a new monthly *Doc Savage* series set in the *First Wave* universe. A back-up feature focusing on new adventures of "Kenneth Robeson's" other pulp hero, The Avenger, made such radical changes to Richard Henry Benson and crew that they were nearly unrecognizable.

In March 2011 DC completed its bimonthly *First Wave* mini-series. The monthly *Doc Savage* series ran until issue #17 (October 2011), when it was cancelled with just one issue remaining in its then-current storyline, along with the other titles which were being published under the *First Wave* umbrella.

That final issue of DC's second *Doc Savage* series was finally published in a digital-only edition almost a year later (cover date August 2012).

What follows is a hopefully-complete listing of Doc Savage comics, listed by publisher, in order of appearance.

Street & Smith

Doc Savage Comics #1–20, November 1940–October 1943
Doc appeared in issues # 1–3 of *Shadow Comics* (1940) and then gained his own title. With issue #5, the character ceased to resemble the pulp version of Doc; he acquired a magic hood with a gem that gave him superpowers. After *Doc Savage Comics* ended, Doc made more appearances in various issues of *Shadow Comics* (1944–1949).

Shadow Comics – March 1940 – "Monk Called It Justice"
Shadow Comics –April 1940 – "The Crimson Serpent"
Shadow Comics – May 1940 – "The Smoke of Eternity"
Doc Savage Comics – July 1940 – "The Land of Terror"
Doc Savage Comics – October 1940 – "Thunder Island"
Doc Savage Comics – February 1941 – "The Polar Treasure"
Doc Savage Comics – May 1941 – "Terror in the Navy"
Doc Savage Comics – August 1941 – "The Angry Ghost"
Doc Savage Comics – November 1941 – "The Peace Clan"
Doc Savage Comics – March 1942 – (title unknown)
Doc Savage Comics – June 1942 – "The Long Lost Treasure"
Doc Savage Comics – September 1942 – "Japan's Secret Oil Supply"
Doc Savage Comics – November 1942 – "The Living Dead"

Doc Savage Comics – January 1943 – "The Giants of Destruction"
Doc Savage Comics – February 1943 – "Minute Men—1943 Style"
Doc Savage Comics – March 1943 – "Doc Savage Fights the Living Evil"
Doc Savage Comics – April 1943 – "The Beggar King of Hate"
Doc Savage Comics – May 1943 – "A Toast to Blood"
Doc Savage Comics – June 1943 – "Death Traps of Hidden Valley"
Supersnipe Comics – June 1943 – "Supersnipe and Doc Savage"
Doc Savage Comics – July 1943 – "The Skull Strikes"
Doc Savage Comics – August 1943 – "Rocket Ship Adventure"
Doc Savage Comics – September 1943 – "The Black Knight"
Doc Savage Comics – October 1943 – "The Pharaoh's Wisdom"
Shadow Comics – January 1944 – "Murder Is a Business"
Shadow Comics – February 1944 – "The Wig Thief"
Shadow Comics – March 1944 – "Water, Water, Everywhere"
Shadow Comics – April 1944 – "The Man Who Hated Miami"
Shadow Comics – May 1944 – "The 'Egg'-centric Mr. Dumptee"
Shadow Comics – June 1944 – "Death Strikes in Mid-Air"
Shadow Comics – July 1944 – "Blind Flight"
Shadow Comics – August 1944 – "X—The Unknown Quantity"
Shadow Comics – September 1944 – "Castles in the Air"
Shadow Comics – October 1944 – "The Villain Too Black to Be Seen"
Shadow Comics – November 1944 – "The Savage Doctor"
Shadow Comics – December 1944 – "Square Deal"
Shadow Comics – January 1945 – "Behind the Eight-Ball"
Shadow Comics – February 1945 – "The Spider Strikes"
Shadow Comics – March 1945 – "The Man Who Wasn't There"
Shadow Comics – April 1945 – "Blood Money"
Shadow Comics – May 1945 – "The Touch of Death"
Shadow Comics – June 1945 – "The Most Dangerous Place"
Shadow Comics – July 1945 – "The Man Who Could Make Lightning"
Shadow Comics – September 1945 – "The Heaviest Metal"
Shadow Comics – October 1945 – "The Impossible Escape"
Shadow Comics – November 1945 – "The Unseen Harpist"
Shadow Comics – December 1945 – "Melting Welding"
Shadow Comics – January 1946 – "To Live is Evil"
Shadow Comics – February 1946 – "Quest of Evil"
Shadow Comics – March 1946 – "Conclave of Evil"

Shadow Comics – April 1946 – "Live, Evil, Veil"
Shadow Comics – May 1946 – "Napoleon of Crime"
Shadow Comics – June 1946 – "Mad Hatter"
Shadow Comics – July 1946 – "The Airplane Spin"
Shadow Comics – August 1946 – "The Stolen Seismograph"
Shadow Comics – September 1946 – "A Most Practical Joke"
Shadow Comics – October 1946 – "Guarding the Atom Secret"
Shadow Comics – November 1946 – "Return of the Skull"
Shadow Comics – December 1946 – "Pursuit of the Skull"
Shadow Comics – April 1947 – "Death's Period"
Shadow Comics – May 1947 – "Zenda—Delilah!"
Shadow Comics – June 1947 – "Doc Savage's Inertia"
Shadow Comics – July 1947 – "The Disappearing Diamond"
Shadow Comics – August 1947 – "One Bad Headache"
Shadow Comics – September 1947 – "Pieces of Fate"
Shadow Comics – October 1947 – "The Touchdown Murder Mystery"
Shadow Comics – November 1947 – "The Man from Mars"
Shadow Comics – December 1947 – "The Puzzling Puzzle Box"
Shadow Comics – January 1948 – "Golden Galleon" and "Doc Savage
    Rents a Gun"
Shadow Comics – February 1948 – "Terror Trap"
Shadow Comics – March 1948 – "Hounds and Hare"
Shadow Comics – April 1948 – "The Million Dollar Stick-Up"
Shadow Comics – May 1948 – "The Devil to Pay"
Shadow Comics – June 1948 – "The Crystal Monsters"
Shadow Comics – August 1948 – "Thunder in a Test Tube"
Shadow Comics – September 1948 – "Ice Age–1948"
Shadow Comics – October 1948 – "The Television Peril"
Shadow Comics – November 1948 – "The Bottle Ghost"
Shadow Comics – December 1948 – "The Robot Master"
Shadow Comics – January 1949 – "The Case of the Heavy Feather"
Shadow Comics – February 1949 – "The Man Who Wasn't!"
Shadow Comics – March 1949 – "The Odd Halo"
Shadow Comics – April 1949 – "Blind Flight"
Shadow Comics – May 1949 – "Moon Madness!"
Shadow Comics – June 1949 – "The Fault Finder"
Shadow Comics – July 1949 – "Limbo of the Lost"
Shadow Comics – August 1949 – "The Flying Serpent"

Gold Key Comics

Doc Savage #1, November 1966
Loose adaptation of the pulp novel *The Thousand-Headed Man.*

Marvel Comics

Doc Savage: The Man of Bronze #1–8, October 1972–January 1974 (color comics)
#1–2: loose adaptation of the pulp novel *The Man of Bronze*
#3–4: loose adaptation of the pulp novel *Death in Silver*
#5–6: loose adaptation of the pulp novel *The Monsters*
#7–8: loose adaptation of the pulp novel *Brand of the Werewolf*

These eight issues were collected by DC Comics in 2010 in the volume *Doc Savage: The Man of Bronze.*

Giant-Size Doc Savage #1, January 1975
Reprint of *Doc Savage: The Man of Bronze* #1–2, loosely adapting the pulp novel *The Man of Bronze.*

Giant-Size Spider-Man #3, January 1975
The Yesterday Connection: although they don't meet in person, Doc Savage and Spider-Man are involved in connected events taking place in 1934 and 1974.

Doc Savage #1–8, August 1975–January 1977 (black and white magazine)
#1: *The Doom on Thunder Isle*
#2: *Hell-Reapers at the Heart of Paradise*
#3: *The Inferno Scheme; A Most Singular Writ of Habeas Corpus*
#4: *Ghost-Pirates from the Beyond*
#5: *The Earth-Wreckers*
#6: *The Sky Stealers*
#7: *The Mayan Mutations*
#8: *The Crimson Plague*

These eight issues were reprinted by DC Comics in 2011 in the collection *Showcase Presents: Doc Savage.*

Marvel Two-In-One #21, November 1976
In *Black Sun Lives*, Doc, Monk, and Renny (in 1936) have a crossover (and cross-time) team-up with The Thing and the Human Torch of the Fantastic Four.

Skylark Publishing

Doc Savage: The Man of Bronze, March 1979
An adaptation of the first Doc Savage novel.

DC Comics

Doc Savage, volume 1, #1–4, November 1987–February 1988
The story, entitled *The Heritage of Doc Savage*, was collected by DC in 2010 as *Doc Savage: The Silver Pyramid*. The storyline involves Doc's forty-year disappearance, his wife Princess Monja, his son, grandson, and his reappearance in the 1980s.

Doc Savage, volume 2, #1–24, November 1988–October 1990
#1–6: *The Discord Makers* (1980s timeframe)
#7–8: *The Mind Molder* (1980s timeframe)
#9–10: *The Golden God* (1980s timeframe; features Princess Monja, from the original pulp novels, as Doc's wife)
#11–14: *Sunlight Rising* (1980s timeframe; features the resurrection of villain John Sunlight)
#15–16: *The Sea Baron* (1980s timeframe)
#17–18: *The Conflagration Man* (1930s timeframe; parts two and four of a crossover with The Shadow; parts one and three are in #5–6 of DC Comics' *The Shadow Strikes!*)
#19–21: *The Air Lord* (1930s timeframe)
#22–24: *The Asteroid Terror* (1980s timeframe)

Doc Savage Annual #1, 1989
The Olympic Peril told the tale of Doc and the Amazing Five's liberation from Camp Loki during the Great War, expanding on Farmer's description of those events in *Doc Savage: His Apocalyptic Life*. This version of the events can, as Farmer would say, be dismissed as completely fictional. He gave the accurate account in his 1991 novel *Escape from Loki: Doc Savage's First Adventure*.

Millennium Comics

Doc Savage: The Man of Bronze #1–4, November 1991–May 1992
A four-issue mini-series, *The Monarch of Armageddon*, featuring Princess Monja and the return of villain John Sunlight.

Doc Savage: Doom Dynasty #1–2, June–July 1992
A two-issue mini-series featuring Doc's battle against Guy Boothby's villain Dr. Nikola. The story has Colonel Richard Henry Savage as Doc's grandfather.

Doc Savage: Devil's Thoughts #1–3, August–October 1992
A three-issue mini-series taking place before the pulp novel *The Man of Bronze*.

Doc Savage: Manual of Bronze #1, August 1992
Not a story, but an illustrated guide to Doc, his aides, some of the villains, and his equipment vest and superfirer pistols.

Pat Savage: Woman of Bronze #1, October 1992
Pat has a solo adventure in *Family Blood*.

Doc Savage: Repel #1, January 1993
One issue of an adaptation of the pulp novel (never completed).

Dark Horse Comics

The Shadow and Doc Savage: The Case of the Shrieking Skeletons #1–2, July–August 1995
Two-issue mini-series with Doc and The Shadow teaming up.

Doc Savage: Curse of the Fire God #1–4, September–December 1995

DC Comics

Batman/Doc Savage Special #1, January 2010

Bronze Night, a tale crossing over Doc Savage with The Bat-Man, launches DC's "First Wave" alternate pulp universe, and leads into the six-issue *First Wave* mini-series.

First Wave #1–6, May 2010–March 2011

Six-issue mini-series set in an alternate pulp universe with modern, 21st century trappings, and featuring alternate versions of Doc Savage and his Amazing Five, Pat Savage, The Avenger and his aides in Justice, Inc., The Bat-Man, The Spirit, Rima the Jungle Girl, Black Canary, and the Blackhawks.

Doc Savage #1–18, June 2010–August 2012 (the final issue was only released digitally)

#1–4: *The Lord of Lightning*

#5–12: *The Two Who Are One*

#13–18: *Raise the Khan*

First Wave Special #1, April 2011

Doc Savage, The Avenger, and The Bat-Man appear in *The Avenger Problem.*

Bonus Addendum 3
WRITING DOC'S BIOGRAPHY

by Philip José Farmer

"Writing Doc's Biography" originally appeared in Pulp #5½, *Special Pulpcon issue, Robert Weinberg, ed., July 1973 (as "Writing the Biography of Doc Savage"). It was reprinted as "Writing Doc's Biography" in* The Man Behind Doc Savage: A Tribute to Lester Dent, *Robert Weinberg, ed., 1974, and in* Pearls from Peoria, *Paul Spiteri, ed., Subterranean Press, 2006.*

JUST AS I sat down to start writing this article, the galley sheets *of Doc Savage: His Apocalyptic Life* arrived. That was the morning of April 19. Not until today, April 23, was I able to return to writing the galleys. Hopefully, all my corrections will be in the book. Such was not the case for *Tarzan Alive*, my biography of Lord Greystoke. For some reason, Doubleday did not incorporate my corrections, and I've never been able to get an explanation out of them why this omission occurred.

Things may be different this time, however. My title for the Tarzan biography was not used nor was I consulted about the dust jacket illustration. I didn't like either. But Doubleday is using my title for the Savage book and is following my suggestion that the "real," the "original," Doc be portrayed on the dust jacket. I had been afraid that the illustration would be based on those that Bama has been doing for the Bantam reprints.

As we all know, however striking Bama's covers are, his Doc Savage has little relation to that described by Dent and illustrated by Baumhofer or succeeding artists for the Street and Smith magazine originals. As a friend of mine, Jack Cordes, said, Bama portrays Doc as he would have looked like if Nazi Germany had won the war. (A cross between the Jolly Green Giant, and a Nazi Stormtrooper!... RW.*) In my opinion, Bama's Doc looks like a middle-aged, habitual criminal, or a 55-year old ex-Mr. Universe down on his luck.

When Ace Books published my Doc Savage pastiche, *The Mad Goblin*, I asked Don Wollheim, the editor, why Gray Morrow had not portrayed Doc as described by Dent and myself. That is, as a man about thirty, handsome, and with straight bronze-red hair. Why was the cover illustration based on Bama's crewcut, widow-peaked, golden-haired monster?

Wollheim replied that the Bama was the only one most readers knew. The Bama-type cover would sell the Ace pastiche much better than a faithful picture of Doc. I replied that I was a purist and preferred the Baumhofer version. Besides, my Doc Caliban is not a Doc Savage imitation, but a pastiche, a continuation of the original. But when I write my next Doc Caliban, tentatively titled *Some Unspeakable Dweller*,** Doc may be shown as he really was. Wollheim will be buying it, and he is now vice-president and editor of DAW Books, and so he can pick his own covers.

Bantam, by the way, sent a note to Ace after *The Mad Goblin* appeared. Bantam objected, not to the book, but to the cover because it was too Bamaish. Wollheim's comment on this was that Bantam did not have a copyright on a torn shirt.

Thus, I was pleased when Doubleday asked me to send them some copies of the Street and Smith Savage magazines, one of which

---

* *Robert Weinberg, editor and publisher of* The Man Behind Doc Savage. *—WSE*

** *Although this book was never completed, Phil did write a chapter for the book which was printed in the World Fantasy Convention Program, 1983, under the title* The Monster on Hold; *reprinted in* Myths for the Modern Age: Philip José Farmer's Wold Newton Universe. *Win Scott Eckert, ed. Austin, TX: MonkeyBrain Books, 2005;* Pearls from Peoria. *Paul Spiteri, ed. Burton, MI: Subterranean Press, 2006. Additional chapters under the title* Down to Earth's Centre *were located in Phil's notes and published in* Farmerphile: The Magazine of Philip José Farmer *no. 12, April 2008. —WSE* would be used on the dust jacket. I made my choice from the Baumhofers. Baumhofer is, in my opinion, the best illustrator of Doc, though Emery Clarke is very good. Doubleday did have on hand the cover for *Quest of Qui* (July 1935), which is a head and shoulders portrait of Doc. I like this, but it has no action, and action is the essence of Doc. After consideration, I narrowed my choice to the covers for *Fear Cay* (September 1934) and *The Spook Legion* (April 1935). The former shows Patricia Savage, Doc, and (presumably) Renny caught in a net. Doc is tearing apart the thick ropes of the net, and we see lovely Pat full-face. *The Spook Legion* cover was my top choice because it shows Doc in a classical pose, riding a running board. Monk is at the wheel of the roadster; New York City buildings form a silhouette in the background. Diane Cleaver and the Doubleday artists agreed with me that this was the best. This made me happy, though I hated to omit Pat.* As I say in the book, I fell in love with her when I was fifteen. (This explains why the chapter on Pat is twice as long as the chapters on the five assistant archenemies of evil. On the other hand, Monk Mayfair was my favorite character, perhaps because being so inhibited myself, I loved my opposite, the noisy, brawling, skirt-chasing, ungrammatical, vulgar, and violent Monk.)

The acceptance of my title and my choice of dust jacket illustration pleased me. I suspect, however, this came about because I was the only one involved in the book who knew anything at all about Doc. The Doubleday staff thought they knew about Tarzan, but Doc was an unknown quantity.

The full title, as it appears on the title page is:

---

* *Phil is discussing the cover art to the 1973 hardcover edition. He would be happy to see Pat on the cover of this edition of* Doc Savage: His Apocalyptic Life *(a first for any edition) and perhaps less so to see the Bama-esque version of Doc by current Doc artist Joe DeVito. The Bamaish version was used on the subsequent mass market paperbacks: Bantam, 1975 (cover by Roger Kastel against the Baumhofer cover of* The Spook Legion *in the background); Panther, 1975 (cover by Richard Clifton-Dey); and Playboy, 1981 (cover by Ken Barr). —WSE*

DOC SAVAGE
His Apocalyptic Life

As the Archangel of Technopolis and Exotica
As the Golden-eyed Hero of 181 Supersagas
As the Bronze Knight of the Running Board
Including His Final Battle Against the Forces
of Hell Itself

The table of contents is as follows:

1. The Fourfold Vision
2. Lester Dent, the Revelator from Missouri
3. Son of Storm and Child of Destiny
4. The Bronze Hero of Technopolis and Exotica
5. The Skyscraper
6. The Eighty-Sixth Floor
7. The Hidalgo Trading Company and Its Craft
8. The Crime College
9. The Fortress of Solitude
10. Monk, the Ape in Wolf's Clothing
11. Ham, the Eagle with a Cane
12. Habeus Corpus and Chemistry
13. Renny, Door-Buster and Holy-Cower
14. Neoverbalist Johnny
15. Patricia Savage, Lady Auxiliary and Bronze Knockout
16. Long Tom, Wizard of the Juice and Misogynist
17. Doc the Gadgeteer
18. Some of the Great Villains and Their World-Threatening Gadgets

Addenda

1. The Fabulous Family Tree of Doc Savage
2. Chronology
3. List of Doc Savage Stories

I give the table of contents so the reader may get some idea of the structure of the book. When I did *Tarzan Alive*, I modeled its structure somewhat after William S. Baring Gould's biography *Sherlock Holmes of Baker Street*. This demanded placing all of the stories in the sequence in which they happened, not in the publishing sequence. They were then summarized and the blanks left by Burroughs were filled in by me. I also tried to reconcile the discrepancies among the various stories and generated various theories or used those of various ERB scholars to explain certain difficult points.

But in writing Doc's life, I wasn't about to summarize all 181 of the supersagas. To do this would not only make the book about three times as long as it is, but it would appall and bore the general reader, who is no Savage specialist. So I structured Doc's biography on Baring Gould's *Nero Wolfe of West Thirty-Fifth Street*. Even this summarized the forty-four Wolfe books published up to 1968. I knew that my summaries would be longer than Baring Gould's and would probably amount to about 181 typewritten pages if I kept restraints on myself.

But there are enough references to various stories throughout the book to give the nonspecialist the feel and color of the supersagas.

The first chapter, "The Fourfold Vision," is a comparison of four writers who have something in common: apocalypticism. These are Dr. E. E. Smith (author of the Skylark and Gray Lensman series), Henry Miller (author of *Tropic of Capricorn*), William Burroughs (author of *Nova Express*, *The Soft Machine*, et al.), and Lester Dent.

The second chapter, "Lester Dent, the Revelator from Missouri," is a biographical sketch of Dent. To get details of his life and to ensure accuracy, I twice visited Mrs. Dent in her home in La Plata, Missouri. She was very charming and helpful, and it was a thrill to see Dent's home, his studio, the Baumhofer originals, and the collection of manuscripts. He was a remarkable man.

Chapter 3, "Son of Storm and Child of Destiny," recounts Doc's immediate ancestry, his birth in a ship off Andros Island, his early training, his World War I experiences, and his deeds just before he moved into the Empire State Building.

(Yes, I know the actual 86th floor of the ESB is the observation floor and never was occupied by an individual, and I know that Dent never named Doc's skyscraper. But I explain this, satisfactorily, I hope, in the book.)

The fourth chapter, "The Bronze Hero of Technopolis and Exotica," sketches Doc and his activities and his character development during his adventures in the big cities and the jungles and deserts.

Since "the skyscraper" and the 86th floor are as much characters as the living beings in the stories, chapters 5 and 6 are devoted to them. Chapter 5, "The Skyscraper," contains a line drawing of the ESB and the Hidalgo Trading Company. Floors prominent in the stories are called out, and the various secret express elevators, the subbasement garage, the giant underground pneumatic tube, the secret tunnel to the Broadway subway, and several other features are shown.

The sixth chapter contains a diagram of the 86th floor. This is to be referred to during the reading of the text of this chapter. This includes many, though by no means all, of the devices, furniture, lab equipment, secret wall panels, doors and various items (including the portrait of Doc's father and the mounted lion, etc.). It wasn't easy making the floor layout or placing many of the items. I had to reconcile the many discrepancies perpetrated by four writers trying to beat a deadline. But, in writing a biography of a "fictional" character, half the fun is in explaining away the discrepancies. It also generates much that wasn't in the originals, and it enables the biographer to fill in the blanks.

I put fictional in quotes because this book, like *Tarzan Alive, Sherlock Holmes of Baker Street, Nero Wolfe of West Thirty-Fifth Street, The Life and Times of Horatio Hornblower, A Gay Adventurer: Being the Biography of Sir Percy Blakeney, Bart.* and *Yankee Lawyer: the Autobiography of Ephraim Tutt*, is based on the premise that Doc Savage was a living person. Of course, his exploits were considerably exaggerated and distorted, some of them being entirely fictional. Doc himself complained of the exaggerations in the memo he sent to Dent in *No Light to Die By* (May–June 1947).

The contents of the remaining chapters are self-evident by their titles, Addendum 1, subtitled "Another Excursion into Creative Mythography," is an extension of Addendum 2 of my *Tarzan Alive*. Doc's ancestry and relatives are described in this and end-paper genealogical charts are provided as aids for the reader of Addendum 1. This chart, unlike that in *Tarzan Alive*, spells out the names of the major characters and gives the initials of the minor people. The names initialed on the chart are spelled out in the text.*

---

* *In this edition, all of the names are spelled out on the chart.* —WSE

Perhaps some, reading this article, will be surprised to learn that Doc is a descendant of Solomon Kane, Captain Peter Blood, Raphael Hythloday (of More's *Utopia*), and Manuel of Poictesme (of James Branch Cabell's *Figures of Earth, Jurgen*, et al). And he/she may also be surprised to discover that Doc is related to Sam Spade, Richard Hannay, James Bond, Richard Benson, Fu Manchu, Carl Peterson, Professor Moriarty, Captain Nemo, and Doctor Caber (of Dunsany's *The Fourth Book of Jorkens*).

On the other hand, if the reader is acquainted with *Tarzan Alive*, he may not be surprised.

Addendum 2 is a chronology of the supersagas, an attempt to put the stories in the sequence in which they must have happened, which was not always by any means, the order in which they were published. I had a hell of a time with this. Some of the problems are described in the foreword to the chronology. Very few of the stories specify the dates or the day and the year of the particular event. A few specify both, and some of these presented additional problems because of this. It's axiomatic that an adventure has to occur before it can be written and published, and in some cases, the dates were too close to the publication date to be regarded as accurate.

Fear Cay enabled me to determine the year in which it took place because of the age of Dan Thunden. *The Squeaking Goblin* refers to a book published exactly one hundred years ago. Both of these adventures can thus be set in 1934, but both had to occur early in the year to have been written up and gone through the publishing process before appearing on the stands. *The Squeaking Goblin* (August 1934) appeared on the stands in July. Though Dent probably only took three or four days to write it, the editing and printing of it even at the speed with which pulp magazines put out issues, must have taken a minimum of a month and a half. I would have preferred to place the story in early spring, but *Goblin* definitely takes place during summer, during vacation time. I settled for the first seven days of June, when the rich could be vacationing early.

Many of the stories contain definite references to the season or seasonal data, and these enabled me to determine if the supersaga occurred in fall, winter, spring or summer.

Doc was often said to have just returned from one of his six month stints at the Fortress of Solitude. This stretched the chronology to impossible lengths, and I determined that only in 1933 could he have spent that much time at the Strange Blue Dome. He could have spent five months there in the first part of 1934.

Another problem was presented by the absence of the five aides on projects which required a very long time. These would also expand the chronology; the times of their absences had to be accounted for. I finally concluded that Doc's assistants couldn't have seen these projects through from beginning to end. Thus, when Renny is building a road or airport in China and Johnny is digging in Inca ruins, or Monk is rebuilding a chemical plant in post-war Germany, they were on these projects only as consultants. They flew in, looked around, straightened out the biggest problems, and flew back in time to join Doc in his latest exploit.

In the early years of the magazine, the stories often ended with a preview of the next adventure. These were supposed to follow immediately the story at hand. But this often just could not be. So I presumed that the editors wrote these previews to intrigue the reader. The facts were ignored. It was evident that Dent and his associates did not write the stories in the sequence in which they had actually happened. Not always, anyway.

It was necessary to classify some of the stories as all fiction. *World's Fair Goblin* was obviously written before the World's Fair at New York opened. And I classified *Land of Long Juju* (January 1937) as fiction, and abominable fiction at that; just as a story, it's ridiculous. But the description of and references to East African customs and peoples are absurd. Donovan knew nothing of this area, made up the whole thing, and committed an abomination. Why Bantam did not save this as the last to be printed in the series, why Bantam picked this one when there were so many better stories to publish, I don't know. But, I suspect that the editor of the Bantam stories does not read them before he chooses which one will be issued. More on this later.

The first three supersagas, *The Man of Bronze*, *The Land of Terror*, and *Quest of the Spider*, occurred in the published sequence. Doc was at the Fortress, but only for two weeks, between *Land* and *Quest*. The fourth story in my chronology, *The Red Skull* (August 1933), was the sixth published. *The Polar Treasure* (June 1933) the fourth published, must have been the eighteenth in chronological sequence.

The Purple Dragon (September 1940), one of my favorites, is definitely set in August 1940 by the text. The "1940" has to be a typo of Dent's or the printer's, and so I put *Dragon* in the August 1–3 slot of 1939. This is a reasonable move, since the stories have many typos, and errors, including the names of characters who are not in the particular scene.

I suspect that some Savageologists will take issue with me on some of my chronology, or will want to know how I arrived at a certain decision. Don't write me about these, because I don't have time to answer such questions. Write an article for *PULP* or some Savagezine and if I happen to have enough time, I might answer the article. Some of the slots into which I put certain stories were the result of many factors which had to be weighed against each other. Where discrepancies which existed were found, I favored that which had the most evidence on its side.

Addendum 3 is a list of the stories in published sequence. Date of publication, author, and Bantam reprint (if any) are given. The list of Bantams stops with the middle February 1973 issue, *The Seven Agate Devils*.

I wrote the Bantam publishers to get their publication figures and also to find out what method was used to pick those stories published. In fact, I wrote three letters, none of which were answered. I mentioned in each that I wanted the information for the biography, which would be published in August by Doubleday. It was to Bantam's advantage to reply, since my book will give the Doc Savage stories some publicity.

It's my opinion that the editor of the Bantam Savage books has a very contemptuous attitude towards them. I doubt that he has ever read any of them, though somebody at Bantam has to have skimmed through them to get the blurbs which are on the back of the books.

This indifference seems to extend to the mail-order department. Some years ago, I ordered a batch of Savages through the mail. The package I received was lacking *Meteor Menace* and *The Monsters*. I wrote three letters asking for the books or a refund. No reply. I gave up.

Interim note relating to "biographies." I just strolled over to the Book Emporium on my lunch hour and looked for copies of the softcover *Tarzan Alive*, which appeared on most stands at least three weeks ago. (But, to my horror, Popular Library had omitted the end-paper charts, referred to in Addendum 2 and essential to help the reader.) I could not understand why no copies had been received by the Emporium. Then, while strolling around, I passed the Biography section. And a certain cover caught my eyes. Yes, there it was, *Tarzan Alive*, nestled in with books on Hitler, Jennie Churchill, Hornblower, Einstein, Lincoln, Louis XIV, Dorothy Parker, et al.

I wonder what the fate of the Savage biography will be in this particular bookstore.

In conclusion, though the biography was hard work, it was also fun. I could have written three novels in the time I took to do it and could have made three times as much money. But, I'm glad I did it. I loved the Doc Savage stories when I was a kid. I still get a charge out of reading them, even if they're not great literature. And, I was finally able to fulfill a boyhood ambition, the writing of a book about my hero, Doctor Clark Savage, Jr.

Philip Jose Farmer
Unreal Estate Agent & Stock Baroquer

CHOICE LOTS: RURITANIA, TROY, KOKOVOKO, POICTESME, KOR
BARSOOM, RAINTREE COUNTY, CARCOSA, NO 7 ECCLES STREET
BUNDELCUND, MIDDLE EARTH, HALLAMSHIRE, OZ AND PEORIA

HIGH-PREMIUM SHARES: COSMODEMONIC TELEGRAPH CO.,
UNIVERSAL BASEBALL ASSOCIATION, HIDALGO TRADING CO.,
B. JONAS, AND THE WHITE COMPANY

ADDRESS: C/O LORD GREYSTOKE, ESTATE OF AFRICA

LESTER DENT
AUTHOR, LECTURER, EXPLORER

Creator of "DOC SAVAGE"
under pseudonym of Kenneth Robeson

LA PLATA
MISSOURI

Bonus Addendum 4

AFTERWORD TO
DOC SAVAGE OMNIBUS #13

by Philip José Farmer

Bantam Books completed reprinting the entire Doc Savage series in 1990, with Doc Savage Omnibus #13. *Farmer contributed this afterword, in which he discusses his forthcoming authorized Doc Savage novel,* Escape from Loki.

"DOC SAVAGE *Lives Again!"*
So declares Will Murray in the last line of the afterword you have just read.

He has told you how Doc Savage came into being as a fictional character. He has also outlined for you what may be in store for the Savage fan after Bantam has reprinted the entire canon.

Thus, if all goes well, we will have more novels about The Man of Bronze and his five aides than we had counted on.

Glory Hallelujah!

Forgive me this outburst. But if joy is a sin, I'm headed for Hell.

Which place, as I understand from recent travel brochures, is not such a bad long-vacation area after all. It's filled with old pulp magazines which were consigned to Hades by the literary critics.

That's another story, and one we'll not tell here.

Will Murray is admirably suited to write Doc Savage stories based on Dent's outlines and notes. He is one of the few top Savage experts and researchers and may be the foremost. At least, he has no superior in that field. I look forward with more than just eagerness to his expansions.

He deals in his afterward with facts (the past) and what may be facts (the future).

I am writing here about the emotional impact of the Doc Savage novels upon me when they appeared in the Street & Smith pulp magazines. Also, I'll speculate a little on the Savage stories which may be written some day (and on one already written) but which are not based on Dent's outlines and notes.

In my biography of The Man of Bronze, *Doc Savage: His Apocalyptic Life*, first published in 1973, I wrote of the day on which the very first Savage novel swam up in all its glory from the dozens of pulp magazines on racks in Schmidt's drugstore and hit me in the eye. That was on a Friday, February 17th, 1933.

Never mind whether or not that day was sunshiny, cloudy, drizzly, rainy, or snowy. I do not remember the weather. It would not have mattered what it was. That day radiated with a golden light. And that is how I remember it, forever and forever and amen!

You might say that my personal alchemy transmuted the bronze into gold.

In other words, the title story, the main one, that about Doc Savage, was "The Man of Bronze." And that became the golden aura still glowing in my memory.

In those days, the Depression was going full blast. Dimes were hard to come by, and ten cents was what the magazine cost. I had one dime, and I was lucky to have that, and I doubt I had more than that. I was looking for a new "Shadow" magazine or a new "Argosy" or some other great adventure pulp magazine. If I found issues of these which I had not read, I would look through them and determine which one appealed most to me. Then I would plunk down the dime.

I was just fifteen and would attend Peoria Central High School in the fall. I was, in fact, the ideal target at which the Doc Savage magazine was aimed. Years later, when I met Mrs. Dent, she told me that the stories were designed for the fifteen-year old youth, though she used the age estimate rather loosely. Elsewhere, it is recorded that they were written to allure the twelve-year old boy.

It does not matter. Essentially, the stories were supposed to attract the adolescent. But, as it turned out, they drew children, adolescents, and adults, male and female. All shared one thing, an active imagination and a love for vicarious adventure and high deeds.

All other magazines forgotten, I carried "The Man of Bronze" home. I read it while I walked slowly down the alley and to my home, less than a block from Schmidt's drugstore. Savoring the text (and the illustrations) I went up the steep steps into the attic and then into the tiny bedroom in the back of the house. It had been made into a room partitioned from the attic. It was too cold in winter and too hot in summer. But I could get some privacy there in a small house holding my parents and my four siblings. I shared it with the oldest of my younger brothers, Eugene Avon Farmer. He is now retired but was once, among other things, a private detective.

As I remember it, while going up the poorly lit steps to the attic, I seemed to be bearing a lamp which glowed strongly enough to banish the shadows and which was like Aladdin's lamp. I only had to brush it well and then summon the genie inside, a spirit who would give me all I could wish for: a flying carpet, palaces, subjects to rule, a roc to ride on when I tired of the carpet, an invisibility suit, a magical belt which enabled me to call in flying monkeys or King Arthur's army, risen from the dead, to aid me. Or a horn like Roland's to notify my paladins that I was in dire straits and could use their swords to battle the heathen Saracens.

That magic lamp was, of course, the magazine containing "The Man of Bronze."

Nowadays, such juvenile thoughts are called "power fantasies." Those who apply these labels use them in a derogatory sense and are not backward in designating them as smacking of fascism. But these labelers have their own power fantasies, of course, because everybody, conservative, liberal, or middle-of-the-roader, has them. The labelers are also intent on pursuing their ideology and unmindful of anything that could negate that. They ignore the immense continuity and the deep mass-unconscious roots of these fantasies.

There are two types of power fantasies. One is that type in which the fantasizer wants to do good for an individual or a community. This community may be that of the entire world population.

The second type is that in which the fantasizer wants to do evil to individuals or certain groups. But this person is convinced that he or she is not committing evil but is doing good. Hitler, Stalin, Chairman Mao, and Khomeini were sincere in believing that their murders and repressions were for a good purpose. The ends justified the means.

Thus, the supervillain, John Sunlight, who appeared in two Doc Savage stories, intends (in "The Devil Genghis") to commit great evil in order to bring about a great good. This is the elimination of national boundaries and, hence, of nationalism, the breeder of hate and wars.

The Doc Savage stories have their power fantasies. The villains have them, and Doc and his aides act out power fantasies in combating the supervillains and the lesser villains. But there is no doubt that Doc and his henchmen (and his cousin, Pat, a henchwoman) act only to protect the innocent and defeat the evildoers. There is not the slightest doubt for Doc or for the reader that the villains are evil.

Children and youths have always had power fantasies. I imagine that humankind has had them since it was able to speak. That is, starting with the emergence of *Homo sapiens* from the hominids just preceding our species. And, perhaps, the immediate forerunners of humankind had the same power fantasies.

Of course, when you grow up, if you do, you see these fantasies for what they are, daydreams about possessing impossible forces which you may use to get rid of all those irritations, frustrations, anxieties, repressions, and unjust and unfair situations which make life so miserable. Not to mention the evident evils in this world and the villains who oppress and exploit anybody and anything they can oppress and exploit.

There is also the desire to have things and do things without working hard for them. That's a thread running through all power fantasies and through the lure of magical and invincible weapons and of devices which summon magical or mystical creatures to your side to sweep away your enemies.

Alas! In this grim and gritty world there is no real magic. That is, there is no physical magic, no cornucopias or witches' mills pouring out gold in vast quantities, no Holy Grails, no invincible swords, no flying carpets, no Tarnkappe or hat of invisibility, no ghost armies to rescue you, no savior to come down out of heaven and redeem humankind or, at least, to save those individuals who are worth redeeming according to certain rules, regulations, and codes.

But there is mental-emotional magic. This exists in our minds and is stimulated by music, movies, and especially by printed stories.

While listening, watching, or reading the mental magic created by others, we are sucked into the depths of a golden whirlpool. Or we fall into the hole which Alice fell into while following the White Rabbit. Or we step through the looking-glass mirror she passed through.

These fantasies made by others then lead us into our own creations, fantasies based on those of others but which, after a time, change enough so that they are our own.

They metamorphose if you have a high imagination.

But when I was fifteen and just entering my bedroom and carrying "The Man of Bronze," I did not know all that. The golden light spread from the magazine and through the room and into my brain.

ZAP!

But I prefer not to think of the golden light piercing through my skull as a beam from a raygun. I prefer to think of it as the shower of gold which was the form taken by Zeus, chief of the ancient Greek gods, when he made the maiden princess of Argos, Danaë, pregnant. From this photonic or auriferous union was born Perseus, hero, rescuer of princesses, and slayer of dragons.

Doc Savage, though thoroughly modern and metropolitan, was a reincarnation of Perseus. Not to mention many other heroes of ancient and modern times.

I did not know all this when I sped through the "Man of Bronze" nor when, a few days later, I reread it slowly. Nor did I know this for many years afterwards while reading the sequels and rereading all the novels from the very first. It did not matter. I was just as well off. The golden joy was unalloyed, not mixed with knowledge of classical antecedents or literary criticism. It was all great fun. Truly, ignorance is bliss! Or something close to bliss, anyway.

However, I realized that here, in the form of Doc Savage, was a hero equal to John Carter of Barsoom and Tarzan of the Apes and Odysseus, the Man of Many Turns.

(I did not read just the pulps then. I was also well acquainted with certain ancient classics at an early age. My reading indiscriminately mixed "trash" with "good" literature. I still do mix them though I am much more aware of the difference in the quality of books. You can't really claim to know English literature if you do not also read "trash" or "poplit." This also holds for the literature of any language.)

Doc and his five aides, a sort of highly scientific d'Artagnan and the Three Musketeers, emitted the golden light of joy which Tarzan and John Carter and David Innes and Allan Quatermain and Galazi and Umslopogaas and Sherlock Holmes and Odysseus and a small number of others emitted. These, along with Alice of Wonderland, Dorothy of Oz, Og the Son of Fire, Tom Sawyer, Huck Finn, Captain Gulliver, d'Artagnan, Hercules, Sindbad the Sailor, Captain Nemo, Leif Langdon, the Snake Mother, the Connecticut Yankee, Thibaut Corday, and several others the names of which the reader may or may not recognize would be lamplights in my mind for the rest of my life.

I was fifteen and very innocent. The year was 1933, and, though those times had their obvious evils, the hidden evils were not as well known then as the evils of now. In fact, unfortunately, things we consider evil now were not then so considered except by more perceptive and humane people, a very small minority. All my peers were innocent, though not as much as I was. But I was somewhat aware of the sufferings and grimness of the Depression, though shielded from them more than many were. My father had not lost his job as an electrical and civil engineer for the local streetcar and power company. But he had suffered a big cut in salary and had lost all his investments in stocks.

I read widely though only what I liked and what I was forced to read in school, but I usually liked the required reading. Even then, I knew I wanted to be a writer. And I wanted to write sequels to the exploits of many of the heroes and heroines mentioned above. Those that shone most brightly in my mind were enemies of evil, foes of villains supreme, and sometimes saviors of the world or of individuals in distress and danger.

In other words, they were slayers of dragons, bad wizards, and monstrous ogres. And they were saviors of the many or of the few. They were reincarnations of Beowulf, Sigurd of the Völsungs, the knights of King Arthur's Round Table, Robin Hood, the Iroquois Indian Hiawatha, the Sumerian Gilgamesh, and Lemminkäinen the Finnish hero-shaman.

Doc Savage was the latest in this line of heroes and, in fact, the last. At least, he is for me. James Bond and his kind are entertaining, but they are not made of the stuff of the archetypal hero. They're ephemeral, and their roots are shallow. They don't cast a shadow that goes back to the Old Stone Age.

However, Savage himself seemed ephemeral as far as durability in literature went. Many of the other heroes I've mentioned survived during the years after 1949, when the final magazine Savage appeared. They were kept in print, and their popularity seemed to increase. But, even though it seemed that Savage had vanished forever from the racks, he would not perish in my mind. I would never forget him, and I did have copies of the early stories (from 1933 through 1940) to reread. These were destroyed by a flash flood in 1967.

Meanwhile, coincident with my move from Arizona to California in 1965, Doc Savage suddenly reappeared. He still lived in print! Rather, he was born again! Bantam had started to reprint the series, defunct since 1949. Though I was much older now, forty-seven, I eagerly read them as they came out and wished that the tempo of publication could be speeded up. Each issue evoked the youthful golden joy, though that did not burn as brightly or as ecstatically as when I was young and still had intimations of immortality. I had lived too long and had learned too much.

Never mind. The Bantam reprints of the Savages were great, and I would eventually have them all, if Bantam did not quit printing them. And here I am, seventy-two in 1990, and the end of the series now seems close. One of the things I hated about dying was that I'd not be able to reread the last of the series, *Up from Earth's Center*.

Meanwhile, I've achieved some of my childhood and youthful ambitions. I've written stories about Oz, Holmes and Watson, Captain Nemo, Raffles, Umslopogaas (the real great black warrior, not Haggard's fictional hero), and others. I've written pastiches about Tarzan and Doc Savage, though I could not use their names.

In 1973, when my biography of Doc Savage came out, I wrote therein that I'd like to write a novel about Doc when he was sixteen years old. In this, to be titled *Escape from Loki*, Doc would lie about his age and join the U.S. Air Service shortly after the U.S. entered World War I. He would be shot down while balloon-busting. After several escapes from his German captors, he would be sent to a supposedly escape-proof camp for incorrigible prisoners. This would be called Camp Loki. Here Doc would meet his future five aides, Monk, Ham, Renny, Long Tom, and Johnny.

He would also, of course, encounter a supervillain, a scientist more or less mad who was working on a weapon to devastate the enemies of the Kaiser's Imperial Germany.

But at that time, Bantam still had years to go before the end of the series was in sight. The editor thought it was best not to buy a brand-new Savage story.

So, when the printing of the final book in the series was not so far off, I asked Bantam if I could now write the new novel proposed about sixteen years ago. Bantam was receptive, and the manuscript is now (April, 1990) in the hands of Bantam.

When it's published, it'll bear my byline, not that of Kenneth Robeson, the Bantam house name for the magazine writers of the Savage stories.

This novel is not what I would have written at the age of, say, twenty or even thirty. It's longer than any Savage story so far printed, and it's more realistic. I'm not bound by the tabus that Dent and other writers had to respect when they wrote their sagas.

But my version of Clark Savage, Junior, who would be Doctor Savage some years after World War I, is still the essential character he was in the magazines. And his aides are basically the same. Nor have I forgotten that the basic interest of the readers (of whom I am one) is to have fun during the adventures. However, their icons, glowing in my mind all these years, have gained a third dimension. Or, at least, I've tried to extend them from length and breadth to depth in *Escape from Loki*.

In any event, they're treated as if they were real people, not fictional characters. As if they did live and did experience those adventures which thrilled me and my generation and then, as Bantam reprints, two more generations.

I also have in my files notes about three more original Docs, stories I'd like to write if circumstances permit.

The one I'd write first would be the sequel to the final magazine novel, "Up From Earth's Center," 1949. This was written by Lester Dent and is a very strange tale. It's the only one in which Doc is both puzzled about the identity and powers of his antagonists and in which he is defeated. He may have fought with supernatural forces or there may be some rational explanation for the enigmatic foes. But he does not know what he has been battling. I would like to write the sequel, solve the puzzle, and have Doc be victorious.

My files have notes about another saga I'd like to work out on my word-processor. This will be about Doc's search for and final confrontation with the supervillain who caused the Stock Market crash of 1929 and, thus, the worldwide Depression and suffering which followed the crash. Tentative title: *Dark Satanic Mills*.

Also in my files are notes about an adventure which takes place in 1930. This is about a group of world-powerful industrialists which hires professional killers to eliminate Doc after he stumbles across evidence of their organization. Tentative title: *Bloody Hands*.

Then there is *Invisible Nation*, in which Doc finds out that a hidden subculture exists in America and forms its own country within the Western Hemisphere. Its citizens, when among themselves, speak a language unknown to him and act both as parasites and symbiotes to the countries within which they live.

I also have notes about the adventure in the jungle of the Amazon basin in 1923. It should be, if it goes as planned, a wild and colorful exploit. Tentative title: *The Crimson Jaguar*.

As you can see, The Man of Bronze is, in my mind, a man as real as you or I and perhaps even more real.

Doc Savage still lives!

TRIBUTES

CALIBAN

by Will Murray

"Caliban" originally appeared in Farmerphile: The Magazine of Philip José Farmer *no. 6, October 2006. It was reprinted in Will Murray's* Writings in Bronze, *Altus Press, 2011.*

IT'S ONE of those interesting coincidences of life that I first discovered Philip José Farmer in the same Boston variety store where I purchased my first Doc Savage novel. Only a year or so had passed, when spinning the wire rack, my eyes fell upon *The Mad Goblin* side of an old Ace Double.

"What is this?" I wondered.

That title sounds like a Doc Savage title. That guy on the cover looks like a cartoony Doc Savage. Years later, I realized that artist Gray Morrow had painted it from an old production still of Steve Holland as Flash Gordon. Holland was the model James Bama used for his Doc Savage covers. He had played Flash in a short-lived 1950s TV series prior to becoming the Man of Bronze.

The other side was *Lord of the Trees* by the same author—unusual for Ace doubles. But this was a very unusual book.

I was slightly put off by the odd, unfamiliar name, but my curiosity was piqued. I bought it, and started reading with *The Mad Goblin* side.

My memory has faded of my exact impressions in my first encounter with Phil Farmer. I recall being bewildered by the interlocking stories, and never suspected both sequeled *A Feast Unknown*, of which I had never heard. No wonder I felt a little lost along the way.

I do remember being puzzled by his choice of name for his Doc

Savage simulacrum, Doc Caliban. The reference escaped me, then a teenager. When I subsequently discovered the derivation (Shakespeare's deformed monster from *The Tempest*), I was just as baffled. It seemed, well, unDent. It was my first inkling that Phil Farmer and I saw Doc Savage—if not the world—through very different eyes.

On the other hand, I like Lord Grandrith better than Lord Greystoke for the Ape Man.

Farmer next came to my attention when he released the fascinating *Tarzan Alive*. I was a big Burroughs fan, although I preferred John Carter to the Ape Man. I admit that Phil's conceit that Tarzan was not only an actual person, but still living, enthralled me with its sheer audacity. I enjoyed *Tarzan Alive* better than I liked some of Burroughs' Tarzan novels.

Then came *Doc Savage: His Apocalyptic Life* in 1973.

I was delighted to read a book on the Man of Bronze. But once again bewildered by some of it. Farmer's mix of history and personal fantasy with its impossibly ever-shifting lines prompted me to write him a letter. He was kind enough to respond to my foolish fan letter which elected to pick some bones that probably can't be picked. I had recently discovered a number of the Docs had been ghosted by unsuspected writers, which accounted for a lot of the puzzling factual discrepancies Phil had wrestled with. Phil sent me an autographed copy of the Corgi edition of the book, and I offered to help him straighten out the authorship issues in any future edition of *Apocalyptic Life*.

After several years I finally tracked down *A Feast Unknown*. Its reputation had preceded it. I wish it hadn't. It spoiled the story for me. I can see how one writer might give Tarzan the edge over Doc Savage. But I'm not that writer.

We fell out of touch until Bantam Books asked me to write new Doc Savage novels in 1990. I had submitted one in 1980, based on a Lester Dent outline. Ten years later, Bantam ran out of original novels and wanted *Python Isle*, and more. But first, they told me, Phil Farmer was doing *Escape from Loki* to kick off the new series.

I'll admit to a mixture of intrigue and apprehension when I learned of his plans. A prequel story set in World War I. Once again, I was struck by how differently we approached Doc Savage. Phil was drawn to the backstory. I wanted to tell classic-style Doc Savage adventures set in the '30s.

I will confess that had I been Phil's editor at that time I would have pleaded with him to please write a science-fictional Doc adventure set in, say, 1936. Make it as wild as imagination can conceive. But no, Phil wanted to tell the wartime tale of how Doc and his men first met. He had planted the seed in *Apocalyptic Life* and it was time to harvest the fruits. Few Doc fans understood that the entire Camp Loki meeting was a Phillip José Farmer myth. But a persistent one.

Although Phil had originally planned to write only one Doc, he caught the bug. He expressed to me an interest in working with Dent material. For a while we were talking about him rewriting an old Lester Dent manuscript, to turn it into a Doc. I selected a novelette set in the North Pole called "The Polar Corsair," as the most appropriate to his gifts. With its Polar submarine and naturalistic setting, it was not only Dentian, but Burroughsian. A perfect fit.

But it was not to be. The series proved to be short-lived, a victim of the great Midlist Implosion of 1992–93.

I finally met Phil at the 1993 Pulpcon, where he graciously consented to an extended two-part interview that ran in *Starlog*. It may be one of the longest interviews with Philip José Farmer ever done. Probably only half of it saw print.

We fell out of touch after the Doc Savage series ended. While I continued to write, I drifted into the frontiers of human knowledge, learning Remote Viewing from one of the Stargate pioneers and going on to teach RV as well as doing related—ahem—non-local operations.

At one point, the spectre of writing a Tarzan novel reared its head. Dark Horse had acquired the rights to the legendary unfinished Burroughs' Tarzan novel. I lobbied for the opportunity to finish it, knowing in my heart of hearts that Phil Farmer was the only man on earth truly worthy to squeeze in ERB's boots.

To my horror, it went to a writer who seemed the antithesis of Burroughs' heroic pulp tradition. My curiosity overcame my skepticism. I gave the finished book a shot. When in chapter 1, I came upon the UnBurroughsian word "Sasquatch," I quietly closed the book forever…

Later, I read a letter in the *Burroughs Bulletin*, where Phil paid me the ultimate compliment of suggesting that only he or I could have done justice to Burroughs. Let me repeat for the record: Phillip José Farmer is the only living writer worthy of ERB's boots.

I was delighted when he got to write a Tarzan novel to call his own.

Recently, I was hurled back into time, back to 1970 and that magical spinner rack where I first saw the name of Philip José Farmer. I was going through the carbon to Lester Dent's early Doc Savage novel, *The Squeaking Goblin*. My purpose was to discover any deletions Dent's editors might have made.

I found one in Chapter IX THREE SKYMEN. It was a modest cut, as those things went. Four words. In the passage below, it follows the word "launch." Four words. But they struck me like a thunderbolt. I will italicize them for you:

Jug took advantage of the respite. He jumped up and down in the launch, *an animated elephantine Caliban.*

Philip José Farmer, how could I ever have doubted you?

Will Murray discovered Doc Savage in 1969 at the age of 15, and grew up to become the leading authority on Doc Savage and the literary agent for the Lester Dent Heirs. He scripted an adaptation of The Thousand-Headed Man *for NPR's* Adventures of Doc Savage *radio program, and has to date written a dozen authorized Doc Savage novels for Bantam Books and Altus Press, all but one based upon Lester Dent concepts. The sole exception,* Skull Island, *pits the Man of Bronze against the legendary King Kong and has been hailed as one of the greatest pulp adventures ever penned. (www. adventuresinbronze.com) Murray's forty years of Doc Savage articles have been collected into one volume,* Writings in Bronze.

DOC AND PHIL:
A HECK OF A RIDE

by John Allen Small

IN CHAPTER ONE of *Doc Savage: His Apocalyptic Life*, Philip José Farmer speaks of the fifteen-year-old in his adult brain who continued to love Doc Savage.

I know exactly what he meant. Because in my own brain—and, perhaps more importantly, in my heart—there is an eternal twelve-year-old that will always love not only Doc Savage, but also Phil Farmer. I met both of them in that same summer of 1975, within just a couple of months of one another, and both have remained faithful and steadfast companions on the many roads I have traveled ever since.

I made Doc's acquaintance first. Not through the books, ironically enough, but through the movie. That seems odd to me in retrospect; I had been an incurable bookworm pretty much from the beginning, a great gift bequeathed to me by parents who both loved to read, and based upon my reading habits even then it seems that my path and Doc's should have crossed much earlier than they did.

But somehow Doc escaped my notice until that afternoon right around the time of my twelfth birthday when one of our TV stations aired an ad for the film *Doc Savage: The Man of Bronze*. I knew producer George Pal through his earlier classics like The Time Machine and When Worlds Collide, films that were standard TV fare for my generation. And I recognized star Ron Ely from having watched his *Tarzan* TV series with my father when I was very small. Based on the scenes included in that ad it looked like it might be a pretty exciting film, so I decided I would have to see it if it came to one of our local theaters in Kankakee, Illinois.

A day or so after seeing that first ad, I was at the store with my parents and happened to spy a copy of the Bantam Books movie edition of the first Doc novel, *The Man of Bronze*, and somehow managed to talk my mom into giving me the $1.25 to buy it. We went home and I read the book in a single sitting—and a lifelong fan was born. There was something about Doc that reminded me a little of Tarzan; I had read my dad's entire collection of Edgar Rice Burroughs novels by the time I had finished the fourth grade, so Doc's books represented a similar treasure trove of excitement and adventure. I was hooked.

I began picking up the other Bantam Docs when I found them (as my parents' pocketbooks would allow, of course). Then one day we were at a local department store when I happened to spot the familiar Doc Savage logo on a book I didn't yet have. This one was different from the rest. For one thing it didn't carry the familiar "Kenneth Robeson" byline; this book was written by somebody named Farmer. Even more surprising, the cover claimed that this book was a "biography" of my new hero. Now I was truly amazed; it had never occurred to me that Doc, Tarzan, Sherlock Holmes, the Shadow and others might have been real people—much less dreamed that they might have been somehow related!

By the time I finished reading *Doc Savage: His Apocalyptic Life* I was hungry for more. I searched in vain for some time for a copy of Phil's earlier biography *Tarzan Alive* before discovering that my father had actually bought a copy a year or so earlier. By the time I'd finished that book Dad had also picked up a copy of the (unbeknownst to me at the time) rare Dell paperback edition of *The Adventure of the Peerless Peer* and I had to read that one too. Tarzan and Sherlock Holmes in an adventure together—wow! I hadn't been that excited since that time Batman and Robin teamed up with The Green Hornet and Kato...

By now I held Farmer in the same high regard as I had ERB, which meant I had to read everything with his byline that I could get my hands on. So over the next few years that's exactly what I did. My father gave me copies of *Time's Last Gift*, *Hadon of Ancient Opar*, and *Flight to Opar*; his brother, my Uncle Tom, gave me *To Your Scattered Bodies Go* and *The Fabulous Riverboat*. Those books filled me with the same sense of wonder that I'd earlier experienced through Burroughs, Wells, Verne, et al.

In time Phil also introduced me to a much different sort of wonder, courtesy of his novel *A Feast Unknown*—definitely not a story for a twelve-year-old, eternal or otherwise, and in retrospect probably not one for a lot of sixteen-year-olds either. A high school friend who knew of my fondness for Farmer's work had smuggled his father's copy of the novel into study hall to loan to me one day, much the same way I suspect some in my dad's generation had surreptitiously shared copies of Mickey Spillane's *I, The Jury* or Henry Miller's *Tropic of Cancer*. By that stage in my life I had read *Frankenstein*—twice—*Dracula*, assorted works by Poe and Lovecraft, one or two of Stephen King's earlier works. None of them gave me nightmares the way that A Feast Unknown did.

I first learned of *Feast's* existence in, of all places, the letter pages of a Doc Savage comic book. It was the first book of Phil's—or anyone else's, now that I think of it—that left me so profoundly disturbed. Years later I bought my own copy, just so I would have one in my Farmer collection, but to this day I haven't quite been able to bring myself to reread it. That's not meant to be a negative comment, by the way. It's a great book—in some respects one of Phil's best and most important—but the lessons it held for me at such a young age regarding some of the darker aspects of humanity still resonate so strongly that, even after all these years, I've simply never found the need to revisit them.

Some of my friends and writing colleagues who are fellow Farmer fans may get a bit of a chuckle out of this. They'll probably tease me over what they no doubt perceive as a sense of squeamishness on my part. That's all right; let them. I prefer to think that my reaction says less about my own personal fortitude than it does about the power of Phil Farmer's writing.

Because in that single novel, you see, he taught me more about the nature of evil than in all the Stephen King novels and all the *CSI* episodes and all the Sunday school lessons that I ever sat through. It's a lesson that has actually served me well over the years in my day job as a newspaper journalist, where from time to time I've found myself having to report about murder and abuse and other activities that have emanated from those darkest corridors of humanity. It's a lesson for which I can never thank him enough.

That, to me, is what separates Phil Farmer from all the other writers whose works I've held so dear for so long. Burroughs, Dent,

Wells, Doyle, L'Amour, et al., were all wondrous storytellers. But Farmer—for me, at least—was also a great teacher. He taught me about the nature of good and evil. He taught me that heroes and villains, for all the good or evil attributed to them, are first and foremost human beings—even if they did spring from the loins of meteorite-irradiated forebears. He taught me that sometimes the "official" story is not always the full story, or even the true story. (That's another one that has stood me in good stead as a journalist.)

He also taught me to broaden my horizons beyond that which was already familiar and comfortable. I was already a fan of ERB, Wells, Verne, Haggard—and yes, of Lester Dent—before I ever heard of Phil Farmer. But I don't know that I would have voluntarily sought out such works as *Raintree County* or the works of William Blake had it not been for their mention in *Doc Savage: His Apocalyptic Life.* I had read a number of the Sherlock Holmes stories and *The Lost World* by the time I was twelve, but if not for Farmer I don't know that I ever would have even known of the existence of Conan Doyle's "lesser known" protagonists, Micah Clarke and Brigadier Gerard.

And you can be sure that I never would have had the slightest interest in *Pride and Prejudice*—a novel that one of my childhood chums still dismisses as "sissy stuff"—had Phil (aided and abetted by our mutual friend Win Scott Eckert) not tipped me off about the important role Pemberley House has played in the greater scheme of things....

"All my life's a circle," Harry Chapin sang—and for me that circle always seems to lead back to Phil Farmer.

While stationed in Athens, Greece, while serving in the U.S. Air Force in the mid-1980s I found new editions of Phil's World of Tiers novels—books I had somehow missed during my initial exposure to PJF in junior high and high school—at the base PX and snapped them up. It was like a grand reunion with an old friend.

Phil's work had helped fuel the dream I already had to become a writer myself—and part of that dream coming true was the publication of an essay in Win Scott Eckert's anthology *Myths for the Modern Age: Philip José Farmer's Wold Newton Universe (MonkeyBrain Books, 2005).* That moment remains for me one of the most exciting achievements in a career that has now spanned over three decades, a few sleepless nights and even a handful of awards here and there. My wife still likes to tease me about the expression I got on my face when my copy of *Myths* arrived in the mail; I guess it really was like being a little kid at Christmas.

I couldn't help it, though. The idea that something penned by one of the least distinguished graduates of Bradley-Bourbonnais Community High School should have been published in the same book as a man three times honored with the Hugo Award—a Grand Master so often mentioned in the same breath as Asimov, Heinlein and Pohl—is something that I sometimes still have trouble processing whenever I happen to catch a glimpse of that volume on my bookshelf.

Three decades after first getting to know him in the pages of his books and short stories, I not only got to meet both Phil and his lovely wife Bette in person but had the opportunity to twice spend time—along with other fans and writers such as Joe Lansdale, Win Eckert, Chris Carey, and others—in the Farmers' home in Peoria, Illinois. I still remember the sense of almost childlike awe that Chuck Loridans and Henry Covert and I shared as we stood there in Phil's basement, gawking at his Hugo Awards sitting there on the mantle, and the twinkle in Bette Farmer's eyes as she told us, "Go ahead, pick them up—that's what they're there for."

For a lifelong bookworm those days at Phil's house were the equivalent of a baseball fan getting to meet his childhood idol. And a memory I will always cherish.

And now I come full circle—not quite four decades after I found that copy of *Doc Savage: His Apocalyptic Life* at the old Belscot store in Kankakee, here I am writing an essay about Phil for a new edition of the book that started me down this road. It's been a heck of a ride. And with any luck, there's a long way yet to go.

Thanks for everything, Phil.

John Allen Small has contributed to several popular anthologies: The Avenger: Roaring Heart of the Crucible *(2013);* The Green Hornet: Still at Large *(2012);* The Worlds of Philip José Farmer 2: Of Dust and Soul *(2011); and* Myths for the Modern Age: Philip José Farmer's Wold

Newton Universe *(2005)*. *He is also is the author of two collections:* Days Gone By: Legends and Tales of Sipokni West *(2007) and* Something in the Air *(2011)*. *An award-winning journalist and columnist, he resides in Ravia, Oklahoma, with wife Melissa, sons Joshua and William, and a house full of books.*

CHASING THE BRONZE
KNIGHT OF THE
RUNNING BOARD

by Keith Howell

I **MUST** admit that I feel out of place and unqualified to be included in this august group of contributors writing about their memories and experiences in the world of Doc Savage fandom—and especially in relation to Philip José Farmer's brilliant *Doc Savage: His Apocalyptic Life*. However, having been asked it falls on me to regale you with my sideways tale of how Doc Savage, and particularly Phil's take on the character, has impacted my lifelong love of adventure fiction and superheroes.

Let's hop into the time machine and wing our way back to the halcyon summer of 1975 on the island of Puerto Rico. My friends and I spent a lot of our days, when not out throwing overripe mangoes at each other, watching movies at the local cinema on Ramey Air Force base. Our favorite repeated films were the European theatrical cuts of the *Six Million Dollar Man* TV movies. We, of course, were unaware that they were TV movies. We were just excited to see a superhero on the big screen. But come the summer of 1975, the big budget *Doc Savage: The Man of Bronze* film, directed with tongue firmly in cheek by George Pal with a bombastic John Phillip Sousa score, hit our theater. Now, I have since learned that the world of Doc Savage fandom almost universally despises this movie, and it tanked at the box office, but I am here to tell you that for this young viewer, it made a profound impact and I loved it. I thought it was hilarious, fun, exciting, and that Ron Ely made the perfect Man of Bronze at that time. I lost count of how many times I saw that movie. And I wasn't the only one. My circle of friends were all running around that summer playing Doc Savage and humming that ridiculous Sousa-based theme song.

When next Doc found his way into my life, he showed up in a comic book where he teamed up with The Thing from The Fantastic Four. This was my first encounter with the usual "widow's peak" look for Doc. Then I came across a hardback copy of *Doc Savage: His Apocalyptic Life* in the library on Fort Hood in Texas. I was fascinated by it as I sat and thumbed through it at the table. I was too young to quite grasp what I was skimming but I was definitely intrigued. I didn't actually check the book out and we moved to another town as my dad retired from the army. A couple of years later, in junior high, I walked into my very first comic book shop and my eyes fell upon a poster on the wall with James Bama's classic cover painting of Doc from the *Man of Bronze* paperback. I couldn't ever get that image out of my head after that.

Now let's move the time machine forward a bit to the summer of 1990. I'm freshly married and into adulthood when I picked up a copy of *Starlog* magazine and read an interview with an author named Philip José Farmer where he discussed at length his writings. I remember asking my wife after reading the article, "Why have I never heard of this guy? Every single book he talks about sounds like something I need to read." And from that point on I made it a bit of a quest to track down his books and read them. The first three I read were *The Wind Whales of Ishmael*, *Tarzan Alive*, and *Doc Savage: His Apocalyptic Life*. I didn't just read them, I devoured them.

I wish I had more to contribute to the broader picture of Doc Savage fandom in the days before the internet, but I was truly walking around in a blind haze oblivious to the fact that there was an active Doc and Wold Newton fanbase publishing Xeroxed-copy fan magazines and corresponding with each other around the world. Other than the Doc Savage comics that DC and Marvel had published, I was unaware of and had no sense of there being a larger following for the character. In fact, most people I mentioned the character to had already forgotten the 1975 movie or, rather, that was their sole point of reference. So, I was a fandom-base of one and I was quickly adding to my new interest (and filling my bookshelves) because a local Friends of the Library book sale had a set of dozens of Bantam *Doc Savage* paperbacks for sale at a quarter a book. I scooped every single one up, including a near complete set of *The Avenger* books. I also devoured these. Probably my favorites were *Fortress of Solitude* and *Brand of the Werewolf*—the latter because it introduced me to Doc's cousin Pat Savage.

There was something about Phil's writing that hooked me, but I completely understand why *Doc Savage: His Apocalyptic Life* (DS:HAL) grabbed me and wouldn't let go. He began the book with his nostalgic memory of discovering Doc and his Amazing Five. By the time I was at the end of the book, I felt like I had to know these characters myself, and not just filtered through Phil's nostalgia, wickedly sharp sense of humor, and desire to "connect all the dots"—essentially setting forth the basic principles and approach (along with *Tarzan Alive*) for his Wold Newton Family stories. My heart was energized by the exciting adventure and the archetypal mythology, but my mind was engaged by the interconnectedness that Phil grasped as he pulled the pieces together to form a puzzle tapestry that made these characters so much larger and more important than their pulp roots ever aspired.

This progression of personal interest, and remember this is still happening without my being in contact with any other Doc fans or even realizing they are out there in the world, eventually led me to track down not only all affiliated Wold Newton books I could get my hands on by Phil, but also works and characters referenced in the family trees of DS:HAL and *Tarzan Alive*. This led me to grabbing copies of the "Professor Challenger" stories by Arthur Conan Doyle because Challenger was listed by Phil as Monk Mayfair's uncle. Had that connection never been made, my online *nom de plume* would never have become "Prof. Challenger." I specifically chose that name in honor of the Doyle character that I became aware of through Phil's family trees.

As our time machine continues trudging forward, we get to my first foray onto the internet around 1993 or so. One of the first things I did was track down a used book service to order myself a copy of Phil's elusive *Venus on the Half-Shell* (with the Kilgore Trout byline). Then I wound up searching for Phil, thinking half-heartedly that I might find a P.O. Box or something that would allow me to write him a letter. And lo and behold I got his home address! I decided to not only write him a letter, but also to draw him an original illustration utilizing some of my favorite characters from his books, including his Doc Caliban (maybe or maybe not actually the "real" Doc Savage) featured prominently. I mailed that off and never really thought about it again until many years later when I wound up making contact with Michael Croteau and Win Scott Eckert through some Phil/Wold Newton web forum I believe—but also I think Phil had mentioned or shown the art I sent him to Mike. Honestly, the info has been lost in the scattered ruins of my mind, but what is important is that I had quit the art profession for a few years. I was totally burned out on the entire thing and had lost my creative spark. So I decided to exercise different mental muscles and go to law school. It was while in law school that I got asked if I would be interested in contributing a quick wraparound cover for a book devoted to those crazy collectors of Phil's work. I was thrilled to do it even though I was severely out of practice. It was crude and done without any access to Photoshop or such programs, but I knocked that out, the book was published (*Collecting Philip José Farmer: The Illustrated Guide, Volume 1* by Michael Croteau), and the rest is history.

Let's bring the time machine back to the present; as we fast forward through the years we can look fondly as we pass through the now frequent contributions I have been able to make to Phil's literary history. Let's remember meeting Phil and Bette and spending time with them in their home. Let's remember designing the art and logo for DocCon. Let's remember the thrill and honor of taking Phil's notes and Win's kibitzing to construct the official "Wildman" Coat of Arms—Doc's family line. Let's take note of how much my personal worldview expanded through exposure to Phil's work and how many times I have gone back to DS:HAL because it holds a special place in my heart. This book is dripping with enthusiasm and fondness for Doc, and his family and friends, to the point that no reader could conceivably finish it and not have a nagging desire to pull out a Doc Savage adventure and get lost in it. Yes, Phil's love of the character rubbed off onto an adult who was prepped to receive it. Superheroes have always had a strong appeal to me. I'm drawn to their innate goodness and the sense of tapping into the higher mythical archetypes that underlie all myths and heroic legends. Doc is the precursor to all other modern heroes. Even "Clark Kent" was named Clark in homage to "Dr. (Doc) Clark Savage, Jr." I'm forty-six at the time of this writing and when I recently tore a sleeve on my shirt, my first thought was of Doc Savage flexing his coiled serpent biceps and tearing through his shirtsleeve. Doc has been a part of my inner world since 1975. He is an example of the best that a man can be. He is smart, strong, loyal, and honest.

I will forever be incapable of listening to Sousa without singing along inside my head with:

> Have no Fear, the Man of Bronze is here.
> Peace will come to all who find
> Doc Savage, Doc Savage.
> He's a friend to all Mankind.
> Pure of heart and mind.
> Who will make crime disappear?
> Doc Savage, Doc Savage
> Part hero and pioneer.
> Thank the Lord he's here.

Thanks to George Pal for introducing me to the character. Thanks to James Bama for intriguing me about the character. Most especially, thank you to Philip José Farmer for making the character real to me and igniting a spark that continues to this day.

Keith Howell has illustrated countless textbooks and contributed to dozens of books and magazines by or about Philip José Farmer, including The Best of Philip José Farmer. *He is a recovering law school graduate, professional artist, occasional blogger, and reviewer of graphic novels who resides in the heart of Texas. He does not have a Fortress of Solitude but does disappear into his subterranean Dungeon of Solitude to refresh his mind and creative spirit. If you hear a certain beautiful, but mysteriously melodic trilling seeping through the cracks in the door, it is best not to disturb him. Have no fear, he will return... when the world needs him.*

THE MAESTRO
OF MYTHOLOGY

by Rick Lai

PHILIP JOSÉ FARMER was one of the greatest mythmakers of all time. Just as everyone in history was united in his Riverworld novels, nearly every major fictional character in literature was united in the Wold Newton Universe. In Greco-Roman mythology, the legendary heroes were descended from the ancient gods. In the Wold Newton Universe, the icons of literature have mutated genes. Farmer updated the classic template of ancient mythology with modern science.

The most remarkable thing about Farmer's Wold Newton Universe is that it was conceived in a pre-internet age. Today it's very easy to go online and find a list of every book in a series. You might even be lucky enough to find free e-texts of those novels. With sophisticated search software, you could find in the text every reference to the lineage of a fictional character. Some critics harp on the fact that one of Farmer's theories may conflict with a statement in one of over scores of novels in a mystery or adventure series. What those critics forget is that they possess research tools that were nonexistent in the 1970s. Farmer's knowledge of literature was astounding.

Philip José Farmer taught me that pulp literature is no different from mainstream literature. Edgar Rice Burroughs and Lester Dent are just as important as Jane Austen and Daniel Defoe. Farmer was my guide to the wonders of Riverworld, the World of Tiers and the Wold Newton Universe. In those realms charted by Farmer, I discovered how to mix historical facts with fantastic concepts and literary traditions. I learned from Farmer how to write speculative articles

and short stories. I wouldn't be a published writer today if not for
Philip José Farmer.

*Rick Lai is a computer programmer. During the 1980s and 1990s, he
wrote articles on crossover universe concepts for pulp magazine fanzines.
Most of these articles have been collected by Altus Press as* Rick Lai's Secret
Histories: Daring Adventurers, Rick Lai's Secret Histories: Criminal
Masterminds, Chronology of Shadows: A Timeline of The Shadow's
Exploits, *and* The Revised Complete Chronology of Bronze. *His short
stories have been collected in* Shadows of the Opera *(Wildcat Books, 2011),
and two upcoming Black Coat Press collections,* Shadows of the Opera:
Retribution in Blood *and* Sisters of the Shadows: The Cagliostro Curse.

DOC SAVAGE AND PHILIP JOSÉ FARMER: THE HERO-ON-THE-HUDSON AND HIS BOSWELL

by Arthur C. Sippo MD, MPH

I GREW up in Union City, New Jersey on the Palisades Plateau in full view of Manhattan. The single most prominent object on the New York skyline was the Empire State Building. I could see it from the back window of my house.

New York in the 1950s and 1960s was a magical place. It was still the printing capital of the United States. Broadway theatre was the best in the world. You had the best in restaurants, entertainment, fashion, and publications. Even the comic books of the time ran advertisements for Palisades Amusement Park which excited the imaginations of kids from other areas of the country who thought it was an enormous carnival with rides and exhibits unmatched anywhere else. (In reality, it was a small attraction that my family would visit once a year "if you are good.") It has long since been replaced by a series of modern high-rise apartments overlooking the Hudson River.

Since I learned to read, I had become fascinated with comic books and superheroes. My Aunt Helen bought me the first issue featuring a re-imagined Flash when it came out in 1956. She read it to me since I was only three years old. Within two years I could read it for myself. And I became hooked.

The Silver Age of comics was filled with four-color splash and white bread heroes. But as time went on, it became too weird and unrealistic. The new Marvel comic lines were much more interesting, but even then the stories were too outside of normal experience. At the tender age of ten years old I was being rapidly disenchanted with my favorite escape literature.

And then I discovered Doc Savage.

Once again it was Aunt Helen who introduced me to the old pulp hero. On a bus trip to Florida in the summer of 1965, I read and reread *The Land of Terror*, and I realized that this was what I was looking for: a larger than life hero, with quirky sidekicks, fantastic plots, and just enough imagination to thrill but not to suspend belief. I read six Doc Savage novels that summer and my comic book consumption began to plummet. At that point new reprints were being published every few months and my collection grew.

I used to walk to the edge of the Palisades down the street from my house and study the New York skyline. I tried to imagine Doc sitting in his headquarters *right there* in the ESB watching over us. I checked out the various waterfront buildings trying to figure out which one was the Hidalgo Trading Company. I became obsessed with all things Doc Savage.

He became more to me than a superhero. He was a role model. Doc was both a physical and mental marvel. He knew everything about everything because he worked hard to study and understand science. And he was a medical doctor first and foremost. The example of my favorite hero would influence the course of the rest of my life.

In 1967, I started high school at Xavier Military Institute, a military school run by the Jesuit Order of Catholic priests on 16th Street in downtown Manhattan, on the edge of Greenwich Village. The school was just two blocks away from the original Barnes and Noble Bookstore at 18th Street and Fifth Avenue.

By this time the reprints of Doc Savage novels were coming every month and a whole new stable of pulp characters followed in their wake. I discovered Conan, The Shadow, Captain Future, the Lensmen, Adam Link, and a host of science fiction from the pulp era. I discovered contemporary science fiction and immersed myself in stories by Isaac Asimov, Arthur C. Clarke, Poul Anderson, Keith Laumer, Kate Wilhelm, and Robert Heinlein, along with the classics by Jules Verne, H. G. Wells, and Olaf Stapledon. But Doc was still my favorite and nothing excited me more than a new Doc Savage story.

The Jesuits were extremely literate men and they introduced us to great literature as a matter of course. We read Shakespeare, Nathaniel Hawthorne, Edgar Allen Poe, Stephen Vincent Benét, James Fenimore Cooper, Aldous Huxley, George Orwell, James

Joyce, George Bernard Shaw, and many others. Since I was going to bookstores to find Doc Savage and science fiction, I branched out into other literature and discovered others works written by authors we were studying in school. My reading tastes became more eclectic and I started reading books on religious themes including the Koran, the Bhagavad Gita, Carlos Castaneda, and Tuesday Lobsang Rampa. I tried some of Ian Fleming's James Bond novels but they were too stark for me. I would not appreciate them until I was much older. Instead I luxuriated in the James Bond films and Sean Connery will always be *the* James Bond to me.

The summer reading list we were given after my sophomore year was incredible. It included *The Adventures of Sherlock Holmes*, *The Hobbit*, *The Lord of the Rings*, and T. H. White's *The Once and Future King*. This increased my interest in fantasy and had me seeking out more adventures of the world's greatest private consulting detective. From there I branched out into the detective genre to seek out stories about some of Holmes' rivals.

I chose to study the French language and as part of the program, we were required to read French novels. The authors included Albert Camus, André Malraux, Jean-Paul Sartre, and Antoine de Saint-Exupéry. A particular favorite was Jean Giraudoux, whose fantastic plays about Biblical themes, gods, goddesses, and ghosts were both amusing and poignant.

My thirst for reading increased exponentially and I eventually discovered the amazing variety of bookstores that 1960s New York had to offer. There was a whole street full of used book stores down on Third Avenue. One of them was Stephen's Bookshop that specialized in science fiction and fantasy. (When his shop closed in 1970, the owner kept up a mailing service through which I received such prized possessions as a first edition of Phil Farmer's Sherlock Holmes pastiche *The Peerless Peer*, and the chapbook containing the greatest air battle in history that had been edited out of Farmer's *Riverworld* series.)

On Fifth Avenue north of 45th Street, there was a series of bookstores carrying things I couldn't find anywhere else. Scribner's had a selection of literature and serious non-fiction coupled with a section that carried speculative fiction from small publishers. It was there where I purchased a copy of Phil Farmer's *Inside Outside*.

Across Fifth Avenue was the enormous Brentano's bookstore

that penetrated through the middle of the block and had entrances on 47th Street, 48th Street, and Fifth Avenue itself. It carried American and International books as well as games, records, and rare books. At its largest extent, Brentano's encompassed five stories and included an art gallery, sheet music, musical instruments, maps, and a special service that would find any book for you anywhere in the world. Sadly, they went bankrupt in the early 1980s and we never saw its like again.

Just down the block toward Broadway was the Gotham Book Mart which had been a favorite hangout for the Beat Generation. Jack Kerouac, Allen Ginsberg, William S. Burroughs, James Joyce, Truman Capote, Saul Bellow, Lillian Hellman, Gertrude Stein, Andy Warhol, Arthur Miller, and so many others were associated with this store. It was said that the Nobel Committee, when it was considering authors for a prize, would order copies of their books from the Gotham. They also had a small section on adventure fiction and detective stories that included the British editions of the Doc Savage reprints and very rare pastiches on Sherlock Holmes and others that could be found nowhere else in New York.

In this dizzying array of modern science fiction writers, there was one who seemed odd and scary. A fellow named Philip José Farmer wrote strange books about deceitful quasi-gods and tiered universes. One of his most famous books, *Night of Light*, seemed to challenge the limits of religious orthodoxy and I shied away from reading his work.

Then on that fateful day in the summer of 1969, in the old Book Masters shop on Times Square, I came upon a strange book in the sci-fi section with two naked men wrestling on its cover. One of those men looked like Doc Savage. The title of the book was *A Feast Unknown*. I was shocked to see that it was written by that "scary" author, Philip José Farmer. I read the blurb on the cover and knew this was a Doc Savage/Tarzan pastiche featuring Doctor James Caliban and John Cloamby, Lord Grandrith. The book appeared very strange, but I couldn't resist it.

A Feast Unknown alternately entertained, horrified, disgusted, and intrigued me. It's most intriguing idea was that Tarzan and Doc Savage were actually half-brothers who had been fathered by Jack the Ripper! It was a book that changed my life and my reading habits. I became an instant fan. That next year, the Science Fiction Book Club offered his book of short stories, *Down in the Black Gang*, which included the first Riverworld story, a two part tale about Fr. John Carmody, and several other gems that fascinated me. From that time on, I began to seek out his work.

I started St. Peter's College in Jersey City in 1970, and lived at home. This was also a Jesuit institution and extensive reading was a fundamental part of the curriculum. I continued my forays into the New York bookstores regularly and was rewarded with the Phil Farmer book *Lord Tyger*, and the tame sequels to *A Feast Unknown*: *The Mad Goblin* and *Lord of the Trees*.

Then, in 1972, after hitting the uptown bookstores all day, I dropped into the drugstore at Port Authority Bus Terminal just to check out their paperbacks. Strange as it may seem, that drugstore sometimes got the Bantam Doc Savage reprints before anyone else in town. I was expecting one at any time but had not found it when I made my rounds that day. The drugstore didn't have it either, but they had something much more interesting. It was a paperback by Phil Farmer entitled *Tarzan Alive* which purported to be the biography of the real man upon whom the character Tarzan was based. This was the book that introduced the Wold Newton family to the world at large.

For three days I devoured the book and looked up every literary reference. The premise of the book was outrageous but exciting: virtually every adventure character from the Scarlet Pimpernel, to Sherlock Holmes, Tarzan, and Doc Savage were all part of a single "family" that had originated at a meteorite fall in rural England in 1795. The simplistic relationship in *A Feast Unknown* became more convoluted, but Tarzan and Doc were still blood relations. The focus of the book was on Tarzan, Lord Greystoke, but Farmer promised that he was working on a biography of Doc Savage himself! That was a book I *wanted*!

I scoured my usual bookstores for months searching for it. There was one particular section in Brentano's that had books about classic speculative and adventure literature, including several books about Sherlock Holmes. It was there I previously found a hardback copy of the British edition of John Pearson's *James Bond: The Authorized Biography of 007*. In the late winter of 1973 I went to that section and there it was: *Doc Savage: His Apocalyptic Life* by Philip José Farmer.

I cannot describe what I felt at that moment. The intensive reading program of the previous decade had exposed me to all different types of literature. And all of it stemmed from the love of this one character. Doc Savage was the lynchpin that united all the books and all the bookstores during the single most informative and enjoyable time in my life.

In his Doc Savage biography, Phil Farmer connected Doc Savage to a host of literary characters from serious literature. Because of this one book I began to read Jack London's work. I reintroduced myself to Jules Verne and the work of Sir Arthur Conan Doyle beyond Sherlock Holmes. It was also through his reference to *At the Mountains of Madness* that I was introduced to H. P. Lovecraft, about whose work I had only heard whispers.

Phil Farmer was the first one to reveal to me the name of the real author of the Doc Savage sagas, Lester Dent, and he confirmed my suspicion that there were several ghost-writers who contributed to the series. He didn't get all the names correct, as later research would show, but this was a serious attempt at discerning the sources that helped shape the character.

Farmer made it clear that this biography was telling the story of one James Clarke Wildman, who was the real life person upon whom the fictional character of Doc Savage was based. From there his imagination took over. He speculated about Doc's origin and training as I had myself. The sections on the five aides, Pat Savage, and the pets drew together material from the entire run of the series that was still in its early stages at that time. In fact, some of the material from the sagas that Farmer quoted in the book was not yet reprinted by Bantam, and it was clear that material inspired scenes in the 1975 movie *Doc Savage: The Man of Bronze*. Farmer also included his own idea that Doc and his aides had met in a prison camp during the Great War. This was used in a Doc Savage comic in the late 1980s.

Farmer made some outrageous—and perhaps tongue-in-cheek—suggestions (e.g., that Doc and his cousin Patricia were lovers) which I did not accept then and which are not followed by most Wold Newton scholars today. But he took the stories seriously, as I did. He was the first person to propose a chronology for all of the Doc

Savage sagas, using research into the weather, current events, and scientific discoveries of the 1930s and 1940s. He even covered the Holy Grail of all Doc Savage sagas, *Up from Earth's Center*, the very last saga published in the series, where Doc Savage enters a demonic realm under the Earth and wrestles with the Devil himself!

Phil Farmer took a pulp hero and turned him into a literary figure. Doc reached almost godlike status in my imagination. Now he was something much larger than that. *Doc Savage: His Apocalyptic Life* marked the end of my adolescence. It was the capstone on my youthful reading period that validated and put into perspective everything I had read and loved in those early years.

Because of *Doc Savage: His Apocalyptic Life*, I read books I would never have known about. I delved more deeply into the literary foundations of heroism and manhood. I recognized that popular literature was not merely entertainment but something much more. There were a series of themes that permeated all of literature (what I would later understand as a metanarrative) tying together the disparate hopes, dreams, and fears of all men.

I owe a great debt to Phil Farmer. I think of him as kindred soul. He was interested in the same things I was. He loved the same stories and characters that I did. The great questions about human life and our place in this mad universe intrigued him, as they did me. He shared his vast literary knowledge with us and in many ways it felt as if he were speaking to me.

Doc Savage: His Apocalyptic Life has given me an integrated vision of all the things I read and loved about books. I cannot turn my back upon that vision without denying a part of myself. For this reason, the Wold Newton Universe remains a passion for me that unites the early experiences of my youth with the adventures I have had in life. I am a retired Lieutenant Colonel from the U.S. Army Medical Corps, who has done both patient care and scientific research. I have served all over the world and spent three years as an exchange officer in the United Kingdom at the RAF Institute of Aviation Medicine. Nevertheless, I am that same boy today who—quivering with anticipation—checked every month for those Bantam reprints and their fantastic Bama covers. I brought that same excitement with me to my work as an adult. I owe much to the work of Phil Farmer, who validated my continued concern for the values of my youth and shared my sense of wonder in human existence and its inherent possibilities.

I hope this book means as much to many of you as it does to me.

Art Sippo is a medical doctor who served in the U.S. Army and the National Guard for over twenty years. He is board certified in Aerospace and Occupational Medicine. Art has a bachelor's degree in Chemistry from St. Peter's College (Magna Cum Laude), a medical degree from Vanderbilt, and a Masters in Public Health from Johns Hopkins. He was a Flight Surgeon for the 101st Airborne Division, Director of the Biodynamics Research Division at the U.S. Army Aeromedical Research Laboratory, an exchange officer with the RAF Institute of Aviation Medicine in Farnborough, England, the Commander of the 145th MASH, the Assistant State Surgeon for the Ohio National Guard, and vice president of the Occupational Care Consultants in Toledo, Ohio. Currently he is the Medical Director of Express Medical Care in Fairview Heights, Illinois. He is also the cohost of The Book Cave *podcast series that covers pulp fiction, comics, sci-fi, and adventure stories. Art has been a fan of Philip José Farmer since reading* A Feast Unknown *in 1969. He has been married to his beloved Katherine for twenty-five years and they have five children.*

AN ARCHAEOLOGY OF DREAMS

by Christopher Paul Carey

IT'S A warm, overcast summer day in 1997 as I tear up the asphalt heading south on Missouri's Route 63. I've just made what in all likelihood is the worst decision of my life, forsaking a hard-won career in archaeology for what is surely a pipe dream. My future looks as stygian as Cthulhu's dark maw. I have no idea how I'll earn a living, much less make a success of myself. But my trunk is full of dog-eared Philip José Farmer paperbacks and the green sign that flashes by says it's only seven miles to La Plata, Missouri, home of Doc Savage author Lester Dent.

This pipe dream feels *right*.

IT'S a few days earlier and I've been working for the past couple weeks as an assistant site director at an archaeological site in western Illinois. It's my dream job, everything I've spent the last few years of my life striving for. I'm out in the field balancing transits and laying out excavation grids, exactly where I want to be, and yet something sticks in my craw: the creeping feeling that no matter how much I love digging into the past, I have something else I'm supposed to be doing. What that calling is, I'm not exactly sure, but a spectral voice from somewhere deep inside whispers that it has something to do with writing and literature. I know too that the eerie susurration probably has something to do with the letter I'd received shortly before I left my home state of Pennsylvania to take the job in archaeology.

The letter is from Philip José Farmer. I've brought it along with me as a talisman of sorts, tucked carefully in a folder between several layers of papers so it won't get damaged. When my spirits sink especially low, I take out the letter and read it. It's Farmer's response to an article I wrote for the Doc Savage fanzine *The Bronze Gazette* on the deeper currents in his novel *Escape from Loki*. In his letter, Farmer writes that he finds my article ingenious, that he believes it might cause as much uproar among the Doc Savage fan community as Rex Stout's essay "Watson Was a Woman" did among the Holmesian aficionados of the Baker Street Irregulars.

I don't know it yet but this letter is some kind of mystical chisel, one that's already split the fabric of space and time and shunted me off into another universe.

I'M back on Route 63. A sign says I'm entering La Plata as I ease my way betwixt cornfields. If there's a town here, I don't see it yet.

And then, there it is on my right. No, not the town. It's The Sign. In this pastoral Midwestern setting—with its farmhouse, grain bin, and outbuildings looming in the distance—the white blocky lettering against a background of blood red spells out an unlikely message:

DOC SAVAGE
COUNTRY
HOME OF LESTER DENT
LaPlata, Mo.

Arriving at The Sign, even as dilapidated as it is, is too much for words. I recognize in my gut that it presages something big. I can feel it palpably in the humid air. I park my 1984 Plymouth Reliant along the hay field, get out, and just gaze, knowing this is a Moment I'll revisit many times in the years to come, no matter how far away life's current carries me from this magical place.

I'M fourteen years old and piling into the back seat of my dad's 1974 Plymouth Valiant. It's a school day, but my brother and I have been granted the day off for a family trip to Hershey Park, Pennsylvania. I've brought along my brand-new Playboy Paperback edition of Farmer's *Doc Savage: His Apocalyptic Life*. As a hardcore Edgar Rice Burroughs enthusiast, I've already read Farmer's other biography, *Tarzan Alive*, but I'm unfamiliar with Doc. I prop my knees up against the black vinyl seat back and read.

I've never been to Hershey, PA. When we arrive, I find the street lamps are shaped like Hershey's Kisses and the air literally smells like chocolate. But it's no big deal. I'm already longing for the two-and-a-half-hour drive back home. I'm eager to read more about the Revelator from Missouri, the Son of Storm and Child of Destiny, supermachine pistols, glass knock-out grenades, autogyros, the "eighty-sixth" floor headquarters that's really located on a lower floor. And I'm even more eager for the weekend to come. I'm pretty sure I recently saw a copy of the first Doc Savage supersaga in the 50-cent stripped-cover bin at the local farmer's market and I'm determined to get it if it's still there.

CONTENT that I've permanently imprinted the image of The Sign onto my soul, and also feeling a bit self-conscious at the local traffic passing by, I hop back in my car and drive on, turning west onto Route 156 and setting off for La Plata's town center.

I don't find much there besides a road running between some houses and buildings, but I spy a small grocery store on the right and stop to get directions to Lester Dent's house. The woman I speak with in the store is perhaps eighteen or twenty years old—she has no clue who Lester Dent is. Yes, I know: THE SIGN. But this is small-town America and I'm sure there are plenty of things I never noticed in my hometown even though they were right in front of me for more than twenty years. Luckily, the young woman *does* know where the local cemetery is and gives me directions.

I find the cemetery on the opposite end of town, turn in, and proceed to drive slowly down the gravel road that loops between the gravestones. It's then that a cemetery caretaker notices me. He rides his lawnmower up to my window and asks me if I'm looking for somebody. The man is Hispanic, his deeply tanned, leathery skin showing he's spent a lot of time out in the sun during his sixty-odd years. I tell the man that I'd like to see the Dent plot. He immediately kicks his lawnmower into gear and waves me to follow.

A largish, upright tombstone bearing the name DENT looms before us. I pull over on the side of the driveway and get out, again feeling that palpable something in the air. The caretaker jumps off his vehicle and points to the big headstone. "Dent," he says. I smile widely, but by then I've noticed that it's Bernard and Alice's grave, not Lester and Norma's. I tell the caretaker I'm looking for Lester Dent, and he replies, "You his grandkid?" I laugh at the thought, and have a momentary fantasy of posing as Dent's grandson or great-grandson. Speaking in a literary sense, there could be a grain of truth in answering yes to the question, though if that's so, then Dent has many thousands of grandchildren. But I shake my head, and say, "No, I just like to read his books and wanted to pay tribute." He doesn't seem to make the connection that Dent was an author.

Though in afterthought, I think he might have been playing me.

I'M lying on my bed on a hot, muggy night in August 1991. I've just finished reading Philip José Farmer's latest novel, *Escape from Loki*. The book has hit me harder than Renny Renwick's quart-sized milk-bottle fists, but instead of being knocked out cold, I feel like a Zen master has struck me with his bamboo stick and jolted my consciousness into satori. In the flash of that metaphysical lightning bolt, I see myriad tentacles writhing up from beneath the novel's surface, though I can't discern the exact form of the beast they're connected to.

I turn back to the first page of *Escape from Loki* and begin reading it again. And then, in the days that follow, I read the novel three more times, back to back. I've got an idea for an article. I wonder if the editor of that Doc Savage fanzine I recently subscribed to might be interested in it.

I call up my friend Karl and ask him if he's interested in taking the bus with me up to New York City for another visit to Doc's HQ. He tells me he is.

After I get off the phone, I fire up my Smith-Corona word-processor and start typing.

THE cemetery caretaker asks me where I'm from, and I say Pennsylvania. This results in a raised eyebrow from the man, who seems to think I'm rather odd for coming all this way. I neglect to tell him about my recent fallout with archaeology and that I've had a layover in Illinois.

The man points to the grave right behind Bernard and Alice's plot, a long, flat headstone flush with the grass. He'd known right where it was all along.

Suddenly sensing the man knows more than he's let on, I ask him what he knows about Lester Dent. He still pretends (?) not to know Dent was a famous writer, but says he knew Dent personally.

Actually what he says is, "Yeah, I know 'im. He full o' shit!"

I am, needless to say, somewhat taken aback by this sudden vociferation. What could this fellow possibly mean? I press him, and I get two or three more variations on his prior statement. Coupled with the fact that the man's English is not perfect, I am quite puzzled. Determined to understand, I throw out some guesses as to what he means. Finally, I venture to ask, "You mean to say that he told lies?"

He nods vigorously, laughing. "He tell stories! Make up stories. You run into him on the street an' he pull your leg."

"Ah!" I say, laughing with the fellow. "He was a trickster, a jokester!" The man agrees, smiling because I understand him at last. The man tells me his father knew Dent, but that he, the caretaker, had only encountered Dent occasionally about town (and had tried to avoid Dent because of his prankster nature).

With his story told, the man jumps back on his lawn mower and leaves me alone at the gravesite. I snap some pictures and spend some time absorbing where I am, standing at the grave of a man who was a link in a literary chain that, I hope, I will one day also be a part of.

I return to my car and retrieve my dog-eared copy of Farmer's *Doc Savage: His Apocalyptic Life* from the front seat. As a bookmark in the "biography," I have a ticket stub from one of my several trips to the eighty-sixth floor of the Empire State Building. I pull this stub out of the book and leave it on Lester's grave. I think he'd probably have gotten a good laugh out of that, jokester that I've just been told he was. Then I'm off to hunt down the Dent home.

I can't find it. But while I'm searching I stop by the local library and discover a Lester Dent collection tucked in a nook in the back of the small building. An elderly librarian is kind enough to give me an overview of the library's Dent holdings, which, in addition to what I believe is a complete run of Doc Savage pulps from the 1930s and '40s, also includes a number of Doc Savage and general pulp fanzines. It's here that I first encounter Rick Lai's wonderful and classic Wold Newton article "The Secret History of Captain

Nemo. "This is the first glimmer I have that someone else is analyzing and expanding Farmer's Wold Newton concept with the same degree of care and intensity that I've striven for in my own work. Though I've seen Win Scott Eckert's groundbreaking *Wold Newton Universe* site by this time, it's yet in its infancy, and I am awestruck as I sit in the little nook and devour Rick's article.

And then I come across a folder, meticulously preserved by Norma Dent, that includes correspondence between her and Philip José Farmer. One item is a postcard Farmer sent to Norma while he was in New York City researching *Doc Savage: His Apocalyptic Life*. Farmer writes that he's just been to the Empire State Building, and though he circled all around it, he saw no sign of Doc, Monk, and the gang. Another item in the folder is Farmer's business card, listing his occupation as an "Unreal Estate Agent and Baroquer" representing choice lots in Ruritania, Poictesme, Ilium, R'lyeh, Barsoom, Middle Earth, Hallamshire, and Oz, as well as holding premium shares in the Hidalgo Trading Company. And then there's the copy of the first edition of the Doc Savage biography, inscribed from Farmer to Norma. It's a magical treasure trove. I use what little change I have on me to make as many Xeroxes as I can. When I get home to Pennsylvania, I'll make duplicates and mail them off to Win Eckert and Farmer's webmaster, Mike Croteau.

I'M sitting in Philip José Farmer's basement having a good conversation with Jack Cordes. It's the summer of 2006, and around us swirls the blissful festivity of the first-ever FarmerCon. Jack, of course, is Phil's longtime friend, who loaned him a complete run of Doc Savage pulps during the writing of *Doc Savage: His Apocalyptic Life*, and who accompanied Phil on his visit to Norma Dent as mentioned in that book. A twinkle in his eye, Jack has just revealed to me that Phil Tuckerized him in *Escape from Loki* as the character named Private Hans Kordtz.

Only a few hours ago, before the gathering, I was sitting upstairs talking with Phil about my progress on *The Song of Kwasin*, the third novel of the Khokarsa series. Phil had started working on the manuscript over thirty years ago and then abandoned it in lieu of a host of other pressing writing projects. Now Phil would like to see the novel finished, but since he's long into his retirement and has had a number of health setbacks, he's counting on me to see the book through to completion.

My life has become surreal.

IN my excitement over the library's treasures, I decide it's best to leave La Plata on a high point and abandon my quest for Lester Dent's house. Besides, it's getting late in the day and I have a long drive ahead of me. What's more, I've now met someone who personally knew the Revelator from Missouri. Or at least who claimed to. But in the strange alternate universe I've slipped into, it's enough.

I head back onto the highway. The future is still uncertain, but something has changed this day in La Plata. A shifting of soul-stuff, a tilting of the planet's alchemical axis, a splintering of the pluriverse, something… I can *feel* it.

FOR some, it's a burning bush. For others, a bodhi tree.

For me, it's a beat-up paperback copy of *Doc Savage: His Apocalyptic* at my side, baking in the summer heat as I speed down a Missouri highway toward destiny.

Christopher Paul Carey is the coauthor with Philip José Farmer of Gods of Opar: Tales of Lost Khokarsa, *and the author of* Exiles of Kho, *a prelude to the Khokarsa series. His short fiction and essays may be found in such anthologies as* Tales of the Shadowmen, The Worlds of Philip José Farmer, Tales of the Wold Newton Universe, The Avenger: The Justice, Inc. Files, *and* Myths for the Modern Age: Philip José Farmer's Wold Newton Universe. *He is an editor with Paizo Publishing on the Pathfinder Roleplaying Game, and the editor of three collections of Philip José Farmer's work. Visit him online at www.cpcarey.com.*

INDEX

Note: The Doc Savage stories are listed under their respective titles; other works are listed under their authors.

A

B

www.ingramcontent.com/pod-product-compliance
Lightning Source LLC
Chambersburg PA
CBHW030409100426
42812CB00028B/2889/J